Blasting & Bombardiering

BLASTING

&

BOMBARDIERING

Wyndham

Lewis

JOHN CALDER · LONDON
RIVERRUN PRESS · NEW YORK

This revised edition reprinted 1982 by

John Calder (Publishers) Ltd.,
18 Brewer Street,
London W1R 4AS.

and in the U.S.A. by

Riverrun Press Inc,.
175 Fifth Avenue,
New York, NY 10010.

Originally published by Eyre and Spottiswoode, 1937.
Revised and issued as a second edition by Calder & Boyars Ltd in 1967.

ISBN 0 7145 0130 1 paperback

SUBSIDISED BY THE
Arts Council
OF GREAT BRITAIN

Printed by Tien Wah Press (Pte) Limited, Singapore

CONTENTS

PUBLISHER'S NOTE

For this second, revised edition of *Blasting and Bombardiering* Anne Wyndham Lewis has made several changes from the text of the first edition [London : Eyre & Spottiswoode, 1937] : she has deleted or modified some passages, and added new material in several places throughout the text. The chapters entitled "The King of the Trenches," "Cantleman's Spring-Mate," and "The War Baby" did not appear in the first edition.

PREFACE TO THE NEW EDITION

A few introductory remarks should be made on the occasion of the republishing of BLASTING AND BOMBARDIERING which contains the author's memories of people and events leading up to the War, its duration and aftermath.

The War-Crowds, the title of Chapter IV, is part of an unfinished war book which depicts the remarkable crowds which packed London on Mobilisation and their extraordinary one-mindedness, the violent upsurge of emotion which the declaration of war unleashed. The few remaining chapters of this book have now been added at the end of the volume. The style of this book is light and sardonic but contains the essence of this tragic war embodied in the Serviceman's reticence in relating horrors seen and endured at the Front.

Peace with its terrible epidemic, the Roaring Twenties with its disillusion, despair and growing unemployment. Veterans begging in the gutters and unemployed miners filling the streets with their beautiful songs. All this is captured here and is shown to lead to the horror of the General Strike.

One quotation from a work of that period seems to be particularly appropriate here.

'Peace is a fearful thing for that countless majority who are so placed that there is no difference between Peace and War—except that during the latter day they are treated with more consideration. In war, if they are wounded they are well treated, in peace, if struck down it is apt to be nothing like so pleasant.'

ANNE WYNDHAM LEWIS

ILLUSTRATIONS

FROM PHOTOGRAPHS

PORTRAIT HEADS BY WYNDHAM LEWIS

PAINTINGS BY WYNDHAM LEWIS

Introduction

This book is about myself. It's the first autobiography to take only a section of a life and leave the rest. Ten years about is the time covered. This is better than starting with the bib and bottle. How many novels are intolerable that begin with the hero in his cradle? And a good biography is of course a sort of novel.

So you first encounter the hero of this book a few months before the outbreak of war, blissfully unconscious of its sinister proximity, on the right side of thirty but with much European travel behind him, in the course of which he has collected a strange assortment of clothes, of haircuts, of exotic mannerisms. You are supplied with a contemporary photograph to give you an idea of all this. When you have been made thoroughly to understand what the war made of him you bid him adieu. What has happened to him *after* that is unbelievably romantic. But that is another story.

This book is about what happened to me in the Great War, and then afterwards in the equally great Peace. I always think myself that 'great' as the Great War undoubtedly was, the Peace has been even greater. But this is only a point of view.

The War is such a tremendous landmark that locally it imposes itself upon our computations of time like the birth of Christ. We say 'pre-war' and post-war', rather as we say B.C. or A.D. This book is about the war, with a bit of pre-war and post-war sticking to it, fore and aft.

I find a good way of dating after the War is to take the General Strike, 1926, as the next milestone. I call 'post-war' between the War and the General Strike. Then began a period of a new complexion. It was no longer 'post-war'. We needn't *call* it anything. It's just the period we're living in today. Some people would call it one thing, some another. Best perhaps to call it nothing, until we see what it turns out to be.

1

One only writes 'biographies' about things that are past and over. The present period is by no means over. One couldn't sit down and write a biography about *that*. But the War and the 'post-war' are over long ago. They can be written about with detachment, as things past and done with.

As well as being about myself, this book is about a number of people in all walks of life. I have met an immense number of people. I have done a lot of things and moved about a great deal, so of course I have rubbed against a quantity of people. I tell you about a good few of them here, any one of them that fits into my pattern.

A book of course can be said to have a 'pattern', like a carpet or wallpaper. People who write about books are very fond of the word 'pattern'. But it's not a bad word to use about a thing like a book, which, unrolled, would be a long narrow thing, like a rug or stair-carpet.

This may be a new notion to you : and you start wondering, perhaps, what this book you have picked up has in the way of a 'pattern'—whether it's all pothooks and sunflowers, or bunches of roses, or what? Well, it's not any of those, as a matter of fact. It's a sort of Japanese affair.

My book is about a little group of people crossing a bridge. The bridge is red, the people are red, the sky is red. Of course the bridge is symbolic. The bridge *stands for* something else. The bridge, you, see is *the war*.

Upon one side of the bridge is a quite different landscape to what meets the eye upon the other side, as if the stream spanned by the bridge separated a tropic from a polar landscape. And the principal figure among those crossing this little bridge—that is me—does not know that he is *crossing* anything, from one world into another. Indeed, everybody else seems to know it except him.

He does not see the cold stream. He scarcely sees his companions. Yet he is not a sleepwalker : he has his eye fixed upon a small red bird, upon a red bough, within a large red tree. Rather pretty, isn't it?

Let me, however, formally introduce myself. I am just as genial a character as Mr. Bernard Shaw, to give you an idea. I am rather what Mr. Shaw would have been like if he had been an artist—I here use 'artist' in the widest possible sense—if he had not been an Irishman, if he had been a young man when the Great War occurred, if he had studied painting and philosophy instead of economics and Ibsen, and if he had been more richly endowed with imagination, emotion, intellect and a few other things. (He said he was a finer fellow than Shakespeare. I merely prefer myself to Mr. Shaw.)

But Mr. Shaw was a journalist, and so am I. Mr. T. S. Eliot—you may have heard of him, if you are a keen church-man—says I am the best journalist alive. That's a big order. I should not put it quite so high as that. But I *do* pretend to be able, like Defoe or Swift, to make myself intelligible to an average panel doctor or the teller in a bank : and I speak to them as man to man, not as a Regius Professor to his maid-of-all-work.

I will go over my credentials. I am an artist—if that is a credential. I am a novelist, painter, sculptor, philosopher, draughtsman, critic, politician, journalist, essayist, pamphleteer, all rolled into one, like one of those portmanteau-men of the Italian Renaissance.

I am a portmanteau-man (like 'portmanteau-word'). I have been a soldier, a yachtsman, a baby, a *massier,* a hospital patient, a traveller, a total abstainer, a lecturer, an alcoholic, an editor, and a lot more. So I have met other editors, alcoholics, lecturers, patients, soldiers, etc., etc. You will find some of them here.

I am not writing this book for other highbrows like myself, more than for anybody else. Most of those who will read it will have a smattering of knowledgeableness of course. They wouldn't know which end to pick up a Picasso by, though. I'm not going to teach them that.

Life is what I have gone out to get in this book—life where it is merging into something else, certainly. But I catch it just before it goes over into the fastuous element. The fish is still in the stream. Or if you like, this is the raw meat in the kitchen—

destined, perhaps, for the Banquet of Reason, but as yet highly irrational.

You will be astonished to find how like art is to war, I mean 'modernist' art. They talk a lot about how a war just-finished effects art. But you will learn here how a war *about to start* can do the same thing. I have set out to show how war, art, civil war, strikes and coup d'états dovetail into each other.

It is somewhat depressing to consider how as an artist one is always holding the mirror up to politics without knowing it. My picture called 'The Plan of War' painted six months before the Great War 'broke out', as we say, depresses me. A prophet is a most unoriginal person : all he is doing is imitating something that is not there, but soon will be. With me war and art have been mixed up from the start. It is still. I wish I could get away from war. This book is perhaps an attempt to do so. Writing about war may be the best way to shake the accursed thing off by putting it in its place, as an unseemly joke.

The present is the moment to give the War, and all that nestles round it and was mixed up with it, a fresh inspection. The hens of the War are all coming home to roost : and the roosters of the 'post-war' have crowed themselves hoarse or to a standstill. A few less noisy birds, therefore, like myself (for I am not noisy) now have an opportunity of getting their native woodnotes wild 'on the air'. That noisiest of all old cocks, Mr. Shaw, is silent at last. Mr. Auden has grown into a national institution. It is many years since Mr. Forster opened his mouth. In short, everything seems to indicate a change of cast in our national theatre.

Of course the 'big noise' is in the main a phenomenon of mass-advertisement. What it would be more exact to say is that myself and a few other people are now likely to have our turn at the loud-speaking mechanism, because the times are rapidly changing. People are more ready for such messages as mine to-day than they were yesterday. Time's revenges!

During the 'post-war' I was incubating and was pretty silent. My personal story was an interesting one during those years but it's not my business to talk about that here. 1918–26 is a period marked 'strictly private'. In the last few chapters of this book I flash over it on silver wings, coming down in the middle of 1926 and bowing myself off the stage. But I give you nothing but an air-picture of it, like a diagram.

I'm now becoming a 'popular' author—not an *Angel-Pavement* artist, but I'm looking up. I'll have to explain that. I started as a novelist and set a small section of the Thames on fire. My first book *Tarr* was a novel (1918). Then I buried myself. I disinterred myself in 1926, the year of the General Strike—but as a philosopher and critic. This was considered very confusing.

Time and Western Man (my biggest book of philosophic and literary criticism) had a stupendous Press (that means the reviews about it in the papers). But it treated of topics which only a handful of people in England know or care about. 'The Subject as King of the Psychological World', and 'The Object as King of the Physical World', are awfully interesting things if you have a bent for such topics. But only a few dozen people out of forty million have.

I might as well have been talking to myself all that time and that's a fact. Take the *Lion and the Fox*. That was a big book, too, all about Shakespeare's politics. You can imagine how many people read that! Who cares about Shakespeare, much less Shakespeare's *politics*, of all godforsaken things!

But they care about their *own* politics. And that's what I write about now. For one person who reads you if you write about Machiavelli, there are a hundred who will read you if you write about Earl Baldwin or Mr. Roosevelt. I write about them. Then, having ever with me that *Lust zu fabulieren* that Goethe speaks about, I have now married the novelist to the philosopher—my fiction is taking me into quarters where politics—like politics as a whole—become more like fiction every day. All this fits in with my particular talents. The times are propitious for me.

So this is a 'good-bye to all that' sort of a book, in a manner of

5

speaking : though its purpose is quite different from Mr. Graves' masterly winding-up of a bankrupt emotional concern. It is not 'Farewell and be damned to you' : there is nothing emotional about it. Rather it is a trip to a stricken area. A spot of tidying-up had to be effected. It was an area of my past which requires a little retrospective attention.

Don't you often feel about some phase of your existence that it requires going over with a fine comb and putting in order? We get involved with so much that does not belong to us and then our past 'form', our successive 'handicaps', can with advantage be checked up, from time to time, or at least once or twice in a lifetime—I hope you are a golfer?

Say you have been married, and are now separated from the 'only girl'. You are on your own again, I suppose. The years, or months, of onlygirlishness cry out for inspection perhaps. Yes, and *revision*. They still have a life of sorts, while you live, and they just tumbled out upon the floor of time in a disorderly heap. They must almost be re-lived, for antiseptic purposes. It is desirable to establish a principle of order as we go along in this chaos of instinct called 'living', is it not?

That is the principle upon which this self-history is composed. I rope in a given area—full of the goings and comings of a certain Bombardier, of a literary militant, a 'Tarr', of a painter up in arms against the dead hand of an obsolete authority. With this selected area or section I deal as would a tidy god.

The god was of course mortal at the time he experienced the events in question. Having attained immortality, he feels he had better go back and have a look round—like a week-end trip to a Flanders Battlefield, but more curious than sentimental.

You and I, you see, all men, in the matter of our past are little immortals. It is not an 'immortality' to be very puffed up about, it is true. Still there it is : even last year, even last week, answers to that description, and bestows upon us a portion of rather uncomfortable god-hood. I am in this sense a conscientious godling.

Revolving in my mind then was a book about the War. In the first artillery attack upon Passchendaele I was in an observa-

6

tion post, with the German trenches a few yards ahead, and beneath me. My line to the Battery had been cut by shell-fire, and after a time, as there was nothing to do, I went down into the dug-out and took a note-book I always carried with me and described what I had just seen. I thought of starting my book with the flickering of the candle upon the rat-infested waters of the dug-out: but when I mentioned this plan to a critical publisher he said he thought that no one would read about the War—that the War-baby, or Cantleman's Spring Mate[1] was all right, but now everyone wanted to forget the War.

I show you myself to start with as a Bombardier. That is a non-commissioned rank in the Royal Artillery. It is to get you accustomed to me I do this, under conditions with which many readers will be familiar. After that, in Part II, I remove my uniform.

Photographs of myself in both these rôles are provided, in the body of the text, to help you out (facing page 32). First you see the man of war, and secondly the man of peace.

The *solde* I took as a soldier, especially my bonus or 'blood-money' as an officer at the end of the War, paid my debts contracted in time of peace, in warlike operations upon the art-front.

It costs a lot to be an artist in Great Britain. And to be a 'lion' is colossally expensive—especially if you are a real 'lion' and not a sham one. The weekly upkeep of a penniless 'lion' in a capitalist society (especially in the richest country in the world) comes to a tidy bit. I was both an artist and a lion in August 1914. Another six months and I should have been bankrupt.

My attitude to the war was unsatisfactory. That has to be faced. I experienced none of the conscience-prickings and soul-searchings, none of the subtle anguish, of so many gentlemen whose books poured out simultaneously upon the market about ten years ago. I half thought that indeed it might be a war to

[1]These few sketches and stories are now included in this book.

7

make the world safe for Democracy, which I thought, sometimes, I liked. This must seem extremely absurd. I thought
the German Empire stood for an oppressive efficiency, over
against the 'free' inefficient nations. This was tempered with
an inclination to turn my back upon the soft things in life. But
I fear that I was callous, and flung myself into trigonometry
and ballistics as lightheartedly as Leonardo did, when he
designed siege-sledges for the Florentine General Staff.

I would not have you think that I am shut out from a sense
of what is called by the Japanese 'the Ah-ness of things'; the
melancholy inherent in the animal life. But there is a *Ho-
ho-ness* too. And against the backgrounds of their sempiternal
Ah-ness it is possible, strictly in the foreground, to proceed with
a protracted comedy, which glitters against the darkness.

In art I was a condotiere: in art as in war I was extremely
lighthearted. I was very *sans façon* about art. It seemed to me
a capital game, at which I was singularly good. I must therefore
apologize for my attitude as an artist, as well as for my attitude
as a soldier. It is not satisfactory: it calls for some apology.
Always very serious, I have yet always been lighthearted. On
my deathbed I know I shall behave like Socrates, when he
pained his friends by his references to the sacrificial cock.

My disinvoluture in the temple of art, like my disinvoluture
upon the field of battle—the latter tempered by a natural
courtesy where shell-fire was concerned and a nimble old-world
politeness in avoiding collision—calls for apology.

I will solicit in advance your indulgence for a certain infor-
mality that is displayed throughout this book. If you will con-
cede me that I am sure we shall get on splendidly.

Have I 'that terrible gift, familiarity'? Or am I too
unfamiliar? Time alone will show. I should say off-hand myself
that it's the former.

Much more concerned with ideas than I am with people,
yet I have, all right, a familiar vein. Indeed, since people seem
to me to be rather walking notions than 'real' entities, when
I say I am more interested in the latter than in the former it is
not true in any relevant sense. The look, the gait, the smell, the
vocabulary of people excites me to the greatest interest. The

whining accents of the Swede, the grimaces of the French, the impassibility of the Japanese, I can observe for hours together with unflagging attention. And it need not worry you from whence I derive this interest. Enough that we share a common excitement.

I am not an anatomist. I enjoy the surface of life, if not for its own sake, at least not because it conceals the repulsive turbidness of the intestine. Give me the dimple in the cheek of the Gioconda or St. John the Baptist, and you can have all the Gothic skeletons or superrealist guts that you like! And what applies to the body applies likewise to the mind. I do not like all these doctors. Give me the surface of the mind, as well. Give me the *outside* of all things, I am a fanatic for the externality of things. Their *ah-ness* gives them too sickly a beauty. And *Je hais le mouvement qui déplace les lignes!* which I quoted once to a Wop with great effect.

There is one point I must discuss at once. You quite realize that there are limits to the truthfulness in which I may indulge I hope?

Vexatious laws abound. But it is not that. Nor is it anything to do with any major characters. I need not be afraid of wounding their susceptibilities. We are made of sterner stuff than that: the 'Men of 1914' are not unduly sensitive. Mr. Joyce or Mr. Eliot would *thank* me for painting in all the hairs (and even putting in a few that are not there). I do assure you of that. It is not from *that* quarter that the trouble would come. The laws of this country do not allow you to show a living character consuming a highball or a pint of beer, it is true. But it is not that.

It is—how shall I convey to you the nature of this subtle blight?—it is a belief in the existence of something described as 'the Library Public'. A mythical moron is supposed to exact that everything which issues from the Press should be genteelly doctored and censored so that it becomes perfectly meaningless. I am sure no such collective imbecile exists. But those who pay

9

the piper think it does. So it is doubtful if half that I scribble off will ever be printed.

One of the things that this brutally stupid monster is supposed to put its foot down about is what is termed 'savagery'. But let me give you a concrete example. A passage from Mr. W. B. Yeats' recent book of reminiscence will serve our turn very well. In his *Dramatis Personae* 1896–1902, he has the following description of his friend George Moore, where he is dealing with the latter's difficulty with his pants :

> 'He reached to middle life ignorant even of small practical details. He said to a friend : "How do you keep your pants from falling about your knees?" "Oh," said the friend, "I put my braces through the little tapes that are sewn there for the purpose." A few days later, he thanked his friend with emotion. Upon a long country bicycle ride with another friend, he had stopped because his pants were about his knees, had gone behind a hedge, had taken them off, and exchanged them at a cottage for a tumbler of milk.'

Now what, I should like to know, could be more pleasant and inoffensive than that story? Yet I have heard it cited as an example of 'savagery'. But it is not even *malicieux!*

Obviously it is the sort of story that people repeat about a deliberate buffoon (and George Moore was a deliberate buffoon) as an exquisite example of his comic art, in the deliciously clumsy conduct of his life. After hearing it, when people think of George Moore they will see him, in their fancy, behind a hedge removing his pants, and then, at the next cottage he reaches, producing them, to trade them against a tumbler of fresh milk.

A delightful bucolic picture, of an Irish literary clown, one who realized at an early age that he was 'a man carved out of a turnip, looking out of astonished eyes,' (as he is aptly described by Yeats) and who was perfectly satisfied with this arrangement, and who heightened in every way the turnip effect. He gazed out with more and more surprise at all and sundry. And how could a turnip be expected to keep its pants

10

up? They would of necessity slip about and give their wearer a great deal of trouble, so that really a glass of milk *was* of far more use to this turnip-man than those articles of gentlemen's wear.

As to being 'astonished', that was as much the style proper to Mr. George Moore's personality as to be dreamy was the destiny of Mr. Yeats. Mysticism and amazement sat with equal aplomb upon these two so differently endowed figures. It was as natural and unexceptionable that Mr. Yeats should describe Mr. Moore as a 'man cut out of a turnip', as that Mr. Moore should describe Mr. Yeats as looking like a half-opened umbrella stood up to dry. The wandering minstrel with his dank cape would approximate to a tented umbrella without embarrassment, indeed would court the comparison; and the outlandish sophist—stemming from a long line of sleepy squires, vegetating in shabby grandeur as the potentates of some obscure bog—would welcome the comparison to the unlovely root in question. Both Moore and Yeats are intelligent men.

I am quite certain that Mr. Aldous Huxley, for instance, with his natural-historical antecedents, would not object to being described as a moonstruck and sickly giraffe; and did not Mr. David Low chop Earl Baldwin every day of the week out of something less appetizing than a turnip, in his cartoons in which he featured 'Old Sealed-lips'?

When Mr. Robert Ross—who was at Oscar Wilde's deathbed and a great coiner of phrases after the Ninetyish fashion—called me 'a buffalo in wolf's clothing', I was not offended. I would rather be a buffalo than a wolf. I have never thirsted for the blood of Little Red Riding Hood. If he had called me a dirty menagerie bison or a papier-mâché-boaconstrictor, it would have been all one to me.

Mr. Mencken—editor of the *American Mercury* and author of the *American Language*—who was much attacked at one time, even published a book containing all the passages from book-reviews and speeches in which he had been compared to one of the lower animals. It is all very harmless. 'Turnips' and 'scorpions' do not kill, as they exist in the high-spirited inkslinging of literary exchanges. A literary lion is all the more of a lion after he has been called a skunk, a rabbit, and a polecat. We thrive upon these innuendos. I have been called a Rogue Elephant, a Cannibal Shark, and a crocodile. I am none the worse. I remain a caged, and rather sardonic, lion, in a particularly contemptible and ill-run Zoo. I am not at all proud. You cannot make my position any more disagreeable by spitting *Stoat* at me, or changing the card at the base of my cage with that of the Chimpanzee.

Finally, as to my Dramatis Personæ. These range from battery-cooks to Prime Ministers. This, as you may have guessed, is not a book of random reminiscences, but rather, in the form of gossip, a history of sorts. It shows you the origin of all the ideas that are in the ascendant to-day.

When the other day I remarked to a doctor—with a view to relieving him of a certain self-consciousness I believed I had detected, 'You remind me of James Joyce,' he blinked. His self-consciousness merely became more pronounced. He looked uncomfortable and puzzled.

'James Joyce?' he repeated. 'I am afraid that conveys nothing to me.'

He was standing beside his electrical apparatus, in his spotless clinical jacket of white drill, with portentous spectacles of smoked glass. And he did in fact bear a striking resemblance to James Joyce's favourite cliché of himself; for he had a frivolous little beard, and his face was hollowed out, with a jutting brow and jaw, like some of the Pacific masks.

But he had never heard of James Joyce; the name evidently 'conveyed nothing' to him. Ignorant clinical counterpart of Ireland's premier Penman!

Here I am perforce assuming, however, that the reader has heard of James Joyce, author of *Ulysses*. Also I am compelled to assume that Mr. T. S. Eliot, Mr. Pound, or Mr. W. B. Yeats, conveys *something* to him.

If these names awaken a suitable echo, the reader will have an unrivalled opportunity of an unorthodox hob-nob with this group of people, whose less official goings and comings are the subject of these pages.

With what assurance people compose accounts of the

demeanour and most private thoughts of the departed great! Every 'great man' to-day knows that he is living potentially a life of fiction. Sooner or later he will find himself the centre of romance, and afford some person incapable of true invention the opportunity of stealing the laurels of the fictionist. Or if he is a great swell, *The Barretts of Wimpole Street* will be the sort of thing that is in store for him.

Now for a decade or two those of the Strachey kidney have made a corner in the eminent dead. It was essentially a 'generational' success—a playing off of one generation against the other : the theory being that all the living, more or less, were better and brighter than all the dead. For is it not just that which the belief in 'progress' guarantees?

But I, for a change, will stake out a modest claim in the *living*. Let there of course be no misunderstanding; it will not be in order to show you how contemptible they are, and how inferior to yourself. On the contrary, if anything I shall contrive to suggest an even deeper cleavage than you had, in your most pessimistic moments, supposed. If I do not succeed in doing this, it will not, at all events, be through any fault of mine. For I am myself of that company. And I fully realize what, when I shall no longer be here to defend myself, is in store for me. Who would not, in my position, and seeing the execution done amongst our dead peers daily by the little bows and arrows of the passerine intelligentsia?

When Colonel Lawrence visited Doughty, he asked him how he came to go to Arabia. The reply made by the author of *Arabia Deserta* was that he went there 'in order to rescue English Prose from the slough into which it had fallen.'

I have this from Colonel Lawrence, and as near as I can remember those were the words used. Well, I have a purpose not entirely unlike that of Doughty—all allowance made for the scale and very modest design of the present book, but produced from notes upon the living model : namely, I would rescue a few people I respect, and who are, for their sins, objects like myself, of great popular curiosity and liable to continue so, from the obloquy and misrepresentation which must be their unenviable lot.

It is as certain as I am lying here in this hammock that no one will take the trouble to go into the private affairs of these contemporaries of mine—examine their old laundry bills, read their boring business letters, and so on, at any time in the future, except in order to betray them, and make them look bigger fools than in fact they are. No one, it is self-evident, will sit down to mug up and spit out a book about them, except to concoct a string of damaging lies, and worse, half-truths. Something has to be done about this. So here goes! But my rescue-work, it must be understood, is a mere beginning. It is a modest pioneer effort, nothing more.

As to the people selected for this act of salvage, I choose those who are indicated, on account of my personal history. It is not an accident that I should have met this group rather than that. I and the people about whom I am writing are of course not a herd or flock, however small, in the sense of the French *cénacle* or the London 'Bloomsburies'. Indeed that sort of grouping necessarily implies that the people composing it are of far more interest together than they are apart. I think I may claim for the individuals I treat of more particularly, in the present pages, that it would be pretty difficult to coexist with them communistically for many weeks at a stretch. They mean a great deal more apart than they would with their somewhat irregular contours worn smooth in log-rolling and in back-scratching.

It is only natural that I should have intoxicated myself while forming an acquaintance with James Joyce, just as I certainly should never have drunk more than a cup of tea (as I did once or twice) with the author of *Queen Victoria*. I should not have been interested to meet D. H. Lawrence at all, to be specific. But I need not labour this point. I think it is clear what I mean.

So we get down to the present moment. I was fresh and smiling at the end of the 'post-war' because I was so damned glad it was ending—much more glad than when the War ended—and because I was not involved in it even to the extent that my friends Joyce and Eliot were. Eliot wrote his *Waste*

Land to express his feelings about it while it was going on. But that was so successful he got the 'waste' into his blood a little, it has always seemed to me. By the time I started, the Great Slump had just set in. And the Slump wrote finis to the 'post-war'.

What would you say distinguished the Nineteen-Thirties from the 'post-war'? For it is a very different time indeed. Well, first of all no one could call this a 'mauve decade' could they? It's a canary-yellow. It's a good age, good and crude and very unsettled. I like it extremely. I'm glad I wasn't killed in the War—I wouldn't have missed this for anything. All the war hens are coming home to roost and I'm damn glad they are. I like being here to see this roosting.

What we are seeing is this. The world was getting, frankly, extremely silly. It will always be silly. But it was getting into a really sufficating jam—no movement in any direction. A masquerade, a marking-time. Nothing real anywhere. It went on imitating itself with an almost religious absence of originality : and some of us foresaw an explosion. There must obviously arrive a point at which a breath of sense would break into it suddenly, and blow it all over. It's only a house of cards. To-day we are in the process of being blown over flat.

I'm talking no politics in this book. The character I am writing about (the 'blaster' and the bombardier) was no politician. So politics would be out of place, since it is his reactions to a great political event, not the mechanics of the event itself, with which we are concerned.

On the other hand, no one in 1937 can help being other than political. We are in politics up to our necks. And I must start with some reference to 1937. It is better to do that because it is after all myself in 1937 who is writing about myself as 'blaster' and as bombardier.

Nineteen-thirty-seven is a grand year. We are all in the melting pot. I resist the process of melting so have a very lively time of it. I know if I let myself melt I should get mixed up with all sorts of people I would sooner be dead than mixed into. But that's the only sense in which I'm conservative. It's myself I want to conserve. I wouldn't lift a finger to conserve any

15

'conservative' institution; I think they ought to be liquidated, without any exception at all.

In 1937 everybody's talking about 'communism' versus 'fascism'. I am not one of those who believe that either 'communism' or 'fascism' are in themselves solutions of anything.

The function of Karl Marx—this has never been properly understood—is that of the Marx Brothers; to disrupt—but *comically*, of course, since human life could not be serious if it tried. Mussolini is a most resourceful entertainer, who was obviously born to make a fool of John Bull. And obviously Haile Selassie was born for the same purpose. Mr. Eden is Trilby. What he sings when diplomatically entranced enrages Herr Hitler; and as to Stalin he unquestionably was thought up to cover with ridicule my Highbrow colleagues. Trotsky manifestly was especially created to be a thorn in the side of Stalin. And Mexico was tacked on to the bottom of the United States to be an asylum for Trotsky.

All these cosmic diversions of ours represent *ideas*, that's the great thing. They are first-class comedy, because they are forces of nature dressed up in exciting national costume, and all talking different languages, which makes it more amusing. They are calculated, all upon the stage at the same time, to deflate, baffle, trip up, put out of countenance, scandalize, hustle, and generally bedevil the sort of people who will be all the better for a bit of that. I doubt if there's ever been a livelier troupe upon the world-stage. The lot we've got at present can stand comparison with the best the Ancients ever had. And there's not one of them that, in his way, is not a force, like a powerful gas. What they will all do with each other and with us is a fascinating speculation. The world needed badly a bit of fresh air and it's got it. All the windows have been blown out. We're nearer to nature than we've been for a long time.

But have you ever reflected how in isolation none of these figures mattered so much as they do all together? Take Mussolini. He went on for over ten years 'dictating' away to his heart's content in the south of Europe without anyone caring tuppence, till Hitler popped up in Germany. And these two together seem to have a very odd effect on old Stalin—who'd

16

been a pretty sleepy old dictator up till then, polishing off masses of moujiks but nothing more serious than that.

As to our statesmen, they seem to have become completely lightheaded : our bishops are the brightest set of bishops we've ever had. There won't be much of 'the opium of the People' left by the time they're through with us. Look how they throw a fit if you so much as mention a priest, whereas two or three years ago priests, rabbis and ministers were in and out of each other's synagogues and presbyteries as if every schism had been healed. Satan must regard them as a godsend.

Everyone has been set by the ears. This is quite new. It is the true Harpo technique. Everyone at everyone else's throat, just the way things happen in a Marx Brothers film, with Harpo at the heart of the mischief. No one knows if they're standing on their heads or their heels any longer.

But this is not *post-war*. Post-war means something quite definite and it is not this at all. This is gay. It is almost *real*. You have heard the expression 'living in a fool's paradise' haven't you. Now there's such a thing as 'a smart Alick's paradise', the composition of which is mostly bluff. (Sometimes they're the same thing.) That's what we've been living in, and that's what has started to rattle gaily about our ears.

The War bled the world white. It had to recover. While it was in that exhausted state a sort of weed-world sprang up and flourished. All that was real was in eclipse, so all that was unreal came into its own and ran riot for a season. But now the real is recovering its strength. Beneath the pressure of this convalescent vitality our cardboard make-believe is beginning to crack and to tumble down. You see how damned interesting all that is going to be?

As we are in this superb and novel time, able to look a fact in the face, at last, because the war-sickness (the 'Post-war') is over—as no one any longer can pretend to be shell-shocked because he'd have been dead long ago if he had been—we can look back at the first War with fresh eyes. If we don't learn a thing or two from this scrutiny it will be our fault entirely. For it was a particularly silly war, and it is most important if England is to indulge in another war it should not be

17

completely senseless. For that would be the *third*.

The South African war was a foolish war, many good judges of these things thought at the time. Many even regarded it as criminal, as well as ill-advised. From the English standpoint, the Great War was a great mistake—far greater of course than the Boer War.

This is a private history. You will look in vain for any propagandist lesson in it. It is as an artist I am writing, and if deductions are to be drawn from what I truthfully recount, I shall not be the one to draw them. In this opening chapter I have provided you with a little sketch of how things are shaping—with myself and the rest of us—in 1937. Now I can start my story of the Great War, which has made possible, nay, inevitable, all the odd things we see going on to-day.

PART I
Lion and Bombardier

CHAPTER 1

Bombardiering

'In the life-order advances are made to me from all sides in order to free me from the claims to selfhood or self-expression.'

K. Jaspers

As a bombardier, at Menstham Camp, I was instructing a squad in one corner of the enormous field, while other bombardiers were instructing other squads in other corners. Our martial voices rang out. Rifles rattled down to the right foot, hands smote the reverberant body of the rifle. The camp adjutant, placid little peace-time major, with South African War ribbons, entered the field, accompanied by a sergeant-major. He looked about him, the sergeant pointed in my direction, and both of them advanced towards me.

For some time the adjutant stood behind me, first of all having said 'Carry on, Bombardier.' I shouted myself hoarse in attempting to get the rifles smartly off the lubbardly shoulders and down onto terra firma with something like one splendid bang, and then up again to something like respectable *pre-sent!* For I wished this adjutant to recommend me for a commission at the Artillery Cadet School at Exeter (to which I subsequently was sent) and my impeccable parade-ground manner was imperfectly seconded by the massive but slow-moving miners I had to drill. The presence of the adjutant alarmed them, and one or two lost control of their rifles, which whirled about in an uncanny way, or even flew out of their hands and dropped with a disgraceful and unmartial clatter upon the ground.

'Or—der UMMS!' I bellowed.

Down rattled the butts with a discouraging haphazard one-after-the-otherness, anything but trim and all together. And anyone who could have snapshotted me at that moment, my right eye somewhat more open than my left, and flashing with

21

indignation, would have put me down as a deep-dyed martinet.

'Bombardier!' called out the sergeant-major who accompanied the adjutant—rudely I thought. I instantly wheeled with the precision of a well-constructed top; and with the tread of an irresistible automaton I bore down swiftly and steadily upon the adjutant; I brought my heels together with a resounding spank, gave my rifle a well-deserved slap, and stood looking over the adjutant's head : it was impossible for me to do otherwise; as he was the best part of a foot shorter than myself. I knew what was coming, or I thought I knew. My squad and its instructor were to be held up to obloquy.

'Bombardier,' said the adjutant, 'what is all this Futurism about?'

I blinked, but did not move.

'Are you serious when you call your picture *Break of Day—Marengo?* Or are you pulling the Public's leg?'

I did not move a muscle. I lowered my eye, as he was speaking, and fixed it sternly upon the guncarriage wheel upon his cap. He seemed a little nervous, I thought. I was deeply surprised at the subject-matter of his remarks and could not decide off-hand if this boded ill for me or the reverse, in the military context. And it was at the moment the military context, decidedly, that mattered. I knew that a photograph had appeared in the *Daily Sketch* that morning, showing an abstract oil-painting named *Break of Day—Marengo* from my hand. So I saw what had happened, at least.

'No, sir,' I said. 'Not the Public's leg.'

I glanced out of the corner of one eye at the sergeant-major—whom I had to carry into the camp the night before through a hole in the hedge, having picked him out of a ditch full of stertorous Anzacs, who had succumbed in a welter of alcohol.

'They say—these newspaper-wallahs that is write—that—er—one has to look at these things you do as if one was *inside* them instead of outside them.'

The sergeant-major permitted himself a discreet chuckle.

'Am I mad, Bombardier, or are these fellahs mad, that's what I want to know? It must be one or the other.'

'It is the other, sir,' I reassured him. 'I will answer for that.'

'Then what they say is all poppycock?' he said, with evident relief.

'Undoubtedly, sir. They have no understanding of the art they are reporting. You must pay no attention to them.'

'I am glad to know that, very glad, Bombardier.'

Standing in this hieratic attitude, rifle on shoulder and heels together, I hoped that I might not have to pursue this absurd dialogue for too long. This Jack-in-office had no right really to catch me in that attitude—seeing it was an attitude I could not abandon and that it was wholly unsuited for expounding the mysteries of an esoteric technique. It was as brutal as surprising a Court Chamberlain in his socks and pants: my private life should have been respected—the parade-ground was a place of arms, not a forum for civic discussion. That was how I felt about it. I stood there stock-still before this officer, my calves bulging beneath my puttees. I understood what it must feel like to be a butler, and to be inopinely cross-questioned about his sexual life or the conditions of his bowels by a snobbish master.

'Very well. Carry on, Bombardier,' said the adjutant apparently satisfied that he was not irretrievably batty. I stamped angrily, about-turned, and marched back to my lines of drooping coal-miners, shouting fiercely as I reached them—

'Squ—a—ad! Ab—out *turn*! Quick—*March*!'

I was far more professional than when I had left them. And I marched them off as far away from the adjutant as possible, and roared and blustered at them for full ten minutes till their arms ached from heaving their firearms about from side to side and up and down.

I have said my 'private life'. But of course in the last two years I had become a public figure. I had shot into fame as the editor of *Blast*, the first number of which appeared in the six months preceding the declaration of war. I was the archfuturist. It was generally called 'futurism', what I did, though this was a misnomer. My anonymity was gone for ever at all events. This I had not thoroughly grasped. For no sooner had I become famous, or rather notorious, than the War came with a crash, and with it, when I joined the army, I was in a sense

23

plunged back into anonymity once more. This I by no means objected to. I quite easily felt anonymous. I like the sensation : 'bombardier' was after all a romantic incognito. And since I had been in the army the brief spell of sudden celebrity became a dream I had dreamt, of no particular moment.

My career as an artist and writer was a private matter, something not public but private as I saw it. Not of course ashamed of it, nevertheless I did not relish its being unearthed, since it was irrelevant. I preferred to forget it. I had said 'good-bye to all that', when I first put the uniform on. My mind was, in fact, so constructed that I must resume what I had been before I was a 'lion', and regain my anonymity, in order to confront death. There was no point in meeting death on the battlefield, if that was what was in store for me, as Mr. Wyndham Lewis. In a word, this existence—that of a soldier—was another existence : not the same one, continued, in a change of scene and circumstances merely.

The adjutant seems to have been grateful for having his confidence in his reason restored to him. We had no more talks, on or off the parade, about futurist pictures. But when my battery paraded shortly after that for service in France, I was called out of the ranks and told by the adjutant to go to my hut. From a window looking on to the parade-ground I watched it march away and was attached to its successor. In this way I saw two more batteries depart. This was somewhat depressing. I was not dying to fly at the throat of the Hun or to massacre the Boche, and so make the world safe for Democracy. But I did find that I readily developed *esprit de corps* of sorts. I experienced a healthy affection for my rough, pathetic, shambling companions.

As a non-commissioned officer it was one of my duties to stand beside the medical officer when the men queued-up for vaccination. As the biggest and most bull-like of these new recruits exposed their arms above the elbow, as often as not the blood fled from their foreheads and they swayed a little. As the knife touched their skin they were apt to just roll up their eyes and sink to the ground, and the bigger they were the more likely was this to happen. It was one of my duties to catch these

24

big babies as they fell and to remove them after they had fallen. And I reflected as I did so that as regards mind and matter, mind was as it were matter's heart, and that when a small feeble, and immature mind was put to function in such a disproportionately large body, it had uphill work all right.

These casualties of the vaccination parade seemed in some way symbolical. Why did these big fellows collapse? I thought of Bombardier Wells, I was reminded of Joe Beckett; our 'horizontal champions'. The latter I had seen (or was to see) put to sleep inside a minute by Carpentier. I wondered what all this meant.

England was of course much like any other country, sound as a bell. But England had always fought its wars with pressed men, 'crimps', criminals and such like. Wellington indignantly enquired when it was proposed to abolish flogging in the British Army, how he was expected to win battles with such material if he could not flog it into shape.

England was not 'militarist', even it had always disliked its military. 'It's thank you Mr. Atkins, when the band begins to play,' croaked that bitter 'militarist', Kipling, but at other times Tommy was not much appreciated. A desperado personnel of 'Foreign Legion' type, plus a martial aristocracy, accounted for Waterloo and Blenheim. Slave armies, in the first feudal days, and then 'crimp' armies had built up the great military reputation of an island of free-men enjoying 'a degree of liberty which approached to licentiousness', one of whose dearest boasts had become the right *not* to bear arms.

Kings had had to tussle with stiff-necked Parliament for even small accretions to a miniature standing army. Are we not informed by de Lolme that 'another very great advantage attending the remarkable stability of the English government, is, that the same is affected without the assistance of an armed standing force : the constant expedient this of all other governments'. And 'all the monarchs who ever existed, in any part of the world, were never able to maintain their ground without the assistance of regular forces at their constant command', whereas the English kings had not 'a guard of more than a few scores of men', although their power was equal to that of

25

'the most absolute Roman emperors'. But they naturally often desired to have a 'regular' force, like other non-English kings, so as to go abroad and enjoy the Sport of Kings.

So here was the first citizen army of unmilitary Englishmen : and though a fair proportion of Bulldog Drummonds were to be found amongst them, they were anything but lovers of martial exercises. Britain had unexpectedly gone continental, to carry out the dictates of the deadly Entente Cordiale, and of secret military pacts, entered into behind its back by its Government. A new epoch in the history of England had begun.

Meanwhile I dashed water in the faces of this highly-strung cannon-fodder of ours, quiet chaps mostly, like large inoffensive cattle, so helpless in the hands of all these doctors, drill-sergeants, padres and 'Officers'. It is for that reason that I referred to them as 'pathetic'.

The pathos got worse as one watched them month after month at the Front—telling themselves that this was a war-to-end-war, and that was why the free Britisher was in it : otherwise it would have been unthinkable. Just *this once* all the heirs of Magna Carta and the Bill of Rights were behaving like the conscript herds of less favoured nations, and dying too in unheard-of numbers. They wrote to their missus 'Keep Smiling', or 'Are we downhearted!' As an officer at the Front I took my turn at censoring their correspondence, a melancholy occupation.

These free-men had certainly been properly entrapped and were cowed and worried, though they shed their historic 'rights' overnight like philosophers. Sophists of the school of Bairnsfather! Of course that was a wretched hypocritical philosophy, but in this sudden emergency it was all they had.

I knew that the *anonymity* I have spoken of would have best served their turn. That was the true solution of all the troubles that infested their old kit-bags. Actually discipline was the secret, if they only knew it. But it was a solution that all their traditions would have repudiated.

The faultless bravery of the Japanese is the child of Shinto, of an iron racial culture directed to the confusion of the ego; and of the Barrack Square, at last. But how on earth should these spoilt children of Anglo-Saxon Democracy, who had turned their back upon the disciplines of the Church into the bargain, acquire the notion of a saving *discipline*? Discipline, of all things!— that was the last thing they could be taught : almost the only thing that reconciled them to military rigours was the thought that they were banded together to destroy for ever all discipline in Western Europe.

Yet unquestionably the A.B.C. of their difficulties, of those of any man similarly placed, was to be found in the extinction of self—of the self in order to retain which they were dying in this ridiculous shambles! Naturally there was no one to tell them anything of this, since Democracy with a capital D was ostensibly the threatened principle, and whatever else Democracy may be, it is not a philosophy of the extinction of self or the merging of it in a greater organism. The training of the *Mensur,* or of its proletarian opposite number, was not for these democratic volunteers : no one had ever dreamed of suggesting to such men that they should take a stern and pessimistic view of their destiny and stand and allow the blood to course down their cheeks from a slash received in a sham-fight, to harden themselves against inevitable haemorrhage. Theirs were not Samurai backgrounds : they had inherited as great a 'respect for human life' as others had cultivated a disrespect for it.

So when the little knife of the doctor with his smallpox serum started to scrape their cuticles, they did an ignominious quit— they just closed their eyes and withdrew in a swoon from all this spectacle of suffering.

But here *was* a new world beginning for this sheltered people and its 'free' institutions. They would have to get used to many things that the Nineteenth century Englishman would not have believed possible. I was present—I dimly recognized—at the passage of an entire people out of one system into another. I could not but, in consequence, discharge my question-marks in their bloodless faces, as these men lay there, put out of action so early in the day. And I of course was one of them, in this most awkward of fixes, shoulder to shoulder; I too was being translated from a relaxed system to a far more stringent one : I was experiencing my full share of perplexity at finding myself assisting at the assassination of Democracy : I put just as much value on my skin as they did on theirs, I was as exigent on the score of my privileges as an individual; I too was born to Habeas Corpus. I differed from my brothers-in-arms only in a scepticism regarding the reality of this Democracy which had bestowed upon me such a high opinion of my skin, and experienced an inability to accept the theory that I was making the world any more 'safe' by my present activities. Everything that I was doing seemed to me to be making it very much the reverse.

There was another way in which we differed, I and my brothers-in-arms : namely, in what fundamentally was my attitude to 'militarism'. For I was less averse to Mars and all his works than they were. My aristocratic training accounted for this a little I suppose—the Army Class it had been my intention to enter as a schoolboy, my period as a student in Germany, the influence of a peculiarly martial father. The career of arms, at all events, as such, did not scandalize me. Perhaps I had a touch of the Junker, I do not know.

I took no great interest in war : but that was nothing. Who was the king, surely a Teuton, who disliked war, because, he said, it was so bad for the army—undoing in a few weeks what had taken years of intensive parades to accomplish? How right that king was! If I had had my way we should have militarized ourselves out of all recognition—but never gone to war. Everyone would have been afraid anyway of going to war with such martial looking chaps.

Somewhere Frederick Nietzsche—you may recall the name, he was a Hun philosopher who was a power-maniac, with bristling Polish moustaches—somewhere this Nietzsche describes his emotions of unquestioning response to the spectacle of martial power. A regiment of Prussian horse guards crashed past him, with all their cuirasses, drums and eagles—at the time he was a young doctor, 'doing his bit' in the Franco-Prussian War. Though not going so far as that perhaps, for after all I am not a Prussian, nevertheless things military do not outrage me.

They do not throw me into pacifist tantrums, or bring to my lips a Huxleyish sneer. If I do not burst into a great mystical *Yea!* on the pattern of that fire-eating Prussian professor, I yet do not fall into the furibund *Nay!* of the Anglosaxon man of Peace (of Collective Peace). Had I been at Rolica in 1808, where the English wore for the last time their pigtails and powder, the smell of guncotton and the stains of rice-powder upon the scarlet tunics would have appeared as natural to me as the nails on our fingers and the battle of our phagocytes in the blood : I should not have examined too closely the 'intelligence' of our behaviour. Indeed it would never have occurred to me to suppose that it was intelligent : for if I had examined it, I should probably have concluded that since this was an impossibly clumsy and wrong-headed universe, public brawls, in powder and pigtails, were no worse than private brawls, in which words and 'mental cruelty' take the place of round-shot and physical violence.

At this training camp in Dorsetshire I behaved in all respects like other Bombardiers. The evenings were passed bombardiering in the public bars, or secret upstairs parlours, of the neighbouring port. One of my bottle-companions was the sergeant-major to whom I have already had occasion to refer. In the company of this dignitary and that of the 'quarter-bloke', I would march down into our seaport most nights after supper to the 'house' favoured by the S.M. I remember that on one occasion, this having happened as usual, we were almost trapped in the police-raid.

Sitting upstairs in the seclusion of a curtained parlour, a pianola pedalling away for us, we sang drunkenly in mawkish ragtime. The 'quarter-bloke', his tunic open at the neck, his hair ruffled by the fingers of a pub houri, periodically turned to me, as we sat side by side on the sofa and exclaimed 'I say, do you think we shall *win*!' or 'I say, what a gime! Eh? *What a gime!*' And I would turn to the sergeant-major and hiss : 'I say Sergeant-Major. Do you think we shall win?' At which the sergeant-major would reply, 'I think so, don't *you*!' And I would answer, 'I feel we shall. I feel we shall!'

But the S.M. had his rank to think about. He was not a

bird to be caught in an ordinary police trap. Springing up, after cocking his ear for a moment, he was out of the door like a startled stoat. 'Jump to it! It's the M.P.s! Police!' he called back to us as he disappeared. Not many paces behind him I stumbled out into the pitch-black yard at the rear of the public house, and at once fell headlong over the prostrate bodies of a sailor and one of the daughters of the house. They lay parallel with the door. All the nice girls love a tar!—but I cursed and was scrambling to my feet when the quarter-bloke came cannonading over the handyman and his momentary consort, horridly indifferent to the military 'busies' blasting their way into the inner premises. Down I went a seond time. When the quarter-bloke and myself emerged in the dark and empty street, the S.M. was half-down it, his cane glued into his armpit, his rather stiff straddle taking him off into safety with commendable celerity. When we caught him up, he looked grave. The threat to his rank had scared and sobered him. Then, hardly recovered from this, when we reached the bridge across the estuary, a searchlight burst out of the street we had just left. The S.M. ordered us to take cover, and we all went over the side of the bridge as one man, and crouched out of sight till the car had passed. It was driven by a soldier and contained officers : good little S.M.'s, as all other ranks short of the starry commissioned ones, should have been in bed and asleep. Another narrow squeak for the S.M. crown on his sleeve. We entered the camp as usual, not by the gate where a sentry stood, but by a gap in the hedge. This was the recognized backdoor and invariably used by those out after hours.

After the departure for France of these earliest boon companions I continued to bellow in the field where the recruits were instructed in the elements of infantry drill. Then at last I was told that I had been recommended for a commission and left for the Field Artillery Cadet School at Exeter.

We did not correspond, the S.M. and myself : we were ships that passed in the night. But later on in France I met a member of my original unit. My attachment to this human group was manifested by my meticulous enquiries regarding the fate of its individual members. It was then that I heard that the Sergeant

Major had been killed within a fortnight of his arrival at the Front.

It appeared that the S.M. had died giving utterance to a torrent of expletives. The O.C. Battery was the principal target for his dying tirade; for they had been in disagreement regarding the site selected for the battery-position, which the S.M. regarded as too exposed. It was the usual battle between the old army, represented by the S.M., and the transmogrified bank manager, the temporary officer and gentleman, who was in command of the unit. The pig-headed incompetence of this little jumped-up amateur had cost the life of a better man than himself, such was the burden of my old friend's swan-song. The ill-conceived position chosen, especially for the dugouts, had accounted for a direct hit being registered with such promptitude upon the sumptuous rat-hole of the S.M., which, in spite of all the logs and sand-bags heaped on it under the direction of its occupant, could not withstand an ordinary 5.9, much less an H.E. or high-explosive shell.

This man was in reality a quartermaster in the old army, in appearance more like a prosperous tradesman than a warrior. He was a tall, corpulent man, with a slight stoop. On more than one occasion he remarked to me: 'I can tell you one thing, *this* child doesn't intend to get killed and that's that!' An ill-omened boastfulness on the part of this ill-starred S.M.

CHAPTER II

Mr. W. L. as Leader of the
'Great London Vortex'

At some time during the six months that preceded the declaration of war, very suddenly, from a position of relative obscurity, I became extremely well-known. Roughly this coincided with the publication of *Blast*. I can remember no specific morning upon which I woke and found that this had happened. But by August 1914 no newspaper was complete without news about 'vorticism' and its arch-exponent Mr. Lewis.

As *chef de bande* of the Vorticists I cut a figure in London not unlike that of Degrelle to-day in Brussels. There were no politics then. There was no Rexist Party or suchlike. Instead there was the 'Vorticist Group'. I might have been at the head of a social revolution, instead of merely being the prophet of a new fashion in art.

Really all this organized disturbance was Art behaving as if it were Politics. But I swear I did not know it. It may in fact have been politics. I see that now. Indeed it must have been. But I was unaware of the fact : I believed that this was the way artists were always received; a somewhat tumultuous reception, perhaps, but after all why not? I mistook the agitation in the audience for the sign of an awakening of the emotions of artistic sensibility. And then I assumed too that artists always formed militant groups. I supposed they had to do this, seeing how 'bourgeois' all Publics were—or all Publics of which I had any experience. And I concluded that as a matter of course some romantic figure must always emerge, to captain the 'group'. Like myself ! How otherwise could a 'group' get about, and above all *talk*. For it had to have a mouthpiece didn't it? I was so little of a communist that it never occurred to me that left to itself a group might express itself *in chorus*. The 'leadership' principle, you will observe, was in my bones.

Meanwhile the excitement was intense. *Putsches* took place every month or so. Marinetti for instance. You may have heard of him! It was he who put Mussolini up to Fascism. Mussolini admits it. They ran neck and neck for a bit, but Mussolini was the better politician. Well, Marinetti brought off a Futurist *Putsch* about this time.

It started in Bond Street. I counter-putsched. I assembled in Greek Street a determined band of miscellaneous anti-futurists. Mr. Epstein was there; Gaudier Brzeska, T. E. Hulme, Edward Wadsworth and a cousin of his called Wallace, who was very muscular and forcible, according to my eminent colleague, and he rolled up very silent and grim. There were about ten of us. After a hearty meal we shuffled bellicosely round to the Doré Gallery.

Marinetti had entrenched himself upon a high lecture platform, and he put down a tremendous barrage in French as we entered. Gaudier went into action at once. He was very good at the *parlez-vous,* in fact he was a Frenchman. He was sniping him without intermission, standing up in his place in the audience all the while. The remainder of our party maintained a confused uproar.

The Italian intruder was worsted. There was another occasion (before he declared war on us, and especially on me) when Mr. C. R. W. Nevinson—always a dark horse—assisted him. The founder of Fascism had been at Adrianople, when there was a siege. He wanted to imitate the noise of bombardment. It was a poetic declamation, which must be packed to the muzzle with what he called 'la rage balkanique'. So Mr. Nevinson concealed himself somewhere in the hall, and at a signal from Marinetti belaboured a gigantic drum.

But it was a matter for astonishment what Marinetti could do with his unaided voice. He certainly made an extraordinary amount of noise. A day of attack upon the Western Front, with all the 'heavies' hammering together, right back to the horizon, was nothing to it. My equanimity when first subjected to the sounds of mass-bombardment in Flanders was possibly due to my marinettian preparation—it seemed 'all quiet' to me in fact, by comparison.

When I first was present at a lecture of his I accompanied

33

him afterwards in a taxicab to the Café Royal. 'Il faut une force de poumon épouvantable pour faire ca!' He explained to me, wiping the perspiration off his neck, and striking himself upon the chest-wall.

Marinetti was a rich man. It was said that his father owned a lot of Alexandria and other ports in the Eastern Mediterranean. I do not know whether this was true. But he certainly had at his disposal very considerable funds.

'You are a futurist, Lewis!' he shouted at me one day, as we were passing into a lavabo together, where he wanted to wash after a lecture where he had drenched himself in sweat.

'No,' I said.

'Why don't you announce that you are a futurist!' he asked me squarely.

'Because I am not one,' I answered, just as pointblank and to the point.

'Yes. But what's it matter!' said he with great impatience.

'It's most important,' I replied rather coldly.

'Not at all!' said he. 'Futurism is good. It is all right.'

'Not too bad,' said I. 'It has its points. But you Wops insist too much on the Machine. You're always on about these driving-belts, you are always exploding about internal combustion. We've had machines here in England for a donkey's years. They're no novelty to *us*.'

'You have never understood your machines! You have never known the *ivresse* of travelling at a kilometre a minute. Have you ever travelled at a kilometre a minute?'

'Never.' I shook my head energetically. 'Never. I loathe anything that goes too quickly. If it goes too quickly, it is not there.'

'It is not there!' he thundered for this had touched him on the raw. 'It is *only* when it goes quickly that it *is* there!'

'That is nonsense,' I said. 'I cannot see a thing that is going too quickly.'

'See it—see it! Why should you want to *see*?' he exclaimed. 'But you *do* see it. You see it multiplied a thousand times. You see a thousand things instead of one thing.'

I shrugged my shoulders—this was not the first time I had had this argument.

34

'That's just what I don't want to see. I am not a futurist,'
I said. 'I prefer *one* thing.'

'There is no such thing as *one* thing.'

'There is if I wish to have it so. And I wish to have it so.'

'You are a monist!' he said at this, with a contemptuous
glance, curling his lip.

'All right. I am not a futurist anyway. *Je hais le mouvement
qui déplace les lignes.*'

At this quotation he broke into a hundred angry pieces.

'And you "never weep"—I know, I know. *Ah zut alors!*
What a thing to be an Englishman!'

This was the sort of thing that was going on the whole time.
And at last this man attempted a *Putsch* against the 'great
London Vortex'. He denounced me in letters to the Press, as
the major obstacle to the advance of Futurism in England. And
this was perfectly true. I 'stood in its path', as Sir Austen
Chamberlain would have said.

Then Mr. C. R. W. Nevinson attempted a *Putsch*. He
selected a sheet of 'Rebel Art Centre' notepaper. The 'Rebel
Art Centre' in Great Ormond Street, founded by Miss Lech-
mere and myself, was the seat of the 'Great London Vortex'.
Upon this notepaper Mr. C. R. W. Nevinson expressed Futurist
opinions; he too, I think, went over into the Press, and I had
to repudiate him as an interloper and a heretic.

I have said enough to show that the months immediately
preceding the declaration of war were full of sound and fury,
and that all the artists and men of letters had gone into action
before the bank-clerks were clapped into khaki and despatched
to the land of Flanders Poppies to do their bit. Life was one
big bloodless brawl, prior to the Great Bloodletting.

There was the next thing to barricades; there was everything short of Committees of Public Safety. Gaudier was spoil-
ing for a fight. He threatened at Ford's to sock Bomberg on the
jaw, and when I asked him why, he explained that he had an
imperfect control over his temper, and he must not be found
with Bomberg, for the manner adopted by that gentleman was

35

of a sort that put him beside himself. I had therefore to keep them apart. On the other hand I seized Hulme by the throat; but he transfixed me upon the railings of Soho Square. I never see the summer house in its centre without remembering how I saw it upside down. Mr Epstein and David Bomberg kissed, to seal a truce, beneath the former's 'Rockdrill' or similar fine piece of dynamic statuary. This was in the salons of the Goupil. And Mr. T. S. Eliot (that was just after the War, but no matter) challenged Mr. St. John Hutchinson to a duel, upon the sands at Calais. But the latter gentleman, now so eminent a K.C., replied that he was 'too afraid'. So he got the best of *that* encounter, as one would expect when a K.C. clashes with a poet.

The Press in 1914 had no Cinema, no Radio, and no Politics : so the painter could really become a 'star'. There was nothing against it. Anybody could become one, who did anything funny. And Vorticism was replete with humour, of course; it was acclaimed the best joke ever. Pictures, I mean oil-paintings, were 'news'. Exhibitions were reviewed in column after column. And no illustrated paper worth its salt but carried a photograph of some picture of mine or of my 'school', as I have said, or one of myself, smiling insinuatingly from its pages. To the photograph would be attached some scrap of usually quite misleading gossip; or there would be an article from my pen, explaining why life had to be changed, and how. 'Kill John Bull with Art!' I shouted. And John and Mrs. Bull leapt for joy, in a cynical convulsion. For they felt as safe as houses. So did I.

CHAPTER III

Some Specimen Pages of 'Blast' No. 1
(June 20, 1914)

It has occurred to me that since *Blast* was the centre of this disturbance, it might not be amiss to reproduce a few specimen pages. With a page-area of 12 inches by $9\frac{1}{2}$, this publication was of a bright puce colour. In general appearance it was not unlike a telephone book. It contained manifestoes, poems, plays, stories, and outbursts of one sort and another. I will not reproduce the major Manifesto (of the 'Great London Vortex') signed by R. Aldington, Aubuthnot, L. Atkinson, Gaudier Brzeska, J. Dismor, C. Hamilton, E. Pound, W. Roberts, H. Sanders, E. Wadsworth, Wyndham Lewis. That would be too long. Instead I will select a few random pages from the 'Blasts and Blesses'.

These manifestoes require, I suppose, in order to be popularly consumed, and at this distance of time, some explanation. Take the first *Blast,* 'Blast Humour'. That is straightforward enough. The Englishman has what he calls a 'sense of humour'. He says that the German, the Frenchman, and most foreigners do not possess this attribute, and suffer accordingly. For what does the 'sense of humour' mean but an ability to belittle everything— to make light of everything? Not only does the Englishman not 'make a mountain out of a molehill'; he is able *to make a molehill out of a mountain.* That is an invaluable magic to possess. The most enormous hobgoblin becomes a pigmy on the spot. Or such is the ideal of this destructive 'humorous' standpoint, which has played such a great part in anglosaxon life—just as its opposite, 'quixotry', has played a great part in Spanish life.

This manifesto was written (by myself) immediately before the War. And of course 'the sense of humour' played a very great part in the War. 'Old Bill' was the real hero of the World

War, on the English side, much more than any V.C. A V.C. is after all a fellow who does something heroic; almost unenglish. It is taking things a bit too seriously to get the V.C. The really popular fellow is the humorous Ole Bill à la Bairnsfather. And it was really 'Ole Bill' who won the war—with all that that expression 'won the war' implies.

Against the tyranny of the 'sense of humour', I, in true anglo-saxon fashion, humorously rebelled. That is all that 'Blast Humour' means. I still regard 'humour' as an exceedingly dangerous drug. I still regard it as, more often than not, an ignoble specific. In a word, I still 'blast' humour. (But then we come to the 'Blesses', and since there are two sides to every argument, you find me *blessing* what I had a moment before *blasted*. And example of English 'fairness'!)

Take my next *Blast*—namely, 'Blast years 1837 to 1900'. The triumph of the commercial mind in England, Victorian 'liberalism', the establishment of such apparently indestructible institutions as the English comic paper *Punch,* the Royal Academy, and so on—such things did not appeal to me, they appeal to me even less to-day, and I am glad to say more and more Englishmen share my antipathy. Boehm was, of course, the sculptor responsible for the worst of the bourgeois statuary which, prior to the war-sculptors, like Jagger, was the principle eyesore encountered by the foreign visitor to our 'capital of empire'. The 'eunuchs and stylists' referred to in this second manifesto would be the Paterists and Wildeites : and lastly the 'diabolics' of Swinburne are given a parting kick. For in 1914 there was still a bad hang-over from the puerile literary debauchery of that great Victorian who reacted against the 'non-conformist conscience'; who was 'naughty' before the 'Naughty Nineties' capped his sodawater wildness with a real live Oscar.

The third of these manifestoes (all of my composition) is 'Bless the Hairdresser'. That will be a little more difficult to understand. This might equally well have been headed 'Blast Fluffiness'. It exalts formality, and order, at the expense of the disorderly and the unkempt. It is merely a humorous way of stating the classic standpoint, as against the romantic. Need I

38

say that I am in complete agreement, here, with Mr. W. L. of 1914?

As to 'Bless England', that requires no explanation. Our 'Island home'! And 'Bless all Ports' is just a further outburst of benediction—more 'Island home' stuff. That winds up the specimen pages of the manifestoes from *Blast*. However, here they are, as far as possible produced in facsimile, though you lose the scale of the 12 in. high *Blast* page.

BLAST HUMOUR—

Quack ENGLISH drug for stupidity and sleepiness.

Arch enemy of REAL, conventionalizing like

> gunshot, freezing supple
> Real in ferocious chemistry
> of Laughter.

BLAST SPORT—

HUMOUR'S FIRST COUSIN AND ACCOMPLICE.

> impossibility for Englishman to be grave
> and keep his end up
> psychologically.
> impossible for him to use Humour
> as well and be *persistently*
> grave.
> Alas! necessity for the big doll's show
> in front of mouth.
> Visitation of Heaven on
> English Miss.
> gums, canines of FIXED GRIN
> Death's Head symbol of Anti-Life.

CURSE those who will hang over this

Manifesto with SILLY CANINES exposed.

BLAST—

years 1837 to 1900

CURSE Abysmal inexcusable middle-class

(also Aristocracy and Proletariat).

BLAST—

Pasty shadow cast by gigantic BOEHM

(imagined at introduction of BOURGEOIS VICTORIAN VISTAS).

WRING THE NECK OF all sick inventions born in that progressive white wake.

BLAST their weeping whiskers—hirsute

    RHETORIC of EUNUCH and STYLIST —

    SENTIMENTAL HYGIENICS

    ROUSSEAUISMS (wild nature cranks)

    DIABOLICS—

        —raptures and roses of

        the erotic bookshelves

        culminating in

        PURGATORY OF

        PUTNEY

BLESS the HAIRDRESSER.

He attacks Mother Nature for a small fee.

Hourly he ploughs heads for sixpence,

Scours chins and lips for threepence.

He makes systematic mercenary war on this

WILDERNESS.

He trims aimless and retrograde growths

into CLEAN ARCHED SHAPES AND ANGULAR PLOTS.

BLESS this HESSIAN (or SILESIAN) EXPERT

correcting the grotesque anachronisms

of our physique.

BLESS ENGLISH HUMOUR
It is the great barbarous weapon of
the genius among races.
The wild MOUNTAIN RAILWAY from IDEA
to IDEA, in the ancient Fair of LIFE.
BLESS SWIFT for his solemn bleak
   wisdom of laughter.
SHAKESPEARE for his bitter NORTHERN
   Rhetoric of Humour.
BLESS ALL ENGLISH EYES
   that grow crows-feet with their
   FANCY and ENERGY.

   BLESS this hysterical WALL build round
   the EGO.
   BLESS the solitude of LAUGHTER.
   BLESS the Separating, ungregarious
     BRITISH GRIN.

BLESS ENGLAND—

which switchback on BLUE, GREEN and
RED SEAS all round the PINK EARTH-BALL
BIG BETS ON EACH.

BLESS ALL SEAFARERS—

THEY exchange not one LAND for another, but one ELEMENT
for ANOTHER. THE MORE against the LESS ABSTRACT.

———————————

BLESS the vast planetary abstraction of the OCEAN.

———————————

BLESS the Arabs of the ATLANTIC.
This Island Must be Contrasted With the Bleak Waves.

———————————

44

BLESS ALL PORTS—

PORTS, RESTLESS MACHINES of scooped out basins
     heavy insect dredgers
     monotonous cranes
     stations
     lighthouses. blazing
       through the frosty
       starlight, cutting the
       storm like a cake
     beaks of infant boats,
       side by side,
     heavy chaos of
      wharves,
    steep walls of
     factories
    womanly town

BLESS these MACHINES that work the little boats across clean
   liquid space in beelines.

BLESS the great PORTS

   HULL

   LIVERPOOL

   LONDON

   NEWCASTLE-ON-TYNE

   BRISTOL

   GLASGOW

BLESS ENGLAND, industrial island machine, pyramidal
workshop, its apex at Shetland, discharging itself on the sea.

BLESS cold

  magnanimous

  delicate

  gauche

  fanciful

  stupid

           ENGLISHMEN.

CHAPTER IV

'Britannia's hard on the Lions'

Blast appeared on June 20th, 1914. There was not long to go until the 'fog of war' came down. The actual blaze of publicity was therefore brief. Before that, for say a year, publicity had been accumulating about my head. *Blast* gave the finishing touch. Then I fell into anonymity. I became the Bombardier. Though even in that capacity, as you have seen, my publicity pursued me.

I didn't become a Bombardier at once. For the first nine months of the war I was *hors de combat*—either with respect to this new description of Combat, or mortal combat, or what still remained of play-boy operations upon the art-front in the preliminary sham-war. I had been poisoned and had got some infection. *Tarr* was written, a War *Blast* appeared. I lived at No. 4 Percy Street, much in the company of Captain Guy Baker attempting to rid myself of this trouble without operations, part of the time in bed. And then I enlisted.

Now especially in the weeks succeeding the publication of *Blast,* and less intensively for a number of months prior to that, I passed my time in the usual way when a 'Lion' is born. I saw a great deal of what is called 'society'.

Everyone by way of being fashionably interested in art, and many who had never opened a book or bought so much as a sporting-print, much less 'an oil', wanted to look at this new oddity, thrown up by that amusing spook, the Zeitgeist. So the luncheon and dinner-tables of Mayfair were turned into show-booths. For a few months I was on constant exhibition. I cannot here enumerate all the sightseers, of noble houses or of questionable Finance, who passed me under review. They were legion. Coronetted envelopes showered into my letter-box. The editor of *Blast* must at all costs be viewed; and its immense puce

46

cover was the standing joke in the fashionable drawing-room, from Waterloo Place to the border-line in Belgravia.

It was extremely instructive. As a result of these sociable activities I did not sell a single picture, it is perhaps superfluous to say. But it was an object-lesson in the attitude of what remained of aristocratic life in England to the arts I practised. This lesson I took to heart; and the war concluded, I have never, except for an occasional outburst of lunching and dining, entered upon for some strictly limited purpose, consorted with what Mr. Arlen called 'those delightful people'.

As a practical person, and devoid of any emotional bias, I can assert that the district south of the Marble Arch but north of the Ritz, and enclosed on the east and west by Regent Street and Park Lane, is strictly speaking useless to anybody, unless they have an appetite for a sort of bogus 'high-life'—or it *was,* I perhaps should say. For at present it is plastered with TO LET notices. The Great Slump delivered the *coup de grâce.* Mayfair is no more.

As ever—for we have literary history to prove it—these good people of the British *beau monde* looked upon an artist as an oddity, to be lion-hunted from expensive howdahs. In the snobbish social sunset of 1914 I did my stuff, I flatter myself, to admiration. As regards the poor results of all this publicity I was easily the most good-natured 'lion' that ever stepped. The people I met entertained me as much as I entertained them. Rapidly I understood that the champagne of luncheon tables and the vulgar paraphernalia of butlers and druggets were all that was to be got out of them. But this nursery of almost mindless spoilt-children was a sort of barren accolade, of a farcical celebrity. Good-humouredly I accepted it; for, indirectly, it might serve the cause of 'rebel' or of 'abstract' art and revolutionary letters, I reflected. I was content to starve on champagne and caviare for a season. And then came down on top of all of us the greatest war of all time: came Heartbreak House, came Red Revolution, came everything that you would expect to come, upon such a long-established blank of genteel fatuity.

Besides, I had been warned. Roger Fry had told me, and

47

what he did not know in that connection was not worth know-
ing, that he had never encountered a rich person of unmitigated
British stock who had been of any service to him as a 'patron'.
Supporters of his ventures in the arts had never been the typical
inmates of Mayfair. Always it had been an American, or
Russian, or Irish, or Jewish importation.

Then again, I remembered a dream which Augustus John
had recounted to me. It was about the time of my first meeting
with that standard celebrity. He had dreamed, he said, that he
was conversing with a society woman of astonishing brilliance,
who was so witty that his dream scintillated with the most
unexpected retorts and sallies. All he could recall of them,
however, upon waking up, was *one* saying, *'Britannia's hard
on the lions!'*

Britannia's hard on the lions! That was what the lion
dreamed! And it was true to the letter. Very hard indeed,
though uncommonly charming of course in the hard-boiled
English fashion.

And if I had benefited from the experience of the living,
the dead had told me the same tale. Voltaire and David Hume,
to take at random two distant figures, had shocks of the same
sort : David Hume returning to the capital of Scotland cursing
the 'grinning barbarians who dwell by the side of the Thames';
Voltaire amazed to find a great man-of-letters ashamed to be
one, and desirous only of being taken as a typical 'man-about-
town'. Or, if Disraeli is considered a more level-headed witness, he may be cited equally well. So let us turn to *Coningsby*.

'Nothing strikes me more in this brilliant city (Paris)
than the tone of its society, so much higher than our own.
What an absence of petty personalities! How much conversation, and how little gossip! . . . Men, too, and great
men, develop their minds. A great man in England, on the
contrary, is generally the dullest dog in company. . . .

There is, indeed, throughout every circle of Parisian
society, from the *château* to the *cabaret,* a sincere homage
to intellect; and this without any maudlin sentiment. None
sooner than the Parisians can draw the line between facti-

tious notoriety and honest fame; or sooner distinguish between the counterfeit celebrity and the standard reputation. In England we too often alternate a supercilious neglect of genius and a rhapsodical pursuit of quacks.'

This is possibly the reason why in England 'genius' is obliged to affect the methods of the quack, in order to survive at all. And it is quite certain that what happened to me, in those first days of furious junketing, was that I was mistaken for a quack; it can only have been that.

However, I was thoroughly prepared as you see : I was not surprised, luckily, when I became a lion, to find this gilded Tamer a tough customer. I began studying her ways with curiosity, this spoilt and cocksure goddess of the ocean wave. I filled a notebook with Stendhalian observations.

CHAPTER V

The Prime Minister and Myself, 1914

In my last chapter I have been describing how the richest society in the world reacts to its lions, and how its lions react for the most part to this society. But all the people I met at that time, before and after that comic earthquake, *Blast,* were not true to type. And all the people I met, as a consequence of my sudden fame, were not the standard inhabitants of Mayfair. Some lived east of Regent Street, and some south of the Ritz. The most interesting society in London was not in Mayfair at all.

There was Lady Ottoline Morrell, for instance; sister of the Duke of Portland, a *grande dame* of Bloomsbury, and whose destiny had been involved with that of so many distinguished people: who has been a friend of D. H. Lawrence, of Mr. Augustus John, of Mr. Aldous Huxley, of Mr. W. B. Yeats. She held crowded receptions in her house in Bedford Square. Those great parties, of fashion and 'intellect' mixed in equal measure, would have satisfied, I am sure, even milord Beaconsfield.

The old Liberal society was then still intact, with Asquith for its political figurehead. And Asquith was of course Prime Minister. So actually the people who were the most alive were the people who were in power. They plunged England into an unprecedentedly destructive and unsuccessful war, they were the people who accepted and worked the *Entente Cordiale* policy of Edward VII. But upon the social side they contrasted very favourably with the Baldwins and Macdonalds who have come after them—and whose policies look as if they might exceed in destructiveness even those of 'Encirclement' No. 1.

It was at Lady Ottoline's that I met for the first time Lord Oxford, then Mr. Asquith and Prime Minister. As to his personality, it was that of a cultivated old clergyman, or he inhabited a borderland where Law and Divinity met. And he certainly had the manners a little (with me) of an investigating attorney, tempered with the courteous mildness of a lettered sky-pilot. I might have been a client of his—a client whom he regarded with considerable mental reserve. And he would sit down beside me and start his questions, as if resolved to thoroughly go into the case, incessantly pulling at his nose, as if he were taking snuff.

Mr. Asquith unquestionably displayed a marked curiosity regarding the 'Great London Vortex', in which he seemed to think there was more than met the eye. He smelled politics beneath this revolutionary artistic technique. I, of course, was quite at a loss to understand what he was driving at. That it should be suspected that an infernal machine was hidden in the midst of the light-hearted mockery of my propaganda was to me fantastic. I was cross-questioned at length about my principles. I remember especially that he asked me 'whether I was in touch with people of similar views in other countries'. Yes, I admitted, I had corresponded with continental painters, critics and men of letters. He nodded his head thoughtfully at this. It was obvious it gave him food for thought. Here was a movement masking itself beneath the harmless trappings of the fine arts, and camouflaged as a fashionable stunt of the studios, but with wide ramifications in all countries, and with unavowed political objectives. It cracked jokes, attached to it was a technical mumbo-jumbo to rattle and hoodwink the fashionable crowd. Its so called pictures looked like plastic cyphers or properties of the magician. And here was its high-priest! A pale, tall, exceedingly romantic looking young fellow, who was civil, good-humoured, and quite impenetrable. This learned P.M. was reminded of illuminism, doubtless. He thought of the *philosophes*. He saw in 'the Vortex' a political portent. His attitude to it, and to me, was that of an expert on his mettle, confronted with a political crossword-puzzle of the greatest ingenuity.

I was, I protest again, completely innocent of all political motives. I saw that if London was to be pulled down (and this

I advocated, and still advocate) that vested interests would be involved. That much was evident, but even of that I was not over-conscious. While I was full of the problem of 'Ancient Lights', the mind of the politician, in the nature of things, was busy with the question of the Royal Prerogative, the Mutiny Act, a Second Chamber : of *coup d'états* and of the Rights of Man. I was thinking of a little tube of paint, of Emerald Oxide of Chromium, with which I had just worked wonders. He was thinking of secret reports of torpedo tubes, say, in 'mystery' U-boats, and of the subtle attack upon the European order by the back-door—of the studio, the study, and the newspaper office. I was turning over in my mind the duel of Otto Kreisler, in my novel *Tarr* : but the politician had a whole nation of Teutons on his hands or knew he soon would.

And to these misunderstandings, which I believe I detected; Mr. Pound, now, he may have been preoccupied with Platonic ideologies, with Fourrierism, or the proto-fascist arguments of Sorel. He may have exchanged letters in code with Lenin in Switzerland, for all I know. But for my part I was an artist, first and last. I was concerned with the externals of life, in conformity with my innate habit of mind, not with its mechanics. I was the expert who had been called in by the Caliph (as is described in my *Caliph's Design*)—or who had called himself in. But the Prime Minister of England in 1914 could not be expected to accept this simple explanation. For the destruction of a capital city is a highly political operation. And these blasting operations, so clamorously advocated, suggested dissatisfaction with the regime as well as with the architecture of the houses. And 'Kill John Bull With Art!' The title of one of my most notorious articles—there was a jolly piece of sansculottism. What could that mean, if it did not point to tumbril and tocsin?

Subsequently I had other conversations with Mr. Asquith, all of which followed the same lines. He would sight me, at a party or reception, an expression of polite intelligence would light up his face, he would come up to me with a flattering purposefulness, he would make a few discreet inquiries about my activities, as if these had been a little secret between the

Prime Minister and myself. Although what he *mentioned* was mere painted 'futurist' absurdities, this was as it were a code. We were in fact discussing matters of far more import. I might almost have been the member of a powerful secret society. I could not have had bestowed upon me a more attentive regard if I had been. It is probably a fact that Prime Ministers never quite know to whom they may not be talking—if half is true what they tell us about these subterranean sects. He may even have thought that I was an *Arch-dragon,* of the Kahal or something, who can say? Anyhow, it was very agreeable.

Not very long before the War I went to lunch at 10 Downing Street. It was in the room decorated under instructions from Disraeli, I believe. All I remember is that there were a great number of Asquiths present. It was perhaps some family celebration. Elizabeth Asquith, now Princess Bibesco (not the Paris one) was very dark and handsome, reminding me of Mr. Augustus John's more aristocratic gypsies, very solemn and upright at the luncheon table.

The last occasion upon which I saw Lord Oxford was in the latter part of the War. I was on leave from the Front, and was invited to be one of a great dinner-party given by Lady Cunard at Claridges Hotel. There was no one there but myself who was not a great political or social luminary, and I was the only one of the guests in uniform—the only one of military age, or not of cabinet or viceregal rank. This was a very great honour, and an occasion from which I drew a great deal of instruction. Lord Curzon, Lord Oxford, Lord Hardinge, were there: Mr. H. A. L. Fisher, the Minister of Education, next to whose very amiable wife I sat.

After dinner all these miscellaneous magnates moved about and talked with one another. Lord Oxford observed me, and crossed the room to greet me and have his usual chat. This time I was a soldier. Unquestionably a suspicious circumstance! What could I be next? And then my rank. A second Lieutenant? Curiouser and curiouser! One star upon the shoulder? Oddly modest!—for one with so many opportunities of pulling strings and getting influence exerted!

I thought I detected a new inquisitiveness. Of course I may

have been entirely wrong, all this is pure conjecture. What was I in? Ah, yes, the Artillery. A pause. (There was much phantom snuff-taking.)—Been at the Front, or was I perhaps—? Yes, at the Front.—Ah, at the Front.—A pause.—Just back from the Front? Yes just back. From the *real* Front (I forget how this was put).—Ay, from the real Front, where shells were bursting all the time and where Death stood at everybody's elbow! (Though I did not say that—that was how the 'non-combatant' who had not 'been there' would think of it.)—Having informed himself as to that, and established the fact that for some reason best known to myself I had gone to live in the Valley of the Shadow, he hastily changed the subject. The most talented of his own sons had been killed in action and death was everywhere. The 'Front' was not a subject upon which one dwelt. One turned one's back on war, upon this unspeakable scandal. And Lord Oxford, though he had got into a war, was not the man to continue in it happily, or to see others 'winning' it with complacency. But I feel sure that there was something about all this that planted the seeds of further inquisitive, idle, question-marks in the capacious recesses of his mind. What was I doing *here*? What had I been doing as an obscure second loot in 'the Trenches' over there? That I was alone, in this hand-picked throng of great personages, in humblest khaki, masquerading as a simple 'gunner'—a sort of Unknown Soldier decorated with one star, no more, representing no great interest, social or political, was an eccentricity of 'Maud's' perhaps. Or perhaps I was not what I seemed, on the other hand. Perhaps I *was* the Boojum!

Lord Curzon I observed at one time sitting by himself on a sofa, with the twisted grimace of painful, staring, rumination which seemed characteristic of him. Afterwards, when this very able administrator and ambitious statesman, with all the typical virtues of the artistocrat, was passed over for Earl Baldwin, I called to mind the pessimistic figure upon the sofa at the party at Claridges. Certainly whenever I saw Lord Curzon he had a fixed look that bordered on distress, as if he had pre-figured what was in store for him. Doubtless he knew all along that the dice were loaded against him. He understood that men of his open and unbending stamp in England are never allowed to reach the highest offices of state. Those are reserved for birds of another and duller feather. Such men are too proud, they are not sufficiently pliant : they do not make ideal servants, and are from the start suspect in the Bankers Olympus. 'Power!' he burst out on one occasion, when some individual who wanted something done reminded him that he had the necessary *power* at least to put it through, if he wanted to : 'Why, I have not the power to send an office boy across Whitehall!' And that was before he was excluded from the supreme office of state, when everyone expected he would receive it, when everything pointed to him as the appropriate person to occupy it.

CHAPTER VI

In Berwickshire, August, 1914

There is one great exception, to everything disobliging that must be said regarding Mayfair. That exception is the embodiment of it in a sense. And yet she is the great exception that proves the rule. I refer to Lady Cunard.

I shall have occasion to return to this celebrated 'hostess' later on. Great last-ditcher that she is, there she bravely holds out, in a corner of Grosvenor Square—in spite of fires, supertax, more and more derelict conditions, in this decaying landscape, with TO LET boards and dusty shutters all about her. Lady Cunard is not only intelligent, of superlative party-wit, a live wire in the realm of music, a keen politician, but a very good-hearted person—a 'classless' virtue. No grim sensations of bored foreboding assail you when you receive an invitation to her house. Credit to whom credit is due! Since I am engaged in such a chronicle as this, I had better effect this little piece of social salvage!

Amongst the people I came across immediately before the War, who were not of Mayfair, or in any case not the standard fashionable article, was a very attractive American, of the name of Mrs. Turner. Since then she has become the wife of General Spears, and is best known as Mary Borden, which was her maiden name. The attractive freshness of the New World, and of a classless community, cut her out in the bogus Eighteenth Century Mayfair décor, as a vivid silhouette.

It was at the house of Mrs. Turner, under the shadow of Westminster Abbey, that I met for the first time Mr. Bernard Shaw. I went with Mr. and Mrs. Shaw to the Opera, I recollect though I cannot for the life of me recall a single utterance for which Mr. Shaw was accountable, to make the meeting other than a dry fact. I just met Mr. Shaw at luncheon. He asked me or Mrs. Shaw asked me to go to the Opera. I went. That is all. We undoubtedly conversed. We must have done so. But he did not say 'Britannia's hard on the lions', or anything striking of that order. He seemed a very faded figure to me. Perhaps at the time he was not well, for I met him later on and he was much more lively. And I suppose, realizing that I took no interest, he took no interest. It must have been as it were a mutual blank.

Some weeks or so before the War appeared on the horizon, I went up to Berwickshire to stay with Mary Borden, or Mrs. Turner, who had rented a country-house across the Border where a large house-party was in progress. Her husband, a Scottish missionary of great charm, was with her, and Mr. and Mrs. Ford Madox Hueffer. Mrs. Hueffer was Violet Hunt, the once famous author of *White Rose of Weary Leaf*.

I do not know when I first became conscious of the possibility of such an immense contretemps as a General War. Not at all, I think, until the war was well under way.

In any case, when I first began to notice that that War, that *Dreadnoughts* meant—England and Germany building ship for ship, against each other—that the effect of that cause was about to declare itself, I felt but a slight tremor of interest. What it portended for me, to go no farther, I had not the remotest idea. 'War', was a word for me only. It was a history-book word.

However farseeing I had been, though, and competent in assessing war-risk, I could not have foreseen the great social revolution in Russia, which lurked behind the 'Great War', as a yet more furibund shadow, and which made even of the European War a bagatelle. And as to *the Peace*—unless the Peace was all plotted and planned beforehand, too, as we are assured the War was, that surely no one could have prefigured. No one—here I feel I must be on certain ground—could have foreseen the vindictive dismemberment of Hungary for instance— the deliberate political annihilation of a strong state to provide an artificial volume for a weak state—everywhere a starving of the healthy organism, and a gorging of the sick, so as to put a premium on the second-rate. The insane attempt to stultify and hamstring *forever* all that was robust, industrious, intelligent, in Europe, and put in the place of the real the unreal. These

57

c

barbarous triumphs of 'democracy' I should have been a seer indeed to imagine. In short, had I been able to see Armageddon Number one, I could at least not have foreseen Armageddon Number two, which is now bearing down on us; a coming home to roost of all the Peace Treaties.

Gradually I became aware, by the greater attentiveness with which everyone read the papers in the morning, and in the evening, too, when they came in from Duns, that something was happening. Without much perserverance, I began looking at the papers, too. And then came the first yard-high newspaper headlines, announcing the first ULTIMATUM.

A conversation occurred at breakfast between Mrs. Turner and Ford Madox Hueffer, to which I listened with surprise, Mrs. Turner was emphatic; she seemed very sure of her ground. I remember admiring her political sagacity.

'There won't be any war, Ford. Not here. England won't go into a war.'

Ford thrust his mouth out, fish-fashion, as if about to gasp for breath. He goggled his eyes and waggled one eyelid about. He just moved his lips a little and we heard him say, in a breathless sotto voce—

'England will.' He had said that already. He passed his large protruding blue eyes impassively over the faces of these children—absorbed in their self-satisfied eras of sheltered peace.

'England will! But Ford,' said Mrs. Turner, 'England has a Liberal Government. A Liberal Government cannot declare war.'

'Of course it can't,' I said, frowning at Ford. 'Liberal Governments can't go to war. That would not be liberal. That would be conservative.'

Ford sneered very faintly and inoffensively : he was sneering at the British Government, rather than at us. He was being omniscient, bored, sleepy Ford, sunk in his tank of sloth. From his prolonged sleep he was staring out at us with his fish-blue eyes—kind, wise, but bored. Or some such idea. His mask was only just touched with derision at our childishness.

'Well, Ford,' said Mrs. Turner, bantering the wise old elephant. 'You don't agree!'

'I don't agree,' Ford answered, in his faintest voice, with consummate indifference, 'because it has always been the Liberals who have gone to war. It is *because* it is a Liberal Government that it *will* declare war.'

And of course, as we all know, a Liberal Government *did* declare it. Within a few days of the period of those country house conversations Great Britain was at war, within a year or so Britain had become so many Heartbreak Houses; and the British Empire, covered in blood, was gasping its way through an immense and disastrous war, upon which it should never have entered.

But I understood as little about all that as the peacocks at the Zoo. Only slowly it dawned on me that something overwhelmingly unsuitable had come to pass; and that my friend, Life, was somehow treacherous and not at all the good sport and 'square-shooter' I had supposed him to be.

After breakfast Ford read the other papers in the Hall. Coming down from my room and going towards the main house-door, Ford put down his paper and held out his hand.

'Help me up, there's a good chap,' he panted, with a pained discomfort. He liked being helped up from chairs by people over whom he exercised any authority, by nobodies or juniors. He got on his feet with a limp, as though he had stuck together. He shook. He stood still, his feet pointing flatly to the right and left.

'When will the car be ready?' he asked, in his soft-panting 'diplomatic' nasal undertone.

'I'm just going to see.'

'I'll come with you,' said Ford.

The car was just outside the door. Ford lit one eye, his teeth appeared through his walrus moustache, he nodded, and went and had a jolly companionable talk with the chauffeur. Soon the guests had collected. They went to play golf: I left them near the town, and went into it alone to get the latest papers.

PART II
Declaration of War

CHAPTER 1

I Hand Over my Self-Portrait to my Colleague of 'Blast'

My life as an artist and my life as a soldier intertwine, in this unaffected narrative. I show, too, going from the particular to the general, how War and Art in those days mingled, the features of the latter as stern as—if not sterner than—the former. This book is Art—War—Art, in three panels. War is the centre panel. But for me it was only a part of Art : my sort of life—the life of the 'intellect'—come to life. A disappointing imitation. I preferred the real thing : namely Art.

So we have, at the end of the last chapter, a breakfast table in Scotland, a few days off war, with a political ignoramus (myself) being instructed by Ford Madox Hueffer in the paradoxical *necessity* of war, just because a liberal government was there, and it is always a liberal government that makes war. In consulting my boxfuls of letters, laundry bills, sketchbooks and articles, dating from this period, in order to get a bit of local colour into this self-portrait, I remarked (with astonishment) that I was by no means a fool. I did see a thing or two that I shouldn't have expected myself to see. Here and there I am staggered by my clairvoyance.

Is it not remarkable how a couple of psyches can inhabit the same body? Have you ever noticed that? I mean, you can be, at the same time, quite acute and quite obtuse. It is possible, for instance, to be perfectly aware that a man is untrustworthy, and yet trust him implicitly. You trust him : and he rifles your drawer and makes off with the fiver you have dropped into it (while he was observing you). You are very surprised. Looking back on it, however, you realize that you never, in fact, trusted him at all. As you popped the fiver into the drawer, you *knew* he would take it. It's odd isn't it?

Life was good and easy, and I called Life 'friend'. I'd never hidden anything from him, and he'd never hidden anything from me. Or so I thought. I knew everything. He was an awfully intelligent companion, we had the same tastes (apparently) and he was awfully fond of me. And all the time he was plotting up a mass-murder. I had been on terms of intimacy with Crippen or Nana Sahib.

It took me some to realize this *fully*. But from the very beginning of the War I got wise to it, in fits and starts. I saw I'd got into rather shady company the moment he pulled out his gun and started shooting.

In the first months of the War I attempted to keep the home fires burning. With the sublimest misunderstanding of the sort of situation I was confronted with I decided on 'business as usual'—along with the *Daily Mail*. I brought out a Number Two of my paper *Blast*. But that, even, was surprisingly intelligent considering. And everyone else being as stupid as I was, it went quite well. It was a 'war number'.

The observations in this War Number were shrewd, considering. In reading it over just now, I rubbed my eyes. And I cannot improve on the account given there of 'how the war came' and how we all took it.

The only trouble about it is that for such an autobiography as the present, it is somewhat highbrow. This is not a potboiling self-portrait. But it is meant to be pretty plain-sailing. And no more highbrow publication ever saw the light in England than *Blast*.

Still, to do a true *self-portrait* one must put in the highbrow, mustn't one, being of that ilk? It's no use cutting down those towering temples to an ape-like shallowness of brow. To get a *likeness* must be our constant endeavour. And since this is a portrait of a great highbrow, at a certain moment of his life, we must not shrink from writing a bit over the head of the Clubman on occasion.

Besides, what I have dug up in *Blast* does register with surprising sharpness first-hand impressions of the opening stages of a great war. You ought to know about the opening stages of a great war. It is a first-hand impression, of butcher-like directness, but translated into what may seem to you horrid language. It makes a dream and a lullaby of those dark happenings, which plunged us like a school of pet gold fish, out of our immaculate 'pre-war' tank, into the raging ocean.

Up in Scotland there was an Olympiad, it seems. Macbeth's witches had gathered at Sarajevo, to preside at a diabolical brew beside which the plots of Shakespeare were storms-in-teacups. Scotland was free of all such presences at the moment, Morpeth living in the golden age.

Meanwhile I watched the papers coming in from London with their crashing headlines. Also I saw the flaming posters of the great Morpeth sporting event. Here, in a sort of diary form, with a fictional character to be the diarist, is my contemporary account of these events.

I will hand over the controls to Cantleman. For a chapter or two I will abandon my narrative in the first person singular. You shall see these things as I saw them, yes, but out of the eyes of a mask marked 'Cantleman'. When he stops speaking (which will be after the declaration of war, in London) I shall take up the narrative again.

C•

CHAPTER II

Morpeth Olympiad

(The account of the British Mobilization from the pages of *Blast*)

MORPETH OLYMPIAD RECORD CROWD

Wonderful Crowds, gathering at Olympiads! What is the War to you? It is you who makes both the wars and the Olympiads. When War knocks at the door, why should you hurry? You are busy with an Olympiad!

Cantleman[1] looked at the perfidious poster, announcing the Olympiad, and reflected as above, in a sombre amazement. The crude violet lettering, distillation of suffragetic years of minor violence! Celebrated for minor violence, too, was *he,* a rough Bohemian—he savoured violence for its own sake, as a coarse joke, or the crepitation of a chinese cracker. He was not a man of blood.—He did not understand—he was very stupid. He was a suffragette.[2]

Eager for news, he went into a shop and got all the big popular London papers, *Mails* and *Expresses*, the loudest shouters of the lot. How they hollered 'War' to a thrilled universe! He found all his horizons, by the medium of this yellow journalism, turned into a sinister sulphur. He was as pleased as Punch.

Ah, the grand messengers of death, the three-inch capitals! With the words came a dark rush of hot humanity in his mind. An immense human gesture swept its shadows across him like a

[1] This was my character, my fictional diarist, the hero of several stories of that time.

[2] I've just put this in. The editor of *Blast* would never have admitted that he was a suffragette. I've had to put a lot more in, too. I've toned him down.

smoky cloud. 'Germany declares war on Russia' seemed a roar of guns. He saw active mephistophelian specks in Chancelleries —'diplomats' like old Leo.[1] He saw a rush of papers, a frowning race. He saw it with innate military exultation. His ancestor had stood beside Clive. His grandfather had served under Outram. The ground seemed to sway a little, as it would with the passage of a Juggernaut, or a proud and ponderous Express. He left the paper shop, gulping this big morsel down, with stony dignity.

The party at the golf links took his *News, Mails* and *Mirrors,* as the run home started. Each manifested his gladness at the bad news in his own inimitable way, every shade of British restraint, *phlegm,* and matter-of-factness.

Would Old England declare War? Leo said *yes,* 'she' would. But Cantleman was all for 'her' not being a silly girl. She would keep out of it, as she always had, said he, the crafty old shop-keeping hussy! But the 'yeas' had it—if you counted in the back of the chauffeur. That back, with the melancholy wisdom of the working man, could only think one thing: namely that whatever was *bad* for the general run of men would probably be done. He knew 'England' better than the others—he had no illusions about 'her'. (He knew there was no 'her' at all, to start with.) His highspirited masters would probably decide to blow his head off—he had learned that in a hard school. If it lay between letting him alone, and dragging him away to death in battle, almost certainly they would choose the latter course. They were like that. The silent back of the liveried servant said all and more than that. His lips were sealed, but his back was eloquent.

The news brought into relief a novel system of things. Everything was going to be delightfully *different.* There was the closing of the Stock Exchange. What would happen as regards the Banks? Would there be a shortage of small change? No sixpence for a shoe-black, or penny to buy a paper! A host of fascinating contretemps presented themselves to the readers of the newspapers as the car rushed along. Food supplies had better be laid in at once. And what of course of *invasion?* What a change an

[1] Leo was Ford of course.

invasion would be! Back to William the Conqueror! The exciting novelties foreshadowed pleased everybody, such a delicious earthquake made children of the party, and Leo was the biggest kid of the lot, in his knowing, fishlike way. For of course *he* ought to have known better! And yet he was a great big *gourmand* for sensation was he not!

The next few days was a gay carnival of fear, or conventional horror. The Morpeth Olympiad poster was secured and stuck up in the hall—an adequate expression, it was felt, of the greatness of the English Nation.

Then the news stopped. All the London newspapers began to be bought up in Edinburgh, and none ever got as far as this remote countryside. The 'cloud of war' had begun to descend already. So the trees and flowers and the bucolic amenities lost all their meaning. Even the Morpeth Olympiad poster began to pall and to take on a silly air and the servants became less wooden as backstairs hysteria developed.

(Note. At this point the heroic Cantleman, of my simple story, abruptly leaves the house-party—just as I did myself, as a matter of fact: though of course the details of this diary must not be identified too closely with its original in life. But as I cannot imagine a better account than that provided by Mr. Cantleman of these events, I will continue with that fictional person.)

CHAPTER III

Journey during Mobilization

C. left Scotland by the night train, on the second day of the
British mobilization order. There was a half-hour wait at Ged-
des station, where he joined the midnight train from Edinburgh.
Upon the platform two English youths in khaki leant upon their
rifles. Several persons arrived in a larger car. One was a very tall
man and rather fat—a man of influence. He moved up to the
stationmaster, who touched his cap with a robust respect. For
some minutes they stood talking; scraps of confidential news, no
doubt, which a station-master might be supposed to know, and
is prepared to impart to an influential traveller.

Cantleman watched the new arrivals with a certain haughty
dislike. In his dress and appearance nautical and priestly at the
same time—a sky-pilot with a master's certificate, gone
Bohemian—he stood guard over a couple of much-labelled suit-
cases. His eye registered with hauteur and distaste the public-
schoolboyish puppy-play of the lesser newcomers.—Officers
packing off southward to their depots a little late? He supposed
so.

'Stupid fat slob!' he reflected, at the tallest and eldest, in
conference with the station-master. 'I prefer the Prussian officer.
He does at least read Clausewitz. He is conversant with the
philosophy of his machine-made moustaches. When he does
something unsuitable he knows what he is doing, and why he
is doing it!' He scowled at the officer-class in the abstract, as
turned out by Arnold of Rugby. 'Arrogant and crafty sheep!'
he said to himself quietly and coldly, as his eye dwelt upon the
fresh and open schoolboy faces. 'Pfui! A la lanterne!'

Talk about conscription being good for the physical health
of the conscripted nation! Better, in the case of *this* nation, to
conscript their mental facilities, say I. See if *they* could be

69

smartened up a bit! Happily the 'masses' are not in such need of it as these monied mutts. Hard conditions keep the souls of the poor in better trim—if not their minds. Doctor Arnold (among others) was responsible for a soul-less nation.

But the train came melodramatically into the station, out of the north, and Cantleman entered it, armed with his bags.

Sailors were sprawled about in most of the compartments. He experienced a brotherly attraction for these coarse sea-animals, and sat down with the curly head of one practically in his lap.

Mobilization was everywhere; the train was quite full. Ten people, chiefly women, slept upright against each other in one carriage. They revealed unexpected fashions in sleep. Their eyes seemed to be shut fast to enable them to examine some ludicrous fact within. It looked, from the corridor, like a séance of imbeciles.

He decided to transfer. The sailors would probably wake up at the hours of the watches: he would sleep better among the vegetative shapes of the women. He forced two grunting bodies apart and joined in the female seance.

He fell asleep. When he woke he was evidently upon a bridge. Newcastle-on-Tyne, he found it was. There were sentries on the bridge. It might be blown up otherwise—we were almost at war, and already spies were speeding towards all bridges with infernal machines ready for use. Stacks of rifles on the railway platform. More 'mobilization scenes', to delight the *Mail* or *Mirror*.

There were no sailors in this carriage, but the ten or so sleeping people, travelling through England on this important and dramatic night, must be connected in some way with mobilization. They seemed quite indifferent, however, to what was afoot. Stuck up against each other, they looked as if they were mobilized every week or so. Disagreeable, no doubt but they had grown accustomed to it.

Newcastle woke them up with a banging of doors. They stared glassily at it, but without disturbing the symmetry of their *tableau vivant*. A squat seafaring figure in a stiff short coat got in. Cantleman made room for him. Six a side made a

70

more massive effect than five, and no one was in a mood of aloofness at this juncture of Britain's history! The newcomer aimed his stern at the fissure between Cantleman's and the neighbouring body. He began a gradual sinking movement, towards the seat. He reached it a short time after the train had restarted.

This was not an attractive man. As he was on the way down to the seat he even showed a certain truculence. As it were defiantly, he announced that he was answering *a mobilization call*. The implication was that such a man had a right to be seated. He must have something to do with the Navy's food, thought Cantleman.

'I'm not travelling for pleasure,' said the fellow later on, in a harsh and angry voice, looking at Cantleman with a bloodshot eye. 'No, I'm called up, I've been called up.'

'I guessed that,' said C.

'You did, did you! Yes, what are we going for—can you tell me that?' That Cantleman could not guess. He shook his head. 'Why, to take the place of other men, as soon as they're shot down!'

The trenchant hissing of the 'soon' and 'shot down' woke up one or two of the women, who looked at him resentfully out of one eye.

'The Kayser ought to be bloody well shot!' he went on.

'He's a bad emperor,' agreed Cantleman.

'Bad! He's worse than bad!'

'He's a wretched emperor,' said Cantleman, soothingly.

'He's bin getting ready for this 'ere for twenty years. Now he's going to have what he's bin askin' for. Hot and heavy— a-ah! Spendin' his private fortune on it, he has. For twenty years. He'll get it where the chicken got the chopper! Shootin's too good for his kind.'

'Who?' asked Cantleman.

'Why the Kayser,' the man roared out suspiciously. 'Who did you think I meant? Napoleon Boneypart!'

This fellow was round fifty, like a hardfeatured Prussian. *Must* be connected with catering, to be so bellicose! thought Cantleman. A sea-grocer? The white apron of the German

71

delicatessen-butcher fitted him, in the mind's eye. Did battleships have sausage-and-snack bars? Too noisy by far to be a
fighting man. Near his pension perhaps. A very savage character.

But the warmth of the woman next to him appeared to
Cantleman at last excessive. Her leg was fat, restless and hot.
It moved spasmodically like a sick thing. Then he detected a
thick wheeze : he remarked a shawl.

The heat was the heat of fever, undoubtedly. He was pressed
very closely against an invalid!

Minutes of stolid hesitation elapsed. He might fall asleep
himself and was not disposed to blend his slumbers with those
of a deceased person. This was not an ambulance! *Why* were
fever patients not discouraged from entering trains?

He had a youthful horror of sickness. A little ashamed, he
rose with stealth, and went out into the corridor, where he
smoked a cigarette. After that he entered the next compartment,
getting in between some slumbering sailors, pictures of health
if nothing else. He expanded his lungs—as if to inhale the briny
freshness of the ocean—and sat down.

The light was uncovered and the carriage not so much packed
as sprawled over. Facing Cantleman a sailor was awake and
filling his cutty : a workman and he were conversing in sober
tones. It was not about the war they were talking, but the
mining industry.

The sailor was a Scot, from near Glasgow, as black as a
levantine, his features acquiline and baggy in the symmetrical
southern way. Eyes brown and animal, lids like brown metal
slides. One black eyebrow was fixed up with a wakeful sagacity.

When the workman left the train, Cantleman took on the
sailor. He was a naval reservist. He had been down to Chatham
for the Test Mobilization a week or two before. No sooner
back, and congratulating himself on no more derangement for
some time to come, then the *real* mobilization arrives. And there
he was; not too well pleased, but sensibly bovine. A great placid
veteran.

'The wife hauns me a letter, the Sunday morr-rening. I tuk a
wee keek at ut, oot o' me richt ee. I see the offeeshal seal in the

72

corrner'—all in the voice of Harry Lauder, if you can do it, with much nodding of the head, and humorous levitation of the eyebrows, the r's rolling, a chuckling drumfire of pawky vocables. 'Then I turrened over and had another wee wink.'

The sailor's conversation gave no indication that he regarded this as a journey to journey's end, or anything out of the way of that sort. Just a freak of irksome duty.

They ran into York. The platform was comparatively empty. It was the emptiest station yet.

A naval reservist got into their carriage. A half-dozen people had come to see him off. His mother, a burly woman, with a kind square face, kept swaying from one foot to the other, with a Johnsonian roll. She was making heavy weather. A contemptuous grin curled her close mouth. With her staring tragic eyes she kept turning and looking at him, with her bitter grinning mouth, then back down the empty platform, into the reaches of the future.

Two girls, the young man's sisters probably, stood crying behind the heavy matron, one wiping her face with a very small handkerchief. An old man, no doubt the father, remained close under the window, deprecatory, distressed, absent-minded.

This was a foretaste of other scenes for Cantleman. But the empty York platform, in the small hours of the morning, and this English family—without the wild possessive hugging of the French at the stations—sending off their young reservist, affected him more. It was the woman; whose sarcastic grin and fixed eyes, and her big body with one shoulder hunched up— almost a grace, like a child's trick—as her eyes wandered, were not easily forgotten. He prayed that the woman might get back her reservist son safe and well; for she was the unhappy child—not he—whose doll was being stolen.

But the family of the young reservist was obscured. A couple of slum-youths, in smart sports-jackets, had jumped in and blocked up the window, talking to a third on the platform.

The train started : the platform with its mourning party was left behind, and the new reservist took his place next to the Scot. The slum-youths stood in the corridor beyond, until the next station, when they left the train with a jerky clatter.

The York reservist was reminiscent of a Breton conscript sailor. He had tobacco-coloured, rather staring eyes: a much developed Adam's apple and jaw muscles. He filled and lighted his pipe, and when that was done turned to the Scot with the question—

'Are you for Portsmouth?'

'Chatham,' said the Scot, with deep solemnity—removing his pipe from his mouth, and leaning towards him as he spoke. 'Chatham,' he said again, and returned his pipe to his mouth.

The York reservist started a conventional grumble, regarding the disturbance to his private life. Both the Scot and he came from the pits. The Yorkshireman had a great deal to say about new German machinery which had recently been installed where he worked. It only functioned properly under certain conditions. The Scot too had seen German machinery. Not satisfactory, must they buy German machinery anyway. For a long time they talked about the pits and the unsatisfactory German machinery.

The Crowd-proof Jack Tars were the first break in the continuity of the Crowd-spirit Cantleman had met with since the war began blowing up.—As sailors of course they were professionals, with a long top-dog tradition that made them proof against nervous excitement. They could not foresee Jutland, any more than Jellicoe. They were still anchored on Trafalgar.

The reservist of Scotland was a Syrian gem of craft and balance. The Yorkshire pitman was a more florid northern sailor.—Referring to the new Crowds, in process of formation, the Scot spoke in his measured way without respect. This new Crowd-spirit did not impress him, as a disciplined man.

'They stood there as seeck as dugs till after twal,' he said. 'I had to go roond by Maryhill. I just gave one luk at the boarrd. *Reserrvists reporrt!* That's settled it, sez I. But they were still thairrr as I went back.'

A young athlete of very heavy build, a coarse lemon blond thatch, but curly, woke up in the corner. He rubbed his eyes

74

with the back of his hands like a schoolboy and grinned at finding himself conscious again. His dreams were realler than he was, probably. Large empty features, with a long pointed nose, lecherously twisted at the nostrils: a mouth of cupid's bow pattern. His hair was going on the temples, but a bunch of curls made a last bold stand in the middle. As he grinned sheepishly from one to the other of those not so newly woken, his scalp retreated and flushed. A painful expression, as if the result of the straining proper to a natural function, never quite left his face. Frequently he sprang up, dashed himself into the woodwork of the door, and sat down again with a bang. At last he rebounded as usual, charged for the fifth time, but straighter, and disappeared. He too was a pit hand, but brought no illumination to the commun fund of talk.

A small wizened fellow, who had been sleeping curled up with his head on his service sack, woke up. He too was a miner. Cross-examined by the first Scot he gave an account of himself, and asked various questions in return. They told him his jersey wouldn't pass muster. Two stripes ornamented the sleeve. Chatham he was bound for. Cantleman began to think of all naval reservists as miners. The Scot, however, began talking of a postman who had been seen off at Ivanhoe or somewhere by the entire staff of the Post Office.

'I could hairrdly squeeze oot o' the cairage cause o' them!' he said, 'I went doon the platforrm to get a wee hauf. When I came back I didn't have to luk for me cairage. The whole of the blamed postal office was collected in front of it.'

The Yorkshireman felt it advisable here to put in a plea for discrimination.

'Yes, when the family comes to see you off, well—your family—'

'That's different, but you should ha' seen those bloomin' post office offeeshuls,' persisted the Scot.

They none of them doubted that the mobilization meant war. The 'Kayser' had made the war, of course. In these simple minds that German Mars, with his imperial helmet, stood delivering Ultimatums. He'd 'cop it this time right enough, the bastard' more than he bargained for.

75

King's Cross was reached—more troops, of course, at this great terminus.

LONDON

A giant canvas by Frith. Or something like a century old print, the perpetual morning of the romantic Coaching highway, fresh and conventional, occurred to Cantleman as he stepped out upon the King's Cross platform. Life had already gone back a century. Everything was become historical—the past had returned. Romance had oozed up and steeped everything in its glamours. Also this was a People's World once more, racy, rich and turbulent.

Cantleman was enthusiastic. Like the others he did not question the credentials of this miracle at first. Soldiers and sailors, an army of porters, rushed and jostled. A big German with scarred face came down from the big gates, looking for his luggage. Acid theatrical concentration behind his glasses. He was another description of reservist.

Cantleman went to his rooms. After a wash he went out to look round and sample the intoxication of this colossal event. He went about in his usual solitary fashion, drifting with the crowd. He enjoyed its enormous depths. The Hippodrome was passed on the other side. He saboted the Bomb Shop, where his bombs sold well. Opposite Crosse and Blackwells he crossed the road, abreast of the Soho Distillery, he went in. The saloon-bar was not very full. Two horse-guards, standing at attention, cane protruding back and front, right elbow up, drained two half pint mugs of 'Four-alf', exchanged a wooden-soldier's painted glance, without moving their lips within their strapped-down jaws, reversed *sur place*, jingling their spurs, and marched out in step, watched by the customers. When they had passed out of sight the other customers looked at each other.

'Fine young fellows!' said one man.

'I suppose they'll be having to stand by pretty soon now,' said the second.

'Ah! I shouldn't be surprised' said the first. 'Looks like it don't it?'

Cantleman sat in silence, drank his Worthington and returned to the Crowd. At Oxford Circus the newspapers were bellowing. He bought a paper. The news-headings that animated the Crowd animated him. The news-sheets were full of gathering climaxes.

War came heavily on with a resolution no one ever credited it with. The unbelievable was going to happen. The Crowd was still blind, with a first pup-like intensity.

The 'great historical event' is always hatching; the Crowd in its habitual infantile sleep. Then the appointed hand releases the clutch, the 'great event' is set in motion : the crowd rises to meet the crash half awake and struggling, with voluptuous spasms. It is the Rape of the Crowd.

Every acquaintance Cantleman met was a new person. The only possibility of renewal for the individual is into this temporary Death and Resurrection of the Crowd, it appears. The war was like a great new fashion. Cantleman conformed. He became a man of fashion. But he was cold in the midst of the Mêlée. In the first days he experienced nothing but a penetrating interest in all that was taking place. His detachment was complete and his attention was directed everywhere. His movements resembled those of a freelance cinema-operator.

CHAPTER IV

The War-Crowds, 1914

THE CROWD

LONDON, JULY, 1914

Men drift in thrilling masses past the Admiralty, cold night tide. Their throng creeps round corners, breaks faintly here and there up against a railing barring from possible sights. Local embullience and thickening: some madman disturbing their depths with baffling and recondite noise.

The police with distant icy contempt herd London. They shift it in lumps, passim, touching and shaping it with heavy delicate professional fingers. Their attitude suggests that these universal crowds are out for some new vague Suffrage—which they may, but only after interminable battles, be accorded.

Is this opposition correct? In ponderous masses they prowl, with excited hearts. Are the Crowds then female? The police at all events handle them with a professional contempt of their excited violence, cold in their helmets.—Some tiny grain of suffrage will perhaps be thrown to the millions in the street. Or taken away.

The police are contemptuous, cold and disagreeable, however.

Already the newspapers smell carrion. They allow themselves the giant type reserved for great catastrophes. They know when they are on a good thing, and it is a good thing they are on.

Prussia should be the darling of the Press. The theatrical instinct of the New Germany has saved the Crowd from breaking up for a third of a century. It has kept men in crowds,

78

enslaving them to the feminine entity of their meaningless numbers.

Bang! Bang!

Ultimatum to you!

Ultimatum to you!

Ultimatum to you!

ULTIMATUM!

From an evening paper: July —.

> 'The outlook has become far more grave during the afternoon. Germany's attitude causes considerable uneasiness. She seems to be throwing obstacles in the way.—The German ambassador in Vienna has telegraphed to his government, etc.'

Germany, the sinister brigand of latter-day Europe, 'mauvais voisin' for the little French bourgeois-reservist, remains silent and ominously unhelpful in her armoured cave across the Rhine.

Do all these idiots really mean—?! An *is it possible!* from Cantleman. To which there is only one answer. YES!

The Crowd, that first mobilization of a country, now is formed in London. It is established with all its vague but profound organs *au grand complet*. Every night it serpentines in thick well-nourished coils, all over the city, in tropic degustation of news.

The individual and the Crowd. Peace and War.—Man's solitude and Man's Peace. Man's community, and Row—or *war*.

Cantleman sees another analogy, to express the meaning of this Crowd. The Bachelor and the Husband Crowd. How about that? The married man as the symbol of the Crowd!—Is it not his function to bring one into being? To create one in the bowels of his wife? At the altar he embraces Death, just as the crowd does, who assembles to shout WAR!

So periodically we shed our individual skin, or are apt to, and are purged in big being.—An empty throb.

Men resist death with horror, it is true, when their time comes. But death is only a form of Crowd. It is a similar surrender. Does not the Crowd in life spell death, when most intensely marshalled? The Crowd is an immense anaesthetic towards death, such is its immemorial function.

A fine dust of extinction, a grain or two for each man, is scattered in any crowd like these black London war-crowds. Their pace is so mournful. Wars begin with this huge indefinite interment in the cities.

For days now wherever you are you hear a sound like a very harsh perpetual voice of a shell. If you put W before it, it always makes *War*. It is the crowd cheering everywhere. Even weeks afterwards, when the Crowd has served its turn and been dissolved, those living in the town's heart will seem to hear this noise.

Cantleman's crowd-experiments began at once. He moved immediately to the centre of London—he dropped out of his taxicab, at hazard—rapping on the window for it to stop where the crowd seemed densest and stupidest.

For some hours he moved forward at a snail's pace. The night came on. He allowed himself to be carried by the crowd. He offered himself to its emotion, which saturated him at length. When it had sunk in, he examined it. Apparently it was sluggish electricity. That was all. As such it had no meaning, beyond what the power of a great body of water has, for instance. It conducted nowhere: it was aimlessly flowing through these torpid coils. The human cables had been disposed no doubt by skilful brains : they might be admirable. But not the electricity.

However, human messages passed up and down. He interpreted the messages. Like the spirit-writing of the *planchette* pencil, they were exceedingly stupid.

He went aside into a Neapolitan café, which was empty. The crowd passed slowly in front of the door. Taking his note-book from his pocket, he wrote in large letters in the left hand top corner of the empty page.

80

An Experiment with a Crowd

What was the experiment to be? Well, he would not only mix with the crowd, he would train himself *to act its mood,* so that he could persuade its emotion to enter him properly. There he could store it, to some extent. Then he would, from time to time, hasten outside it. In isolation, he would examine himself in the Crowd-mood.

This experiment would require a great deal of suppleness, needless to say. He went outside into the crowd again. He sank like a diver. He disposed his body in a certain way, slouched heavily along, fixed his eyes ahead of him. Soon he had become an entranced medium, or the next thing to it.

Then he began to think of things very remote from the herd. There was a bogus countess who was eager to finance a review. He was to be editor. Bogus countesses were a sore trial.

He proceeded to the office of this paper-to-be: he prepared his first number: he composed his prospectus: he defined his policy.

Suddenly he experienced a distinct and he believed *authentic shock*. It could only come from the crowd! Evidently he had penetrated its mind—the cerebration of this jelly-fish! Hence the sting! He had received his first novel sensation. What was it exactly—could he define it? Well, it seemed to be that he was a *married man.*

Unquestionably he possessed, and with extreme suddeness at that, *that married feeling.* He had never had it before—so he knew it must be genuine. Immediately he withdrew from the crowd. There was a public house, he entered the saloon bar, ordered a bitter beer, and, sitting at a table, produced his note-book once more.

Experiment with a Crowd

(1) Single man experiences sensation of married state. The Family. The Crowd.
   [question : Do married men (in crowds) feel single? Feel

like *irresponsible* married man. No sensation of children. Perhaps Crowd-matrix full of children?]

He read this through. He was disappointed. He returned to the Crowd.

For some time, as mechanically as possible, he tramped forward. He reached Charing Cross, then the end of the Strand. Trafalgar Square was an extensive human lake. He moved towards the Nelson Column. He might obtain a valuable note if he climbed up, upon the plinth. Hoarse voices were muttering all round him. He felt the pressure of the visible ghosts whom he was inviting to inscribe their ideas on the tabula rasa he offered them.

Their messages continued to be extremely confused. He noticed he had lost ground, even. He felt more and more solitary. Then free—*single*; and so divorced.

Upon the plinth of the Nelson Column he strained for a distinct sensation. It must this time be distinct. Nothing came at all. He strained again. He felt as detached as the stone Nelson. What a change from Trafalgar! he thought. What a change! Lady Hamilton floated into his mind. She had scent upon her limbs, which were sheathed in tight-fitting bathing drawers. She was going for a dip. She was Britannia. A wave slapped her, roguishly. *Elle faisait le culbute.* Immediately a sensation occurred. Cantleman produced his notebook.

Experiment with a Crowd

(2) A sensation of immediate bawdiness occurs, in contact with Nelson. 'England expects every man to'—yes, *what*? To sleep with Lady Hamilton, apparently. Violets and brine. There's nothing else for it.

(note.—*Plutôt par snobisme que par vice.*)

And the imperial votaress passed on,
In maiden meditation, fancy free.

82

I see her drying thighs, in a virginal pavilion.
Nelson adjusts his blind eye to the keyhole.

Cantleman descended from the plinth, and stood uncertainly gazing to North and South. He turned northwards and made his way round the drab circular fountain, on the sides of which couples squatted, up the shallow steps, over to where the bronze signs set in the granite plinth of the National Gallery by the government, provide a public test gauge. So to the right, to the northern bus-route. He was in St. Martin's Lane. He thought he felt something. Swiftly he withdrew into an Italian café, and yanked out his note-book.

Experiment with a Crowd

(3) The English Crowd is a stupid dragon. It ought not to be allowed out alone! I have lain in it for hours together and have received *no sensation worth noting*. As Crowd it is a washout.

(*Postscript.* Up, the King's Navy. Lord Nelson although on a column now like a gymnosophist, gave me my one sensation.—He had forgotten Trafalgar. He is now quite blind. He had retired into his needle. The wild ass stamps o'er his head but cannot break his sleep.)

CHAPTER V
The 'Author of "Tarr"'

So much for Mr. Cantleman. Need I repeat that this hero of mine is not to be identified with me? But to some extent, in the fragments I have just quoted, you get the lowdown on the editor of *Blast*. That is why I used them.

Remember that I wrote that in 1914. It was written *on the spot*. It was almost as contemporary as the notes jotted down by Cantleman in his cafés, into which he went aside, out of the Crowd, to report his *sensations,* as soon as he got one.

You have read what Cantleman felt. Well, that is *pretty near* to what I felt.—*Great* interest. *Great* curiosity. But no identification of my personality with that collective Sensation. The war-crowds who roared approval of the declaration of war in 1914, were a jellyfish, in my judgement. For some they were a Great People in their wrath, roaring before the throne of the God of Justice, for the blood of the unrighteous. That was not my view of the matter.

This 'Cantleman' fragment (which as I started by saying appeared in *Blast*) was entitled '*The Crowd-Master*'. Deliberately autobiographical up to a point, it is the best possible material for an *Autobiography*: and what was meant by 'Crowdmaster' was that I was master of myself. Not of anybody else—that I have never wanted to be. I was master *in* the crowd, not master *of* the crowd. I moved freely and with satisfaction up and down its bloodstream, in strict, even arrogant, insulation from its demonic impulses.

This I regarded as, in some sort, a triumph of mind over matter. It was a triumph (as I saw it then) of the individualist principle. I believed a great deal in the individual. And I still prefer him to his collective counterpart, though recognizing his shortcomings.

84

Now you will probably see without my telling you what follows from all this. My attitude to War is complex. *Per se,* I neither hate it nor love it. War I only came to know gradually, it is true. War takes some getting to know. I know it intimately. And what's more, I know all about war's gestation and antecedents, and I have savoured its aftermaths. What I don't know about War is not worth knowing.

When first I met War face to face I brought no moral judgements with me at all. I have never been able to regard war—modern war—as good or bad. Only supremely stupid.

Certainly I understand that almost all wars are promoted and directed by knaves, for their own unpleasant ends, at the expense of fools, their cannonfodder. And certainly knaves are *bad men,* very bad men. But the greatest wickedness of all—if we much deal in moral values—is the perpetuation of foolishness which these carnivals of mass-murder involve.

But now I will take up the narrative in my own person again. The War has started. That is the main point. I have shown you how it started, for me. The next step is to tell you what I did next. All Europe was at war and a bigger *Blast* than mine had rather taken the wind out of my sails.

My health was impaired. It gave me a great deal of trouble. For a long time I lived at No. 4 Percy Street treating myself, sometimes in bed for ten days at a time. Percy Street is a short street off the Tottenham Court Road—it would be called Soho by a careless guide. It is principally noted for Stulik. There are other people in it, but he's the one who counts.

Alcohol was an inadmissible indulgence in my poisoned state. But I had most of my meals next door, at the Eiffel Tower Restaurant. There the wines were good. Supposing myself on the way to recovering, I would have a bottle, perhaps, of one of Stulik's less celebrated marks. My symptoms would reappear. Then I would retire to the hospitable comfort of Mrs. Pierce's apartment, at No. 4. Captain Guy Baker, whose acquaintance I had just made in the restaurant next door, would bring me up newspapers and cigarettes, and we would curse together the micro-organism and all its works, discussing Mr. Churchill's escapades at Antwerp, and waggling our old school ties at each other, for we had been at the same school.

During this peaceful period—war was all round us, but I was at peace, with my pestilential complaint—I wrote, practically, the whole of my first novel *Tarr*, which I was under contract to finish.

The question as to whether immediately to attest or not, did not arise, therefore, as I could not have done so had I wished. Any violent movement or exertion redoubled the septacaemia. I had to get well first, before my King and Country could benefit by my martial intervention. Probably the micro-organisms saved my life.

That I would 'join up' as soon as I was well I accepted as a matter of course, though I hoped that I might, without too much difficulty, obtain a commission. Later on, by the time I was fit, that was not so easy.

Meanwhile, I had never done anything considerable in the art of writing—or of course in painting for that matter. I said to myself that if I was going to be killed in battle I should like first to finish this first book, so that the world might have a chance of judging what an artist it had lost. Under the circumstances a not inexcusable vanity.

I did not carry through the piece of work as well as I should. I was hurried (I always thought I was about to get well, then slipped back). Since, I have had to rewrite every line of it. Even in that early form *Tarr* brought me much attention as a writer —though I should be sorry to have gone down to posterity as 'the author of *Tarr*' in its unrevised first version. A gratifyingly large and flattering Press marked its appearance. It was hailed as the first book of a new epoch, 'a date in literature'.

'The prose style is original. . . . A book of great importance, because it will become a date in literature … because here we have a forerunner of the prose and probably of the manner that is to come, a prose bare and precise, a manner hardly ever general, never diffuse, usually concentrated and penetrating. The new writer takes definite and lasting leave of the romantic movement. . . . We are at last spared the illogical impertinence of a set plot in a world where nothing happens according to set plot but by the natural development of character.'

I have no record of who wrote this: it appeared in the *New Witness*.

'*Tarr* is a thunderbolt,' said the *Weekly Dispatch*. '*Tarr* is just *Trilby*—but it is *Trilby* written, elaborated, done, and worth reading,' said the *Outlook*. 'A painful commentary on modern morals,' said a provincial paper. 'But it has a powerful fascination,' it added. Whether the 'fascination' lay in the morals or in the manner of presentment the writer does not say.

A notice in the *Nation,* from the pen of Rebecca West, was a more serious matter, and it was the intelligent support of one or two such influential critics as Miss West which assured this first book the respectful attention of the world at large. It must always be remembered that notices in those days were not the mere clowning that they have become at the present time. So what such a writer as Miss West wrote carried weight.

This, as you can see, is literary history, as well as my personal history, so I need not tell you that there is no vanity in reproducing these opinions of persons at present justly eminent in our literary world.

Miss West's generous tribute to this first book was characteristic of a critic who has never sold her pen, as others have, and who therefore to-day still occupies the position that she always has, as one of the two or three people who remain above the commercial mêlée into which writing has been led.

'A beautiful and serious work of art that reminds one of Dostoievsky only because it too is inquisitive about the soul, and because it contains one figure of vast moral significance which is worthy to stand beside Stavrogin. The great achievement of the book, which gives it both its momentary and its permanent value, is Kreisler, the German artist.'

You can see that with such champions as this, the 'author of *Tarr*' had nothing to fear from critical misunderstanding, and his 'bombshell' was not treated *merely* as an explosive novelty : and the fact that it had in England such a publisher as Miss Harriet Weaver assured it the best treatment a book can receive, on that side. Mr. T. S. Eliot, in reviewing it, remarked that 'In the work of Mr. Lewis we recognize the thought of the modern and the energy of the cave-man.' So, since even then Mr. Eliot was influential, I was launched as a 'caveman', as well as an editor and an author.

Before *Tarr* I had been a painter—though I never had time to paint. I had been so busy massaging the British Public, as it were—in preparation for the effort of understanding that would be required if it once I *did,* in fact, begin.

Now I was 'an author'. I had a first novel to my credit. What fun! you will think, if you are a Boots Subscriber. But, you know, I was a quite different sort of 'author' to the sort you're thinking about. It's never any fun being the real thing!

I was perhaps more of a portent as 'an author' than as 'a painter'. The English will never regard painting as anything but a joke, or a chocolate-box. Whereas whatever else you may say about the English, they are a great literary nation, and in an uneasy way they feel it is up to them to take some notice of a book. They are after all *supposed* to understand books, even if they don't.

I need not describe my first book, otherwise than to say that the attitude of mind that presided at its composition seemed highly original at the time. It would not seem so now, the attitude has been too often imitated. The *statement*—the narrative technique—was denuded of those rhetorical ornaments to which the English critic had become accustomed in a work of fiction. It was not a world of gentlemen and ladies that was unfolded in its pages, nor yet of love's young dream, nor of the 'kindly' emotions. But it was not (if you cared to cross the Channel) the first book in European literature to display a certain indifference to bourgeois conventions, and an unblushing disbelief in the innate goodness of human nature.

Tarr was not 'constructed', as the commercial pundit calls it. It did not conform to the traditional wave-length of the English Novel. There was not a lot of soft padding everywhere,

MR. WYNDHAM LEWIS

THE MOTHER AND FATHER OF THE AUTHOR

THE BOMBARDIER

THE BATTERY OFFICER

in other words, to enable the eggs to get safely to market, to Boots and to Mudies. Indeed they were *not* eggs. They were more like bullets. As Mr. H. G. Wells once remarked to me: I did not write novels as he'd been brought up to think of them. But *Tarr* was only the first: and there have been many since then—of my own, for that matter. To-day *Tarr* would be accepted as a pretty straightforward narrative. Then it looked queer.

As the 'author of *Tarr*', at all events, and as 'the Editor of *Blast*' I was henceforth to be known, until 1926. Then I began writing a lot more books. I had to make a list of them the other day, and found I have by now written twenty-three. This was up to May 1937.

But in 1926 this autobiography ends, as you will remember. So for the purposes of this autobiography I am 'the Author of *Tarr*'. The curtain goes down upon *Tarr*.

Later in the War I was, when on leave from the Front, in Lady Cunard's box at Covent Garden. Next to me sat the General commanding the American troops in England. This was the month in which *Tarr* had made its appearance: and my hostess introduced me as 'the author of *Tarr*—a *novel*, General! Mr. Lewis has been compared, General, to Dostoievsky! *The Times* says he has taken Dostoievsky for his model. Dostoievsky, General!'

'Dostoievsky—Dostoievsky!' exclaimed the gallant officer. 'And a very good model too!'

As a fact, I had not taken Dostoievsky for a model, though *The Times* may have said I had. But this is just to show the sort of form my early lionization as an 'author' was to take. Lady Cunard has much more than her share of mother-wit: and having to make contact quickly, in the midst of the surging pandemonium of a Wagner opera, between an American General officer and a British subaltern, she just shouted the name of a sort of field-marshal of letters (Marshal Dostoievsky as it were) and announced me as the latter's chief of staff— about to step into his shoes: though in the tented field, of course, a mere bottlewasher—not even a brasshat; a battery officer, one amongst thousands popping off stupid guns.

In the years immediately succeeding the War I was 'the

author of *Tarr*' more than anything else, with 'the editor of *Blast*' as a secondary title to fame. The War had washed out the bright puce of the cover of the organ of the 'Great London Vortex'. Too much blood had been shed for red, even of the most shocking aniline intensity, to startle anybody. And upon my literary labours of the first six months of the War I stood or fell, for seven long years. Mostly I stood, pretty securely. Which is surely a tribute to *Tarr*. It is remarkable how well that hasty piece of workmanship supported me until I decided to start building a better pedestal. For a pedestal is as essential for an artist as it is for a statue.

I was, I believe, suspected of painting still (though such an expert in those matters as Mr. Herbert Read assures the Public that since the War I have never been guilty of that offence). But my painting was merely an oddity about 'the author of *Tarr*' which it was rather amusing to recall. Like the landscapes of Mr. Winston Churchill.

CHAPTER VI

The Sitwells, a 'Book-Dictator', and Mr. Richard Sickert

Have you ever heard of the Sitwells? If you *have,* I do hope you won't resent this question. Or rather I hope you will overlook my telling you who they are.

Sir George Sitwell is a baronet in the north of England, and he has three children. Two of them are men, and one a woman. The latter is one of my most hoary, tried and reliable enemies. We are two good old enemies, Edith and I, *inseparables* in fact. I do not think I should be exaggerating if I described myself as Miss Edith Sitwell's *favourite enemy.*

Once I shared that distinction with Mr. Noel Coward, but Noel Coward has somehow dropped out. Why? Oh, I don't know—I suppose you can't go on getting excited about *Cavalcade* forever even if you are Miss Sitwell. Then Mr. Coward has recently become a member of the Athenaeum. It's time to drop an enemy when he does that.

It is just possible that my friend Mr. Geoffrey Grigson may feel that *he* is the favourite. Since the newspaper correspondence in which he referred to her as 'the old Jane', and she asked what *a grig* was and looking it up in the dictionary found that it was 'a small eel', he may feel that his claims should not lightly be brushed aside. All the same, I believe I shall always be the apple of her eye—now Noel's dropped out.[1]

Osbert Sitwell I have always liked, rather in spite of myself— for those foxhunting men I can never really respect. The very name *Sitwell* is suggestive of the horsemaster, the hereditary 'foxhuntingman'. But Osbert is a 'hearty' who has taken the

---

[1] Noel Coward is not an enemy of *mine,* I should perhaps say. In that capacity he belongs to Miss Sitwell, and I am not butting in. I had to make it clear why I should be the favourite, and not him, that was all.

wrong turning—he has looked at pictures, he has listened to music much too much—he has loved the Ballet not wisely but too well. I doubt if he could catch a fox to-day for all the equestrian aplomb of his patronymic.

But Edith Sitwell is another matter. Edith—she is a poetess by the way—is a bad loser. When worsted in argument, she throws Queensberry Rules to the winds. She once called me Percy.

Although I don't like Edith quite so much as I like Osbert (she said I 'wanted to be loved' on one occasion, so I need make no bones about saying that I do not love her) for all that Edith does liven up the English literary scene considerably. And I hope Geoffrey Grigson will stop knocking her about in public. He should remember that although as brave as a lion, she is only a woman.

(By the way, all this is merely doing my stuff. No autobiography of me—1914-1926—would be complete without the Sitwell family. They are one of my comic turns. I assure you that if the above seems to you a bit rough in places, it is nothing to what Miss Edith puts in, once we get into a clinch in the newspapers. You should watch out for that. This book ought to bring her out, and then all the toupets will be on the green. But I'd a damn sight rather have Edith than those cowards[1] who skulk beneath a *nom de plume*, and peashoot you from ambush.)

But back to Osbert now. Osbert was once a minor Maecenas. He had *le bel air,* so much prized by the Baroness Bernstein—a Hanoverian hauteur and a beautiful lisp—which helped him out as a *raconteur,* and he was one of Chelsea's best. He threw quite a good dinner-party, in his salad days, and he was about the last person in London to mix 'mind' with his Mayfair. He would have been a 'baronet with a butterfly', under happier circumstances.

Not long after the War I was at his house for dinner (in Carlyle Square, Chelsea, it was) and Arnold Bennett and Walter Sickert were present.

Walter Sickert is of course Richard Sickert, the great Ex-Royal Academician. It would be in vain for me to tell you all the other things he is—the R.A. is the least of them. And

[1] No, not Noel.

Arnold Bennett was an Edwardian novelist, who wrote about the Five Towns.

I am telling you here about *Tarr*. This preparation (and all that knock-about stuff with the author of *Wheels* was part of it) has been to show you how *Tarr* sometimes got 'the author of *Tarr*' into difficulties.

At this dinner-party Sickert began talking about *Tarr*. I could see Bennett didn't like it. I think Sickert saw that too, for he went on talking about it more and more, at every moment in more ecstatic terms. I did not engage in the conversation. I saw that Bennett was extremely annoyed; and when at last Sickert said : 'Here we've been talking about it for a quarter of an hour. The author has said nothing. But I don't think it matters *what* we say about it. *Tarr* is such a book that it doesn't matter what we say about it, one way or the other!' Bennett threw himself back in his chair at this, and stammered out crossly, 'Oh, I shouldn't say that. I shouldn't say that!'

Naturally it was aggravating of Sickert to make Bennett talk about a 'young author's' book for half an hour. For I saw only too well that as an old hand he had resented this ordeal. So much irresponsible generosity had been more than he could stomach. *Tarr* had been made to stink in his nostrils. Bennett had an age-complex as big as a house. I knew that Sickert had made me an enemy though he had not meant to, for he is the kindest man in the world.

Afterwards it looked as if my forebodings had been confirmed. I say *looked,* because I cannot believe that that episode accounted for what followed, though I dare say it did not help matters.

For a number of years Arnold Bennett was a kind of book-dictator. Every week in the pages of the *Standard*, he 'dictated' what the Public should read. And more or less the Public obeyed. He was the Hitler of the book-racket. The book-trade said that he could make a book overnight. If he praised it on Thursday evening, by the week-end it was selling like hot cakes. And he became inordinately proud of this accomplishment. He loved power in the way that a 'captain of industry' loves power.

He was reported to have sold fantastic quantities of a book

entitled, I think, *The Bridge of San Luis Rey*. But there were hundreds of them. He 'made' one a week. *C'était fou* as Sickert would put it. It was hair-raising.

The 'author of *Tarr*' under this Dictatorship spent his time in a spiritual concentration camp—of barbed silence. No one ever heaved a heartier sigh of relief at the death of a Tyrant, than that the 'author of *Tarr*' heaved when Bennett passed from this scene to a better and even more resplendent one. For living beneath that boycott was no joke, for a person who depended for his living upon what he could get out of his books.

Of course I realize that this particular Dictator probably disliked *The Lion and the Fox, The Childermass, Time and Western Man,* and so on, from the bottom of his heart. Also—as this is after all a democracy (in spite of our local Dictators), and seeing that I had an undeservedly splendid Press everywhere else—'the author of *Tarr*' survived the rigours of this solitary boycotteer. All the same, whenever I see the *Standard* (which thank God only has a mouse-like shadow of a 'dictator' to-day) I shudder. Whatever the reason, it meant a tidy bit out of my pocket. This John Keats would have had much more porridge if this particular Hitler had not taken a dislike to the cut of his hair. If Letters were Life, I am persuaded, I should have been beheaded. My head would have 'rolled in the sand'. But I should never have understood *exactly* why.

As Sickert and I left the Sitwells that night (in 1922 or 3) I reproached him for having been so vehement with Bennett. But Sickert exclaimed against my retrospective objection. 'Nonsense! Why shouldn't he hear it! Of course he should be told—that and a lot more! *Quel comédie*—that such people as Arnold Bennett should be in a position of that sort—it is only in an age like ours that they could be! That one should have to talk to such people about *books* at all! Why should one be asked to meet such people? It is absurd that a Bennett should be referred to, for anything except the time of a train or the cost of a bicycle lamp! Pfui!'

94

CHAPTER VII
The 'Bull-Gun'

I will return to Percy Street, at a later stage. I always return to Percy Street. Suffice it to say that at last 'the author of *Tarr*'—though he was not that yet, but still 'the futurist artist'—'the editor of *Blast*' regained his health—about the same time that he wrote finis to the sad story of Bertha Lunken—and attested.

My first week as a soldier was at Dover. It was on the parade ground of the castle there that I learnt how to fall-in and to dismiss : and in public houses on the quays that I got so drunk with mandoline-playing sailors that I was compelled on one of my first nights as a gunner to crawl up the hill to the castle upon all fours. In the upright position, I discovered, on this steep incline, I either fell to my knees and struck my forehead on the ground like a moslem, or reeled over backwards and struck my occiput like a British heavyweight.

The army hut where I slept was in a little wood. When I reached it, on this occasion, I grasped one of the trees, and rose slowly to my feet. Fixing my eye upon another tree a few yards away, I marched upon it and embraced it. Embracing it I revolved, until I leant against it with my back. Then I retraced my steps, and supported myself against the first tree for a while. So I marched and countermarched a number of times.

Satisfied with my form, I turned my face towards the hut. The corporal in charge occupied the left hand bed beside the door. As I reached it I turned the handle slowly and pushed it inwards. I entered, manoeuvred round it, and walked back with it until it was closed again. Then, averting my eyes from the direction of the corporal's bed, I marched over to my own, sat down a little precipitately, coughed, removed my boots and tunic. *Then* I turned my eyes, with a casualness there was no mistaking, in the direction of the door. I allowed them to skim the bed that stood beside it. There was no one there! There was no corporal. But a little later he came, or it would be more accurate to say *spun* in. He subsided upon his bed, without, however, removing his boots. I laughed drunkenly and went to sleep.

After Dover, with its alarm-sirens announcing Taubes, its hoarse Irish drill-sergeants, its alcoholic A.B.'s, I went to the Camp at which you have already seen me. I had enlisted as a gunner, and that was a trade which required to be learnt. But it was not that which prolonged my training. It was the getting of a commission.

The 'Bull-gun', an article which I wrote at the time, speaks of 'the romance of the big guns, which has boomed loud for over a century'. Napoleon was a gunner. From the day when he first drove the mixed force of British and dagos out of the naval base of Toulon with his guns, he won his battles as a gunner. He always thought in terms of guns. But the romance of those great guns to-day is rather that of the monsters of the Big Bertha type, than of the small howitzer, with which I mainly had to do.

The '6-inch How' is not one of the big imposing machines, nor yet one of the graceful swan-necked ordance, which you see on battleships and in coastal forts. 'The recoil of that gun—its sweep backwards, and its return to the "firing position"—is probably the most graceful thing about the gunner's life,' I wrote while I was serving my apprenticeship to the 'bull-gun'. It was a 'bull-gun' of sorts I tended, yes, but a very diminutive bull. It was the smallest 'siege' ordance, in short. And its habits, in a 'war of position', were very similar to the 'Field', except that one, thank god, was not bothered with horses.

It was rough and heavy work, however, and it required rough and heavy men. On the whole we recruited the *biggest* men of any branch of the service. Mostly they were coal-miners, Rugby footballers, heavyweight boxers and outsize navvies.

There was nothing graceful about our performance as you may imagine. Often it partook of the grotesqueness of a knock-about turn. During my first firing course at Lydd, for instance, when I was an acting-sergeant, it required two of us to fire it. And my mate and myself, gripping our lanyard and pulling on it violently together, we rolled over and over upon the ground, as if engaged in an all-in wrestling match. It was more like pulling out an elephant's tooth than firing a gun, to look at, I expect.

So much for 'the graces', where the 'bull-gun' is concerned. But I soon learnt this strange trade, and should in the normal course of things have gone out to France to shoot at Fritz, but I had set my heart on the commissioned rank. I felt it was due to the editor of *Blast* to be his own master to some extent. Once I had a 'pip' I could go on being a 'crowd-master', without interfering with anybody, or anybody interfering too much with me.

At last I got a 'pip'. I went first to the Field Artillery cadet-school at Exeter, where I nearly lost my life in the riding school. Several people were killed while I was there, trying to ride. It was a weekly—perhaps a daily—occurrence.

Dean Swift never betrayed the essential shallowness of his understanding more grievously than when he selected the Horse as the animal most suited to show up man. I met dozens of his Houhynhnyms at Exeter cadet-school. And a lousier set of four-footed Yahoos I hope I may never encounter. There was one whose tail I had to clean with a sponge (for I had to clean these disgusting beasts as well as ride them) whose behaviour left me speechless and almost lost me a leg. The same outrageous devil nearly broke my neck in the riding school.

However, I escaped from this inferno of horseflesh. It was in the comparative repose of Trowbridge Cadet-school that I got my 'pip'. This I acquired with some degree of brilliance. The examination involved considerable mathematical ability, and I revealed myself as a natural master of the Calculus. A sort of mute, inglorious Pascal. Indeed a senior wrangler who was sitting next to me at the exam—a man of, I suppose, comparable attainment to Earl Russell—cribbed my results over my shoulder, and saved himself the public disgrace that awaits all these star-performers, when they descend into the market-place and attempt to compete with the plain man, once the latter's blood is really up, as mine was. I was fifth from top.

But I have lingered enough in these ante-chambers of war. I have no illusion that I was a valuable officer. I rapidly lost

D*

interest in the 'bull-gun', once I had learnt how to fire it. And it never fell to my lot to apply my mathematical ability at the Front, so as to hit a distant cross-roads on a map, or lay down a barrage on a trench. The O.C. Battery, or the second-in-command did that. I got my 'pip', and in doing so I became a figurehead. I rolled no more upon the earth with a perspiring companion, as I fired the gun. I never fired a gun again, in fact. Successive gun-crews did that for me. I bought two well-cut suits of old-gold khaki, in Savile Row, a cane, a revolver, and a sumptuous British Warm. I was now 'an officer', whom hundreds of thousands of men still living have saluted—have trembled at the sight of, if they were half-seas over. I passed into a more abstract class.

CHAPTER VIII

'Hulme of Original Sin'

Before turning my back upon England, I will first refer to a few of the figures prominent in the literary world and in art, in 1914, who became soldiers. Principally two: namely T. E. Hulme and Gaudier Brzeska. They were both killed, the former within a quarter of a mile of where I was standing. We were in neighbouring batteries.

I did not see him hit, but everything short of that, for we could see their earthworks, and there was nothing between to intercept the view. I watched, from ours, his battery being punched full of deep craters, with large naval shells: and from the black fountains of earth that spouted up, in breathless succession, occasional débris hurtled around us as we looked on. I remember a splintered baulk of wood sailing over and striking the dugout at my back.

Hulme is pronounced *Hume*. Don't ask me how Brzeska is pronounced—I prefer to call him Gaudier, the name he adopted very sensibly to overcome precisely this difficulty.

T. E. Hulme was a remarkable man and posthumously has been much appreciated. He was an art-critic, of a philosophic turn. Although he has been called 'a philospher', he was not that, but a man specializing in aesthetic problems. Theory of knowledge, theology, or anything else he dabbled in, was as the groundwork merely for the philosophic understanding of art.

Neither Bergson (Hulme's master) nor anybody else at the time regarded him as more than that, though sometimes, very naturally, in a Bohemian backwater, he would affect the laurels of the Stagirite, he was not above doing that. I have seen him in the clutches of a little university professional, with Kant at

his finger-tips, whom he had provoked by his dialectical truculence. The spectacle was unedifying. Hulme floundered like an
ungainly fish, caught in a net of superior academic information.

His mind was sensitive and original, which is a better thing
obviously than the routine equipment of the teaching profession : but he was a journalist with a flair for philosophy and
art, not a philosopher. Of both these subjects he was profoundly ignorant, according to technician-standards.

'Mr. Hulme should do useful work in the field of art-criticism,'
or words to that effect, was in Bergson's testimonial, when
writing to someone a letter introducing him. It was mainly as a
theorist in the criticism of the fine arts that Hulme would have
distinguished himself, had he lived. And I should undoubtedly
have played Turner to his Ruskin.

All the best things Hulme said about the theory of art were
said about my art. This remark is altogether without conceit.
The things to which his pronouncements would not apply—
or to which my own pronouncements, which influenced him,
would not apply—may quite well be more important. We happened, that is all, to be made for each other, as critic and
'creator'. What he said should be done, I *did*. Or it would be
more exact to say that I did it, and he said it.

In England there was no one else working in consonance with
an 'abstract' theory of art to the same extent as myself. Neither
Gaudier nor Epstein would in the end have been 'abstract'
enough to satisfy the requirements of this obstinate abstractionist. He would have had to fall back on me.

Epstein, is, I need not tell you, a very fine artist. His superb
busts are among the real achievements in art of our time. But
I (as an abstractionist) prefer his lifelike busts to his other
less lifelike work. And a life-like bust is 'naturalism', as seen by
the puritan-eye of the abstractionist.

Epstein was, if I may say so, more 'literary' than myself. He
was unquestionably Hulme's man (or perhaps I should say
Hulme was Epstein's man) upon the social plane. They were
great friends, where I never stood in that relation to Hulme at
all.

Hulme wrote at great length about Epstein, he had a great

personal admiration for him, almost, I daresay, a big doglike devotion. Me, he did not like so well. But—and this is no criticism of the distinguished sculptor of the 'Christ'—I believe that the pronounced romantic strain in the great Jewish craftsman would in the long run have made things difficult for such an uncompromising theorist of 'abstract art' as Hulme.

He had not had time to write much. Even the short time there had been was mostly spent in nervous talk. His literary remains, edited by Mr. Herbert Read, are incredibly badly written. They are reminiscent of his delivery as a lecturer, which was crabbed and harsh to the last degree, and rendered grotesque by the presence of the sort of accent that has made the fortune of Gracie Fields. When he had occasion to say 'abstract art', for instance, the word *art,* as it was wrung out of his mouth, had a nonsensical quality to the English ear. He read from notes, and never looked up at his audience, and seemed contemptuous of the whole boring performance. These few rough essays and notes all the same show that he was an able and enlightened man, and he was therefore a great loss to England—more perhaps than Gaudier, since he was thoroughly English.

Hulme is mainly distinguished as a 'thinker', for having heard of the theological doctrine of Original Sin. No one else in England at the time had ever heard of it, or would, I am persuaded, have done so since, had it not been for him. So all those who, successively, have persued his literary remains, when they have come across it have been overcome with astonishment. They have been so permanently impressed, that even afterwards they have felt that Hulme must have been a very extraordinary man to have heard of it. Original Sin is such an *original* thing to have taken any notice of.

If men of letters had *sobriquets* or nicknames, in the way that some painters have (like 'Robert les Ruines' for instance, a painter who was always painting ruins), then Hulme would probably be called 'Hulme of Original Sin'. As it is, no one ever thinks of Hulme without thinking of Original Sin.

For my own part, I have always considered that the *discovery* of Original Sin was the least of his achievements. After all, he might have heard of it anywhere. Probably he came across it while reading some primer of Scholasticism. The importance of Original Sin, as a doctrine, *apart from its theological bearing*, is that it puts Man in his place. This can be explained in a few words, and I will do so.

There are two ways of regarding mankind. One is Mr. H. G. Wells's way, which is summed up in the title of one of his books, *Men like Gods*. The other way is that of the theologian, who, believing in a High God, has no very high opinion of Man. For the latter, Man is a pretty poor specimen, who requires a great deal of brushing up before you can make him at all presentable.

A famous French writer, called Jean-Jacques Rousseau—the 'father of European Socialism'—taught that Man was essentially *good*. Mr. Wells, Mr. Shaw, and most people in fact in England, believe that.

Christian theology teaches the opposite. For it, Man is essentially *bad*. But, in theology, there is a reason for Man being bad. He is bad because he 'fell'. The doctrine of Original Sin is the doctrine, of course, of 'the Fall'.

You may believe that Man is bad without being a theologian. And then of course you mean something different by the term 'bad'. How much Hulme's terminology was theological I do not know. I should not have supposed it was very theological.

Now why everyone was so impressed with Hulme's discovery of the doctrine of Original Sin was because that doctrine contradicted the unpleasant idolatry of Man (which you do not have to be a theologian to get a bit sick of). It refuted the modernist uplift. It denied that Man was remarkable in any way, much less 'like a god', or capable of unlimited 'advance'.

For people who had definitely become queasy, after listening for a good many years to adulation of the mortal state—of man-in-the-raw—this theology acted as a tonic. The atmosphere had become fuggy with all the greasy incense to Mr. Everyman. And here was somebody who had the bright idea of throwing the window open. There were the stars again! And even if the Star of Bethlehem *was* amongst them, well what matter!

Some of those who were delighted, however, were theologians, more or less, themselves : though there is every reason to suppose they had never heard of Original Sin, else they wouldn't have made so much fuss about it when it was brought to their notice.

The notion of 'progress' is also involved, in this advertisement of Original Sin. And our world, of 1937, is greatly agitated by the warfare of those who believe in 'progress', and those who do not. It is the principle of 'humanism' versus that of discipline and 'authority'. The doctrine of Original Sin has its uses quite outside of Christian dogma.

When Mr. Baldwin, now Earl Baldwin, talks about the blessings of 'democracy', for instance, he is declaring himself a believer in progress and evolution. When Mussolini talks about the iron disciplines of the Roman soul—or Maurras says 'Je suis Romain, je suis humain'—he is declaring himself a believer in 'authority'. He is basing himself upon the past, instead of upon the future (which is where Mr. H. G. Wells's eye is ecstatically fixed). He is denying that the average man, left to himself, has a divine spark, which will eventually enable him to become a god (as thinks Mr. Wells, and as, in the main, the Anglo-Saxon is disposed to think).

I must apologize for this disquisition. But without a little lecture of this kind I could not possibly have explained to you why it was that this fellow Hulme did everybody such a good turn by discovering the doctrine of Original Sin, or why everybody was so grateful to him and said what a fine fellow he was in consequence.

It would be quite out of the question for me to show you in such a context as this how all this sort of thinking resulted in Hulme and myself preferring something anti-naturalist and 'abstract' to Nineteenth Century naturalism, in pictures and in statues. It must suffice for me to say that Man was not the hero of our universe. We thought he required a great deal of tidying-up before he became presentable; both he and I preferred to the fluxions in stone of an Auguste Rodin (following photographically the lines of nature) the more concentrated abstractions-from-nature of the Egyptians.

We were a couple of fanatics and of course I am still. We preferred something more metallic and resistant than the pneumatic surface of the cuticle. We preferred a helmet to a head of hair. A scarab to a jelly-fish.

But I can see all this will seem so much gibberish to you, unless by good luck it has been your hobby to instruct yourself in all these highbrow goings-on. All I can really tell you is that it *was* extremely original of this Mr. Hulme—especially living as he did in Mr. Polly's England—to pick out this stuffy old doctrine of Original Sin and rub everybody's nose in it. He was a very rude and truculent man. He needed to be. And he greatly relished rubbing his countrymen's noses in the highly disobliging doctrine in question.

CHAPTER IX

The 'Savage Messiah' is Killed

Physically—and to get back to the personal once more, after the foregoing excursion into highbrow regions—T. E. Hulme was a very large and imposing man, well over six foot, broad-shouldered, and with legs like a racing cyclist. He had an extremely fine head, which it was his habit to hold on one side, as if listening (a bird-like attitude) really rather reminiscent of an antique bust. Mr. Epstein's bust of him is an admirable one, but scarcely severe enough.

In private life there was no 'severity' about Hulme. He was a very talkative jolly giant, arrogantly argumentative, but a great laughter. He laughed painfully, coldly, but heartily, always wringling his nose as if about to sneeze, and as if he had a bitter taste in his mouth. And among other things he was very fond of the girls. His conversation mostly bore upon that subject, indeed, and he was a most didactic amorist. He had very hard and fast notions as to how the sexual life should be conducted, and much philosophy was brought in to assist at his abstruse devotions to Venus.

I think that in his management of the sexual impulse he was a pure Bergsonian (as indeed he remained in other fields; too much, to my taste). So we may say that St. Thomas Aquinas presided, when it was a statue, and Bergson when it was the living flesh. Not a bad arrangement.

He had designs, I remember, upon a young lady who worked in a small bookshop. The proprietor of the bookshop worked upstairs. But unfortunately he had had a hole cut in the ceiling, and whenever this discoverer of Original Sin was getting on rather nicely with the beautiful assistant, there would be a frantic stamping, as of an enraged horse, upon the ceiling overhead, and a Mormon-like eye would appear in the aperture.

105

This was for Hulme a maddening experience. It dominated his life for some time. He sneered, with a painful twisting of the nose, whenever he spoke of it. He was held as if in a vice by a concatenation of circumstances. To start with, he could obtain tick at this bookshop. Nowhere else. So he was compelled to go there. He was exposed incessantly to this dilemma—his purse, his sex, his intellect all contributing. The lot of Tantalus was his, a cunningly-contrived frustration : and he could see no way out of it at all.

Had the bookseller been less trustful as a bookseller, and refused him credit, obviously the ordeal would have terminated at once. Or had he became more trustful *as a man,* abolished his spyhole, equally there would have been an immediate solution. Hulme would have found release had the bookseller's policy *as a bookseller* been suddenly modified, under the stress of competition, or as a result of the deterioration of the public taste. Had his stock taken on a more frivolous character, had he ceased to cater for the philosopher, Hulme's trials would have been at an end. Similarly, had the beautiful assistant taken on a more frivolous character, that would have been that. But no, he was condemned to suffer perpetually, to all appearance. This awful stability of things appalled him. No Heracletian flux. An implacable *status quo* reigned in the bookshop—dominated the world. And he would discuss this problem—sandwiched in between the doctrine of Original Sin and the Fascism of the Frenchman, Sorel, whose *Reflexions sur la Violence* he was translating—in his nagging, nasal, North-country voice, until he induced in his listener a sensation of the cussedness of things that really was in its way a novel cocktail. He was an excellent gossip.

He nagged away at the spyhole in the ceiling, with his head stiffly bent to one side. One eye into the Ewigkeit, and there was that look as if he were listening for some response to his obstinate questions. He nagged away, with short sharp bursts of frustrated sneering. *Where* could he make a breach in this inexorable stability of things? Or was this in fact one of those problems set by life that was strictly insoluble, so neatly devised to checkmate the sexual instinct? And was not this instinct itself a trap for the intellect—as the intellect was undoubtedly a trap for sex, only too often upsetting its applecart?

As Hulme would argue tirelessly about his own adventures as an animal, he would not hesitate to suggest that one should reciprocate. He would cock an eye, sneer, and throw out an inquisitive hint. But I was recalcitrant to communism. My technique on such occasions was to retreat into a Tartuffian wonderland, where he would solemnly pursue me with a charlatanesque inquisition. Chased by this clownish sophist into the cardboard fastnesses I had run up for the occasion. I would fight a homeric battle of falsewits. As a rule, honours, I think, were even.

Hulme was not a 'master-mind', or anything of that sort. Some of his friends were far stronger-minded than he was, and he was highly influenceable. Bergson dominated him, of course, with great facility : and anything tainted with Bergsonism could not help being suspect to me. Others would act *through* him. He was not one of those people who when you talk to them you know that at least it is to *them* you are talking. You might quite well with him be talking to somebody else.

I think we must say that T. E. Hulme was one of the most promising intelligences produced by England since the Shaw-Wells-Bennett vintage. That he should have been killed in one of England's stupidest wars was therefore a symbolical happening.

I should perhaps have said that I had quarrelled with Hulme. That in no way affects my estimate of him. I should not have allowed myself to get into a dispute with him if this estimate had not been what you see it was—respectful, but no more than that.

That I have devoted so much attention to Hulme is on the same principle as the 'Cantleman' passages I have quoted. My contacts with this contemporary is one of the best ways of reflecting myself. I am describing myself in describing him, just as in describing me he would be revealing his own peculiarities.

I had no great liking, I mean personal liking, for Hulme's circle of friends. But Gaudier, though I knew him very little, I always liked. This little sharp-faced, black-eyed stranger amongst us, whose name was a Polish city, but who for some reason was a French subject, or had a French name, was an extremely fine artist.

So many excellent books have been written about him (I have not read them, but the names of their authors indicate their quality) that it would be otiose to draw upon my slender knowledge of the facts, and tell you how this young sculptor lived under a railway arch, with a middle-aged Polish sister who was not a sister (so since we have learnt). From the passport point of view, he must have been a walking enigma. I cannot imagine what his passport would look like: if he was married, or Polish—single, or French; or perhaps technically a Briton and mildly incestuous; and whether really liable for French military service, or for English conscription or a little of both. All I know is that he went to France when the war started, to join the French army, but was immediately arrested when he presented himself to the military, put under lock and key, and bundled back to Great Britain. But he was determined to take up arms for a country that was not his. And I among others saw him off. Hulme and I believe Epstein were among those who did so. I remember him in the carriage window of the boat-train, with his excited eyes. We left the platform, a depressed, almost a guilty, group.

It is easy to laugh at the exaggerated estimate 'the artist' puts upon his precious life. But when it is *really* an artist—and there are very few—it is at the death of something terribly alive that you are assisting. And this figure was so preternaturally *alive,* that I began my lesson then: a lesson of hatred for this soul-less machine, of big-wig money-government, and these masses of half-dead people, for whom personal extinction is such a tiny step, out of half-living into no-living, so what does it matter?

Ezra Pound told me after that how Gaudier had rapidly become a sergeant in the French infantry: and very shortly after that, again, how he had been killed in action.

Gaudier has been written about under the heading 'Savage Messiah'. There must be some claptrap about that. To be brave is not to be savage, not what the French describe as *exalté*—

and that he certainly was—messianic. He was gentle, unselfish, and excitable, and probably struck some people as fiery, uncouth, and messianic. No artist so fine as Gaudier could be a Messiah, as a matter of fact. Messianic emotionality and Art are incompatible terms. But the stones that he carved are there to prove that Gaudier was a placid genius, of gentle and rounded shapes, not a turbulent or 'savage' one at all.

PART III
A Gunner's Tale

CHAPTER 1

The Romance of War

Arrival at 'the Front' for us was not unlike arrival at a big Boxing Match, or at a Blackshirt Rally at Olympia. The same sinister expectancy, but more sinister and more electric, the same restless taciturnity of stern-faced persons assembling for a sensational and bloody event, their hearts set on a knock-out. Somebody else's, of course.

We arrived at railhead at night and a battle was in progress. For a long time, as we moved slowly forward in our darkened coaches, the sound of guns had been getting louder and nearer. There was no moon or stars—all lights had been turned down for the performance. Only the unseen orchestra thundered away, before an unseen stage. We had to imagine the actors which we knew were there, crouching in their sticky labyrinths.

From the crowded carriage-windows, at last, sudden bursts of dull light could be discerned, and last of all an authentic flash had been visible, but still far away—angry and red, like a match struck and blown out again immediately.

We left the train, and finally we reached, I forget how, the fringes of this battle. We reached it unexpectedly. We were collected upon a road, I seem to think. Perhaps we were waiting for lorries to take us to billets—for we of course were not going into action then. We were not for this battle. We had no guns either. They could not be made quickly enough. We were just the *personnel* of a battery, with no guns, who had come to stand-by, or be parcelled out as reinforcements.

With great suddenness—as we stood, very impressed as new-comers in the midst of this pandemonium—in a neighbouring field a battery of large howitzers began firing. After this particular picture I can remember nothing at all. It is so distinct everything in its neighbourhood is oblitereated. I can only remember that in the air full of violent sound, very suddenly there was a flash near at hand, followed by further flashes, and I could see the gunners moving about as they loaded again. They appeared to be 11-inch guns—very big. Out of their throats had sprung a dramatic flame, they had roared, they had moved back. You could see them, lighted from their mouths, as they hurled into the air their great projectile, and sank back as they did it. In the middle of the monotonous percussion, which had never slackened for a moment, the tom-toming of interminable artillery, for miles round, going on in the darkness, it was as if someone had exclaimed in your ear, or something you had supposed inanimate had come to life, when the battery whose pretence we had not suspected went into action.

So we plunged immediately into the romance of battle. But all henceforth was romance. All this culminated of course in the scenery of the battlefields, like desolate lunar panoramas. That matched the first glimpses of the Pacific, as seen by the earliest circumnavigators.

Need I say that there is nothing so romantic as war? If you are 'a romantic', you have not lived if you have not been present at a battle, of that I can assure you.

I am very sorry to have to say this. Only a care for truth compels me to avow it. I am not a romantic—though I perfectly understand romance. And I do not like war. It is under compulsion that I stress the exceedingly romantic character of all the scenes I am about to describe.

If your mind is of a romantic cast, there is nothing for it, I am afraid. The likelihood that you will get your head blown off cannot weigh with you for a moment. You must not miss a war, if one is going! You cannot afford to miss that experience.

It is commonly remarked that 'there is no romance in modern war'. That is absurd, I am sorry to have to say.

It has frequently been contended that Agincourt, or even Waterloo with its 'thin red line' and its Old Guard of Napoleonic veterans, was 'spectacular': whereas modern war is 'drab and unromantic'. Alas! that is nonsense. To say that is entirely to misunderstand the nature of romance. It is like

114

saying that love can only be romantic when a figure as socially-eminent and beautiful as Helen of Troy is involved. That, of course, has nothing to do with it whatever! It is most unfortunate : but men are indifferent to physical beauty or obvious physical splendour, where their emotions are romantically stimulated. Yes, romance is the enemy of beauty. That hag, War, carries it every time over Helen of Troy.

The truth is, of course, that it is not what you *see*, at all, that makes an event romantic to you, but what you *feel*. And in war, as you might expect, you feel with considerable intensity.

The misunderstanding goes even deeper than that, however. Knights in armour, with plumes and lances, are not, even in the visual sense, the most *romantic* subject-matter for a romantic painter.

You only have to think a moment : the dark night, with the fearful flashing of a monstrous cannonade—all the things that do not come into the picture, which *are not seen,* in other words, but which are suggested in its darkest shadows—what could be more technically 'romantic' than that, if it is romance that we must talk about?

But even if the pictorial subject-matter were insignificant, it would still be the same thing.

Romance is partly what you see but it is much more what you feel. I mean that *you* are the romance, far more than the romantic object. By definition, romance is always inside and not outside. It is, as we say, subjective. It is the material of magic. It partakes of the action of a drug.

Place a man upon the highest passes of the Andes, and what he *sees* is always what he feels. But when *on joue sa vie,* it is not so much the grandeur of the spectacle of destruction, or the chivalrous splendour of the appointments, as the agitation in the mental field within, of the organism marked down to be destroyed, that is impressive. It is that that produces 'the light that never was on land or sea', which we describe as 'romance'. *Anything* upon which that coloration falls is at once transfigured. And the source of light is within your own belly.

Of course it would be impossible to overstate the contribution of the guns to these great romantic effects. Even in such an essentially romantic context as war, they are startlingly 'romantic' accessories, and help to heighten the effect.

It is they who provide the orchestral accompaniment. It is they who plough up the ground till it looks literally 'like nothing on earth'. It is they who transform a smart little modern township, inside an hour, into a romantic ruin, worthy of the great Robert himself, or of Claude Lorrain. They are likewise the purveyors of 'shell-shock', that most dramatic of ailments. And lastly, they give the most romantic and spectacular wounds of all—a bullet-wound, even a dum-dum, is child's play to a wound inflicted by a shell-splinter.

I have slept soundly through scores of full-dress bombardments. It is very few people who don't, in a war of positions, where bombardments are almost continuous. Through a long artillery preparation for an Attack—a hoped-for 'breakthrough', with the enemy retaliating at full blast—in the very thick of the hubbub, with things whizzing and roaring all round—I have slept for hours together as peacefully as if I were in a London garden suburb.

Rapidly one ceases to notice this orchestra. But although one forgets about it, one would miss it if it were not there. These are the kettledrums of death that you are hearing. And you would soon know the difference if they stopped.

CHAPTER II

Howitzers

We had been hanging about some time, when I was posted to a battery to replace casualties. It was a 'six-inch How' battery, not far from Bailleul. My own battery disappeared : later on I joined it, in another part of the Line.

I arrived at the battery mess and made the acquaintance of the other officers. Our 'battery position', that is, where the guns were, was only a short distance away from our sleeping quarters and the officer's Mess. There was not a great abundance of dugouts. I was given bedroom in the dugout of another junior officer. It was very small but he took me in temporarily. And it was with him that I received what would have been called in the old days of war my baptism of fire. This is how it occurred. It happened straight away, on my first night.

We went to our dugout and got into our respective campbeds. My brother officer was in a very nervous condition I thought, and he unburdened himself to me on the subject of a certain observation post, which was very much in his mind. Twice in the last week he had passed a couple of very unpleasant days in it, 'I *dread* going up to that O. Pip do you know—I dread it! It's the most bloody awful death-trap. You wait till you see it!' he told me with a commendable frankness, though I believe he could not help himself. And after he had described the sort of health-resort it was, I confess that I felt in no hurry to visit it myself. However, he was very exhausted, and soon he turned over to addresss himself to sleep.

No sooner had he done this, than something unpleasant began to happen. There was the unmistakable sound of a shell, which I then heard for the first time, and the explosion followed, not far away outside our dugout, I took it be.

'They've started shelling again!' he groaned in disgust, mov-

117

ing restlessly in his bed. 'This happens every night. They shelled us for an hour the night before last. They've spotted us, I think —they'll never let us alone now.'

No sooner had he uttered his complaint, than a second shell came over. As he heard the sound start, of its whooping approach, his bed gave a violent creak. I watched him heel over on one side. As the shell descended—with its strange parabolic whooping onrush—an anal whistle answered it, from the neighbouring bed. This response was forced out of him, by unrestrained dismay.

That was my first encounter with 'wind-up', as it was my first experience of shelling. In fact, it was the most perfect specimen of wind-up that it would be possible to find I think. And at each successive shell-swoop it was repeated. He raised himself slightly; and he answered the frightening onrush of the cylinder of metal with his humble gaseous discharge. He did not seem to mind at all my seeing this. I suppose he thought I would put it down to indigestion.

After a few shells had come over, we sat up in bed, and he gave me his opinion of the architecture of our dugouts. I was glad, as it seemed to take his mind off the shells.

'This dugout is a joke!' he told me. 'It wouldn't stop an india-rubber ball! These dugouts are washouts.'

'Are they?' I said, glancing up with considerable uneasiness at the mud roof a foot or two away from my head.

Like most military novices I had innocently supposed that a dugout—any dugout—was there to keep out shell-fire, and was reasonably secure. I had felt as safe as houses in this earthen igloo. But he rapidly disabused me.

'A five-nine would go through this as if it was paper!' he assured me. 'If one of those shells happens to hit this dugout— well, it's all up with us. We should both of us be dead within a second.'

As he spoke another shell plunged down outside, very much nearer this time. Indeed it seemed to me that it had come down a few feet off—for at first it is very difficult to judge the distance of a 'burst', from the sound, if you do not see it but only hear it.

'That was pretty near wasn't it?' I asked.

'No, they most of them fall in the next field. But it's quite near enough.'

'Quite,' I said. 'Oughtn't we to go out and see what's happening?'

'Nothing's happening,' he said. 'This goes on all the time. This might stop a splinter. But *a direct hit!* Then we're for it!'

I saw if we went outside we should be inviting a splinter. I supposed the chances of a direct hit were so much less that he was wise to stop where he was.

He went on instructing me in the futility of dugouts, however —especially *our* dugouts. They were champion death-traps for unlucky subalterns.

'There's nothing on top here,' pointing up over his head, 'but a little loose earth. Just a few shovelsful of loose earth and a log or two.'

'Is that all?' I muttered indignantly.

'That's all. What's the use of that? There's a piece of corrugated iron!'

'Is there?' I asked, looking up with expectation.

'Somewhere I expect. A lot of use *that* is! The sandbags at the side are a foot thick if that. A shell goes through that like butter. It likes sandbags. Shells like making holes in sandbags.'

I tossed up my head, in scandalized silence.

'I don't know why they take the trouble to make them. They're useless. We might just as well be sleeping in a Nissen hut. It doesn't even keep the rain out. It drips on my face when it rains.'

'I suppose,' I said for the sake of something to say, 'there is a slight chance. The logs might interfere with the burst.'

'Don't you believe it! It would come clean through and burst in our faces. We'd be full of splinters inside a second.'

I found subsequently that he was quite correct. As regards the surface dugouts, of sandbags, baulks, and earth, they were useless. Later on I was given a bedchamber of my own. It was a shack of corrugated iron, without any pretentions to being a parabellum. It was even a less desirable residence than the sandbagged one, seeing that it was most conveniently placed upon the edge of a road. And whatever else is shelled or not shelled, a road is *always* shelled. It had a further thing to recommend it, namely its position immediately behind a battery of big heavies. These naturally attracted the enemy fire, apart from the banging that they kept up all night.

As time went on, I found that there was one situation in which I did not at all enjoy finding myself. I did not like to be subjected to indiscriminate shell-fire when undressed. Lay me to rest in a flea-bag and I jib at shelling. Most of the shelling was at night. In view of the particular position of my sleeping-shack I never knew, when it started, whether it was (1) the road that was being shelled, or (2) the gun in front of me, or (3) our dugouts behind me. Not that it mattered a great deal, from my point of view. But if it was the gun in front, my companions behind would regard it as no business of theirs (though it was of mine—seeing the electric nature of my position) : whereas if it happened to be *us* who were to be bombarded, then it was our habit (the officers) to collect in the officers' Mess and have a whisky and a smoke. What the men did was somewhat their own affair.

The men's quarters were big and of course unsafe dugouts. Life in them cannot have been pleasant. In my own battery— which as I have said I joined later—there was a gunner whom I had noticed before we came out to France. He was very 'nicely-spoken'—much too nicely-spoken to be comfortable in such a class-conscious country in England, and seeing that none of the officers were particularly nicely-spoken except myself. Later on in France he became the victim of panic. He nursed a shell-shock. Huddled at night in the men's quarters, in a position that was constantly shelled, the other men complained that he kept them awake at night by his shivering. They said his tin hat rattled against his dickie all night long. At last he had to be sent back to England.

The disadvantage of these conditions of the siege-gunner's service is obvious. He was always 'in the Line', he had no spells of rest 'behind the Line'. Where he slept, often for a year on end, was in the midst of nests of batteries which were one of the main objectives of the enemy shelling.

THE AUTHOR OF *TARR*

Wyndham Lewis. 1932.
portrait of Augustus John

Flight-commander Orlebar

Rev. M. C. D'Arcy, S.J.

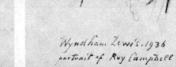

Wyndham Lewis. 1936
portrait of Roy Campbell

Of course my tin house—rather like a suburban garden-coal-cellar—was a palace in comparison with what I should have got as a gunner. When it had been stuck together, the O.C. remarked casually that it was awkwardly placed. I said that was all right : one place was much the same as another.

When the first shell would come over, I would roll swiftly out of the flea-bag and pull on my trenchboots. That is really all I worried about. I think *the whole* of his feet are man's 'Achilles heel'. I would hate to face a firing squad in my stocking-feet! Clothing and its part in the psychology of war is a neglected subject. I would have braved an eleven-inch shell in my trenchboots, but would have declined an encounter with a pipsqueak in my bare feet.

From my standpoint the worst shelling here was road-shelling since I was more or less *in* the road. I preferred a bad shelling of the dugouts at my back, when we were assembled in the mess, which was more matey. It doesn't matter a bit if *everybody's* being shelled.

This battery had among its officers—he was I believe second-in-command—an eminent young mathematician. I knew he was a good mathematician because he was unable to do a simple addition sum, and as to the august operations of subtraction and division, they were entirely beyond him.

While I was reading in my flea-bag by the light of a candle one night—it was the *Chartreuse de Parme* I had just begun, and I was for the second time upon the field of Waterloo—down came the shells, and there was no mistake that this time it was *us* they were after. All were going back of my shack. As I made for the mess I came upon the mathematician. Shells were coming over pretty fast, but he had placed himself in as exposed a position as possible, and was watching them narrowly, as they arrived. With a look of eager surprise he was darting his head round as one fell behind him, and back again to the front as one fell ahead. Something was amiss in his calculations, it seemed, and the position of the bursts was profoundly puzzling, if not unsatisfactory. I could not imagine what he was doing. The laws of probability, or something of that sort, were at stake, I deduced. Nature was behaving eccentrically, affronting, per-

121

haps, laws with which I was totally unacquainted. *Something* was undoubtedly wrong; for he ought by all the rules to have been hit by this time, as a shell splinter had nearly hit me, and I had only just arrived.

The mess was a long open dugout, high enough to stand up in, and was reputed to be a *good* dugout; the only good one we had. I don't know why it was supposed to be good, but we were all persuaded that it could be hit by a five-nine with impunity. (The 'five-nine' shell was the German equivalent of the six-inch English. And practically all the shelling we had to expect was from the five-nines.)

After a bit the mathematician came slowly in, looking very disquietened, sat down and rolled a cigarette. I did not like to question him, though I saw the shells had been falling in a very unorthodox sequence; and I longed to ask him why a shell *never* hit the Mess. That was what puzzled *me*. Indeed they never hit a dugout. They made holes all round them, but never got a bull's eye. But I suppose it is like a game of darts in a pub.

CHAPTER III

How the Gunner 'Fights'

You may have asked how it is, now that I was at the Front, I was not at least firing a gun or doing something except reading *La Chartreuse de Parme* by candlelight, to earn my handsome salary. What did I do in the *daytime*? All that I have told you about happened at night. Was I fighting the German from sunrise till nightfall? Well, as a matter of fact I was doing nothing at all, most of the time.

First of all, I was a supernumary officer, come in as a replacement for a casualty, and there was very little for me to do except hang about and smoke cigarettes.

Probably the casualty, in his turn, was a quite futile and irrational casualty—this is no reflection upon his competence, but he probably got hit while he was performing some entirely useless routine function. He would have been better employed, it is quite likely, house-agenting or clerking somewhere in England, rather than shrouding himself in military mystery 'somewhere in France'.

The trouble about all these batteries was that they were over-burdened with officers. The Germans arm a 'five-nine' battery —our opposite number—with one officer and two or three N.C.O.'s. If the officer became a casualty, it didn't matter. While waiting for another officer, the N.C.O.'s carried on.

We had six officers in this battery. Five too many. We had no more casualties while I was there in spite of a good deal of desultory shelling. It is astonishing how many shells it takes to get one casualty.

The next battery to us, on the other hand, lost a couple of officers a week after I arrived. As usual, 'reinforcements' were available almost at once, in the shape of a buxom little subaltern with cane and kitbag complete, who stepped briskly out of the

123

battery sidecar, before their Mess dugout, took a couple of steps forward, and was hit in the jaw by a splinter from a 'five-nine', which had unexpectedly landed a few yards away. He was put back—but this time in a recumbent position—in the sidecar, and returned at top-speed to the base from which he had arrived. He had spent exactly twelve minutes and a half in the Line, and would probably never see it again, as he was badly wounded.

Such are the chances of this sort of war. I was in the Line for about a year, on and off. I had shells burst within a couple of feet of my head. Splinters of every possible size have whisked around me, at every possible angle and at every variety of speed, grazing my coat, and smacking my tinhat, but I was never wounded. Yet I did not 'bear a charmed life', as our fathers called it, I was just difficult to hit, like most other people. Only a few were easy—I mean with a shell.

I see however that in order to understand this part of my life-story, as many readers will not have first-hand acquaintance with even the simplest facts regarding war, it is probably desirable to give you a little explanatory data.

Most modern war seems destined to be what is called a 'war of positions', or what is technically siege-warfare. A Civil War is no exception to this rule, events in Spain suggest. Endless positional or trench warfare appears to be unavoidable. The Western Front, at the time of my service, was purely siege warfare. We might as well have been before a city which we were investing—except that we were both besieging armies, as it were; besieging each other.

On this principle what would be the 'Assaults', if it were a regular old-fashioned siege of a *place-forte,* were the 'Attacks'; namely the infantry-attacks. These were interminable attempts to put an end to the 'Stalemate'. Throughout 1917 when I was there this was what was happening. Passchendaele—at which I was present—was the culmination of this. The British Army sustained enormous losses, to no purpose. It was the worst battle of the War, and the stupidist, which is saying a lot.

Serving as a 'combatant' in a modern war is referred to as 'fighting'. But of course the only people who *fight* in the most rigorous acceptance of that term are the infantry. A gunner does not fight. He merely shells and is shelled. He discharges a large metal cylinder, aiming it by means of a delicately-adjusted mechanism, to fall at a certain spot which he cannot see, in the hope that he may kill somebody he hopes is there. He himself suffers from the desire of the other, enemy, gunners, a long way away, to achieve the same object with respect to himself.

The gunner rarely if ever sees the enemy, except prisoners, when the infantry succeed in capturing some, and they are sent behind the Line, in small herds. The exception to this rule is the gunner-officer, who as an 'observer' sometimes sees the animal he is opposing in a free state—that is not in captivity. For instance I have seen Germans in their natural state, walking about behind their lines, and even popping about in their trenches. But that was only because I was an officer.

It is one of the tasks of an artillery officer to go up to *observation-posts*, as they are called ('O.Pip', for short). But I have never engaged in personal combat with a German in a trench or anywhere else. So I have not 'fought' the Germans, except in the more abstract sense that I have been responsible for the dispatch of unlimited numbers of shells in their direction, and as a result of the explosion of these shells (when they were not duds) I may have done these foemen more injury than I ever could have done them, I am sure, with my strong right arm.

In the old days of open battle, gunners did on occasion come into personal contact with the enemy—never with the infantry, but sometimes with the cavalry. These cavalry must have been extremely unpleasant customers, prancing and plunging about upon excited horses and waving over their heads long shining knives that they called 'sabres', or armed with barbarous spears, like an intoxicated picador.

You may have read accounts of how a cavalry charge—say in the Indian Mutiny or in the campaigns against the Mahratta Princes—carried these impetuous horse-soldiers right amongst the guns, where the gun-crews were peaceably blazing away, as defenceless as civilians—never dreaming of any unorthodox disturbance, or anticipating strong-arm tactics on the part of the Nosey Parkers on horseback. How they 'cut down' the Sepoy gunners may have been represented to you—it probably was in your history-book—as a dashing and praiseworthy exploit.

My feeling about horses extends to those who sit on them. And whenever I read of the cavalry doing as above, I experience, I am bound to say, much fellow-feeling for the unfortunate gunners. Cavalry should not interfere with gunners in that way, is my feeling. And the exploits of Lake or of French are spoilt for me by these unseemly attacks upon unarmed Sepoy and Boer artillerymen : though on occasion the gunners have given these curvetting musical-riders a warmer welcome than they expected. The old-time ramrod was at times as good at jousting from the ground with, as the sabre was for 'cutting down' from up above.

Still, it *was* done, now and then, in the past—the mounted-arm did run amok among the artillery, having cut its way through the infantry. Apart from Tanks and of course the machine-guns of the air-arm (but this hardly applies at all in the war of 1914-18) the gunner has nothing to fear with regard to personal encounters with the enemy. He is a fighting-man only in name. The infantry do the common-or-garden *fighting*. They are the gladiators.

It is my business here to give an intelligent record if possible of the sort of war I know about. An infantryman's experience is of an entirely different order. A sapper has again a different tale to tell. An airman's is so different that I could not guess at much that he would have to recount. This is a gunner's tale, under conditions of siege warfare, in the commissioned ranks.

Where the officer's experience differs from that of the rank and file is that he leaves the guns and goes up to what is called an observation post. It is in the course of this latter duty that his experience merges somewhat with that of the infantry. A bombardier in a battery, for instance, could go through numerous campaigns, and be wounded a half-dozen times, without ever having been near a front-line trench.

As a battery officer at the Front my main duties were to mouch about the battery, and to go up before daybreak with a party of signallers to an observation post. This was usually just behind the Front Line trench—in the No Man's Land just behind it. For there were blanks behind as before.

This O. Pip work was hard and often very dangerous. The former, the work at the battery position, was not work at all, and was only spasmodically dangerous.

Nearly half the time of a siege-battery subaltern was spent at the observation post. Quite ninety per cent of that time was wasted. In an active part of the Front the telephone wires would never remain intact for long, as they would be cut by shell-fire. It might have been quite useful if the enemy had not persisted in destroying the wires, or if they had left the observation post itself in peace. But this they *would* not do. They spotted an observation post within a half-hour at the outside and would shell it to pieces. They even shelled anything that *looked like* an observation post. A half-dozen stumps of trees in what once was a wood they would never let alone. When I said ninety per cent of 'O. Pip' duty was liable to be time wasted —at the climax of the War, on the Western Front, that is—I was not exaggerating. Usually one would have been as well occupied picking one's teeth at the rest billet or reading *La Chartreuse de Parme* in a café at Bailleul.

When I attested, I selected the Artillery. Afterwards I concluded that I could not have been in the infantry : I am not nearly bloodthirsty enough. You can, I know, have seen a good deal of service as an infantry officer without ever having been called upon to do anything bloodthirsty. But as an infantryman you have to be prepared to behave with savagery, if the occasion arises. And I am the opposite of a savage.

There is no rule about the position of guns, except that the smaller guns, with a shorter range, have to be nearer the front line. The Field Artillery is placed as near behind the infantry as is considered desirable, or the nature of the ground suggests, and behind them come the smallest howitzers. These are the six-inch howitzers, like ours.

If a six-inch howitzer battery found itself 'up amongst the Field', it considered it was being exposed to unnecessary risk.

Often the casualties were extremely heavy when this occurred, as it did quite often in the crowded conditions of the intensive warfare of the last two years. Naturally a larger gun firing too near 'the line' would attract undue attention from the enemy. And when you consider that the Germans had their sausage-balloons practically over the Front Line, and that they would be looking down into a battery of troublesome howitzers placed beneath them in this way, and directing fire on it all the time, you can imagine how undesirable a prominence this might be considered, for those whom it most concerned.

We were 'up amongst the Field' on the Flanders coast, for instance. But this was because we were there for an Attack (which never materialized) and ours was a silent battery at the time, so we were not exposed to aggressive shelling.

In a war of the type with which I am acquainted, therefore, a gunner is a very dangerous type of spectator—without inter-mission throwing murderous missiles into the bullring below (to illustrate what I mean), and over at the banks of equally active spectators opposite, who are of course doing the same thing. It *is* 'active service' all right. But it is not strictly speaking 'fighting'. I have said that I am no friend of war, and I am not. What is more, I never discovered in myself any of those instincts that go to the making of 'the perfect soldier'. When from above a front-line trench (at Passchendaele) I was 'regis-tering' batteries on what was left of a village, I was glad to think that none of the enemy were in it. As our shells fell, and I watched them through my field-glasses, it was a satisfaction to me to know (as we had been told) that it was only brick-and-mortar that was being 'strafed'. By no means a soldierly reflection! I should add, perhaps, that of course this was par-ticular to myself, and that many of my companions were, I am quite sure, the most bloodthirsty people, and determined to wash out Fritz's sins in his own blood.

After all that has been written about the War it seems absurd that all this mere information should be necessary. But I have not so far seen a book in which the gunners' habits have been described. And if such books exist, I will be prepared to wager that at the end of them the reader would be little more able than when he started to know exactly what the gunners' life entailed, or what sort of 'fighting' he'd been doing. If I have debunked the gunner, forgive me, if you are a gunner.

E*

CHAPTER IV

A Day of Attack

It was a Day of Attack—'somewhere in France', and the O.C. Battery had himself decided to go to an observation-post, and observe a bit of what was going forward. He took me with him. It was a reasonably distant one, and we saw what we had come to see without too much interference. We saw the battle : there had been no break-through, but a push-back. When it was evident that *something* had happened, and that the new front line would not be where the old front line had been, he turned to me and said :

'Well, that's that. I'm going down there, to find out where the new front line is now. Would you like to come with me?'

I expressed my desire to find myself at the the side of my commanding officer.

'We shall have to fix on a new O. Pip.'

That, I agreed, would undoubtedly be one of the disagreeable things we should have to do.

'Yes, I think I'll go and see what's happening. Besides, I should like to have a look!'

'I should, too,' I answered.

'You're sure you'd like to come? God knows what it's like. There may *be* no Front Line.'

'In that case we shan't be able to find it,' said I, circumspectly.

'If there's one *there* I'll find it!' said he with great soldierly resolution, as he got up. So we started off, first returning to the battery to explain what we intended to do.

This O.C. was more alive than most—a small commercial gent (perhaps a garage proprietor, I thought, or employee in a Shipping Office) blossomed suddenly into a Major, R.A. Slight in build, about thirty, lightly moustached, he was able and very collected when other people were the reverse. I concluded from what I saw of him that he had set his mind upon taking back a Military Cross to Balham. I was under the impression that he would deserve it, if he could extract it from the donors of such things. Not exactly the man for an unambitious subaltern, more interested in blasting than in bombardiering—and whose most coveted crosses were not military—to go hunting for the Front Line with, in a new No Man's Land, upon a morning of attack.

But I laid it down for myself that two principles should co-exist for me, in my conduct of this war-game. As a 'crowd-master', it was my business not to succumb to the lure of a transitory military laurel: it was on the other hand my business to observe at first-hand all of war's bag-of-tricks. Therefore I allowed myself a pinch of inquisitive pleasure at the prospect of a trip to this problematical place of battle.

Going through the lines of 'the Field' the shelling was heavy—though on the whole there was every evidence that the enemy were not replying with their customary aggressiveness. Their artillery was being moved back.

A Field Battery beside which we were making our way was having a rough time, however. There were several casualties while we were passing its guns, but my little O.C. might have been taking a walk with his dog for all the notice he took. Good boy, I thought! He knew his stuff.

But at this point civilization ended. At least so far, we could be sure of our bearings. Beyond this battery was a short stretch of shell-pitted nothingness—for we had entered upon that arid and blistering vacuum; the lunar landscape, so often described in the war-novels and represented by dozens of painters and draughtsmen, myself among them, but the particular quality of which it is so difficult to convey. Those grinning skeletons in field-grey, the skull still protected by the metal helmet: those festoons of mud-caked wire, those miniature mountain-ranges of saffron earth, and trees like gibbets—these were the properties only of those titanic casts of dying and shell-shocked actors, who charged this stage with a romantic electricity.

Picking our way across the first hundred yards of rugged wilderness, we reached a little ridge and stopped. What had we expected to see? Something, at all events. Whereas we gazed out over a solitary and uninhabited steppe. There was nothing. It was entirely empty and silent, except for a slight movement away to our left in the middle distance and the occasional door-banging effect of a shell-burst.

The battery behind us clamoured, as in duty bound. The thunder of the hammering artillery never stopped at our backs, and for miles on either hand. But before us stretched, terrible in its emptiness, the land we had come to explore.

What we were standing on the edge of was in the nature of a hollow, of cratered nothingness. For it was a hillside, terminating eventually in another ridge, which, with the ridge on which we stood, shut it in, whereas immediately in front of us the ground fell away somewhat. So it was a sort of one-sided valley.

From beyond the opposite ridge came the distant banging of the German artillery. Otherwise this was the most thrilling solitude that the most particular of explorers could have wished for. No valley in a tropical steppe could have been better, from that point of view. The inner fastnesses of the Sahara could not have developed a more inacessible air of unearthly remoteness. Give this wilderness a palm, and make-believe that the artillery outside was some strange mirage-effect of desert-thunder— an aural in place of an optical phenomenon—and this could have been the bleak centre of Africa.

But the O.C. battery pointed a little way ahead of us.

'Our old Front Line,' he said.

'Where is our new one?' I asked him, for I knew he wanted me to ask that.

'God knows!' he answered. 'Let's see if we can find it. There's a barrage on that ridge. It's somewhere there I expect.'

Some distance to our right, upon the skyline, there was a succession of shell-bursts. That would doubtless be it.

For some time we stumbled and leapt, advancing into this

extremely debatable ruin of what was until an hour or two before an underground fortress, under a rain of shells. We crossed what had been our own Front Line and entered the German. It was profusely lined with fresh corpses. We picked our way amid scores of green-clad bodies. Newspapers in Gothic type were a feature of this scene, and I put one into my pocket, to see what Berlin said about these events.

We got out of this—I hated all these bodies, but put that impression away, to be pondered at a later time—and were hurrying forward when my companion dropped into a trench with the suddenness of a collapsing Jack-in-the-box. Simultaneously I heard a sharp tap-tapping—unfamiliar then, but I guessed its import : and dropped too, with a creditable celerity.

'Machine-guns,' he said, as we hurried along—keeping for some time now to the trenches. 'They've left machine-gun posts I expect, or perhaps redoubts. They always do that. I doubt if we've got a proper line yet.'

We continued our breathless and sweaty tramp, always along the abandoned German trench-system, bearing to our right all the time. We were moving over till we got before the line of bursts upon the ridge, a matter of a quarter of a mile. At last my leader stopped. He mopped his brow, and I mopped mine. Then we came once more to the surface and looked round. No machine gun chattered at us this time. We were at the foot of the gradient which led up to the line of bursts.

Now we were in the heart of this sinister little desert. Despite the angry hammering from the world of batteries we had left, and that from the world of batteries whose frontiers lay not so far ahead, but still not near enough to sound very loud—in spite of that agitated framework to our 'mystery land', nothing could have been more solitary. I should not have been surprised to see an Atlas vulture or some desiccated African goat. For it was definitely a red desert, more African than lunar in appearance.

Most of the explorers who have trod those deserts have either left their bones there, or if they have come back to tell the tale, never have told it. For in restrospect they mostly have believed that they must have been dreaming. But a new war is probably near at hand. A new generation will be setting out for that

Never-never Land. So it is that these dreams become topical, alas!

To make a reconstruction of this landscape for a millionaire-sightseer, say, would be impossible. The sightseer would be the difficulty—for the reasons I have given already in my dissection of romance. This is a museum of sensations, not a collection of objects. For your reconstruction you would have to admit Death there as well, and he would never put in an appearance, upon those terms. You would have to line the trenches with bodies guaranteed freshly killed that morning. No hospital could provide it. And unless people were mad they would not want—apart from the cost—to assemble the necessary ordnance, the engines required for this stunt landscape-gardening.—Except that they were mad, they would not have wanted ever to assemble it.

To obtain this parched, hollow, breathless desert you have to postulate madmen.—It was the hollow centre of a madman's dream we had got into. As our feet struck the ground they seemed to be echoing faintly from end to end of this mysterious place of death.

Two men were brewing an inky coffee over a brazier—I have always regarded it as an odd occupation. They half-sat, half-crouched, behind a fragment of wall—a wall borrowed from that other system of domestic peace to be a stunted property of this inferno. The barrage began a few yards away from their blackened nook.

They were the only human beings we had encountered so far. In an exhausted lassitude they attended to their brazier. We had reached the summit of the incline. Along this crest or ridge went a road, terminating in this fragment of wall, behind which we now stood. For fifty yards the road was visible and every inch of it was being shelled.

There was no regular front line yet, the two men thought. There were Germans just the other side of the crest, or they just thought there were. They'd heard a machine gun just now but to whom it belonged they didn't know. Meanwhile Battalion Headquarters was a wee bit along the road. Yes, where that shell was bursting.

'I'm going to Battalion Headquarters,' said the O.C. pointing towards the shell-burst, but every two seconds others were coming down in between. 'You stop here.'

I obeyed. There was nothing I wanted this dark game could give, but my O.C. had his plans. He was not a romantic person. What he did was methodic and in pursuance I am sure of business—plus patriotism, that is understood. Every step of that walk he took was a gamble with death, and he was a hardy gambler to whom I wished luck.

I call it a walk, but it was quite different to a walk. No sooner had he stepped on what was left of the road, than a shell rushed at him, and only just in time he flung himself upon his face. He got another two or three yards at most, and down crashed two more; and down he went for the count. But he was only lying low and resting. I would see his alert little figure rise from the dust of one shellburst, step briskly along and disappear in the spouting of the next. At last with a rush he made what was apparently the entrance to the subterranean headquarters of some invisible battalion.

He stayed down there a while. I sat drowsily nodding in the lee of the fragment of wall, only half-conscious of the whooping and thumping of the shells. The two men and myself became a wax-work trio in this wilderness. I suppose they continued to brew their infernal chicory, at my back. Suddenly I became aware of the imminence of my commanding officer's return. I stood up and after a half-dozen imperative prostrations, and as many headlong rushes, there he was before me, as cool and collected as ever, pointing back over his shoulder.

'As soon as they've got the front-line fixed, there's an old German dugout there,' he pointed to the roadside, between us and Battalion Headquarters, 'which would make an excellent O. Pip. I'll come up to-morrow again with some signallers—there may be something better, but if not that will do.'

Our return journey was less peaceful. More German batteries were firing now, and a number of shells intercepted us. We met an infantry party coming up, about ten men, with earthen faces and heads bowed, their eyes turned inward as it seemed, to shut out this too-familiar scene. As a shell came rushing down beside them, they did not notice it. There was no sidestepping death if this was where you *lived*. It was worth *our* while to prostrate ourselves, when death came over-near. We might escape, *in spite of* death. But *they* were its servants. Death would not tolerate that optimistic obeisance from them!

I heard that our commanding officer got into hot water about this expedition. He sent reports in at once, but they were ill-received. Artillery officers going down before the Front Line was organized—what next! What, to select observation-posts before the 'mopping-up' was over—before anyone knew where we were going to be, or where the Germans were going to be! Preposterous! Supposing, sir, you had run into a German counter-attack! What then, sir!

One can imagine the dudgeon of the staff, at so much officious zeal, the true motives of which they would not be slow to detect.

Whether my O.C. got his M.C. in the end or not I do not know. He was a man it would be difficult to stop. He would probably have contrived to have me hit, and have carried me into the nearest approach to a front line he could find, if the two coffee-makers had not been there.—But I daresay they gave him an M.C. anyway, just to keep him quiet.

CHAPTER V

Trench-fever and 'Hell-Fire Corner'

My days with this battery came to a close when I contracted trench-fever—whatever that may be. All I knew was that suddenly I felt exceedingly unwell, was advised to go and lie down, and was accommodated with a couch upon a clay shelf in a dugout next to the Mess. I got no better. The O.C. came in and looked at me suspiciously once or twice. Had I been a mere gunner I should probably have been sent back to duty; though I doubt if I could have got upon my legs. At length a doctor turned up. Luckily by this time my neck and face were so swollen, in a mump-like magnification, and my tongue was so green, that it was obvious something was the matter with me. Even the doctor could see that.

The side-car was sent for, to take me to Bailleul. It was a gala-day in the sky. All the way along, before my swimming eyes, a futile agitation was in progress up aloft. I watched what was passing idly: from my horizontal position my field of vision was naturally overhead. British sausage-balloons were being brought down in droves. Their occupants, the 'Blimps', would take to their parachutes. But the German airman would plunge under the expiring balloon, and hunt the parachutists with his tracer-bullets. I was in no mood for fun in the air. But I never saw such a massacre of Blimps.

After many vicissitudes I reached the fever hospital at Etaples, near Boulogne. For three days I was the star case in my part of it. My condition was regarded as so critical, that in the morning the doctor directed his steps to my bed first. So I was told, when I recovered consciousness.

Later I went to the convalescent hotel for officers at Dieppe. From this paradise I was prematurely expelled. Trainloads of gassed officers arrived. I was sent back to duty, to recuperate in the Line. And as a matter of fact it was not such a bad idea. Of course I was pretty weak, but the infection seemed to have left me. In this state I reached Dunkerque; for I was now to rejoin my own battery—the one with which I had originally come to France.

Dunkerque, as you may know, is the last big coast-town in France before you get to Belgium. The next big coast-town is Ostend. Half-way between these two places is Nieuport (a bit inland) and that was where we were. Behind Nieuport.

I know nothing about this war—I am writing blind, as it were. I know what caused it—I know who got what they wanted out of it. But it was too vast and dull a dogfight to be technically interesting, I have found.

I have not the slightest idea why my battery should have found itself where it did, except that both the German and the English were always toying with the notion of outflanking movements along the Coast—the English because amphibious warfare is their speciality; the Germans because they are so used to being 'encircled' themselves, that they naturally always hope for a change, to be able to encircle somebody else.

We were told that there was going to be an Attack. Guns were being massed for a big Attack along the coast; and four naval guns, of large calibre, had been landed and brought up as far forward as possible, and it was left for us to do the rest.

As a result of the nautical nature of these guns—or of the semi-nautical nature of this proposed coastal operation—we were handed over to the Navy. And a very breezy period of my military history this was.

With considerable difficulty, and after many wayside diversions, I found my way to Naval Group Headquarters. I was amazed to find myself in the presence of a type of man I had never set eyes on before—pukka navy captains, or commanders, or whatever they were, resplendent in blue and gold, and conducting land warfare in a manner all their own. With a fine disregard for the fact that they were no longer on the deck of a ship, but instead in the 'cockpit of Europe', they deviated very little from what must be their habits when afloat.

They had succeeded in giving the appearance of a sort of ark to their Mess-hut. It shared the characteristics of a house and a boat. Flanders is, as you know, a mere drain. It's about a foot above sea-level. This hut did not wallow in the water, but was lifted into the air a little way, like a boat before it is launched. An immense log-fire roared at the end of it, in an open fireplace, before which an equally huge land-animal—a wolf-hound I think—lay stretched upon a rug; while a bright side-table glittered with glasses, bottles and decanters, cigarette boxes, revolvers, cutlasses, sextants, and new baccy tins.

It would be quite out of the question to give you any idea of the spotlessness of this place. A dozen naval ratings must have scrubbed it every morning. Compared to our noisesome dugouts it was a Ritz.

Much dazzled and considerably perplexed by all this, I asked for the whereabouts of my battery. With royal (naval) hospitality I was given a bumper of navy-rum. I was blown about by the breeziness of my host—a little off my course, I think. Then I was despatched in a trim little side-car to the Battery position.

Have you ever tasted navy-rum? If it has not deteriorated, in these days of Potato Jones, it is stronger than any brandy. It *is* brandy, only 100 over proof. In my weakened condition, I entered the sidecar with the air of a Bulldog Drummond who had taken the wrong turning, my cap at a Beatty angle and my chest stuck out. I have never felt so fine. And when the adjutant sang out in parting, 'Easy, round Hell-fire Corner!' I said, 'To hell with Hell-fire Corner!' and we sailed away—it *was* sailing —with a flourish from the boatswain's whistle. I believe we got that.

Would it be the boatswain? At all events an old salt was always outside the Mess door, and 'piped' off the premises any person of commissioned rank.

The cars of these naval brasshats all had names—like 'Bellerephon', or 'Hood'. And when, say, the senior wardroom panjandrum would drive off in his state-motor, for a spot of play, say, at the Dunkerque Casino, the boatswain, piping with great vigour, would cry 'Away Bellerephon!' as it drew out— or whatever happened to be the name of the superb machine.

Every sector on the Western Front had its 'Hellfire Corner'. Our sub-Nieuport one was as good as most. A hundred yards beyond it lay our battery position. All day this road was bombarded without intermission, or rather with lifts of ten minutes or so at stated intervals. We found a considerable amount of traffic waiting for the 'lift'. At last the 'lift' or pause seemed to have come. Hellfire Corner had been at peace for over a minute. We all rushed forward in a *sauve qui peut* before the next shell should come down.

The motor-cycle stopped at the side of the road, and its driver indicated the remains of a small whitewashed cottage. It stood back about fifteen feet from the road. A familiar face appeared at a crack in the wall. It was the battery cook. The crack in the wall was the back entrance. The faithful cook gave me a discreet Irish welcome from inside the crack. As I approached a shell came down on the road at my back with a wallop, and the splinters smacked the cottage and flew on beyond it : which of course explained the unostentatious nature of my welcome. The cook felt it would have been illogical to welcome me with too promising an effusiveness.

'You've come to a nice place, sir!' he said, as I entered the fissure. 'It's like this all day. They never stop shelling that road. You've come to a hot place. It's a little hell away from hell.'

'Have you had a bad time?'

'We've had six direct hits on this.'

He indicated our humble headquarters.

'Pretty good,' I said.

However, inside, the cottage was a three-room residence— mess, dormitory, and kitchen. And it was not so undesirable as some. The *poilu* had lived there before us. Unlike the English the French were concrete addicts. They mortared themselves in—they built for safety first. They had not altered this cottage outwardly, but had given it eight foot thick concrete walls to its one big room, and at least a ten foot thick roof. This room was a shell that would take some cracking. I was in it when it was hit. It was as firm as a rock. It was a pleasure to be shelled in it.

This was to be my home for some time—two months, I should think. Apart from the fact of its proximity to the road, it was a splendid place.

CHAPTER VI

Our Home in a Pillbox

Whenever we had been shelled, especially if there had been casualities, the Navy would arrive on horseback. This may seem strange to you, and it seemed strange to me. But there would be a clatter of hoofs, and his brasshat at a rakish angle, up would canter the naval pasha. As often as not a salvo of splinters would be whizzing round the stern-sheets of his mount —a naturally rather jumpy steed, for to its surprise at finding itself bestrode by so paradoxical a horseman, was added an aversion to the buzzing of fragments of metal.

I never got used to the sight of a high naval dignitary on horseback. He would sit, his arm akimbo, and look down into my gunpit at my piece of naval ordnance, which no doubt made him feel at home. I always supposed that it was the expression 'Hellfire Corner' which acted as a magnet to this mettlesome personage. It was a standing challenge to the Nelson Touch, that must have been it.

To come back to our shelter from the wintry blast. Our main room was a pillbox, really, built inside a cottage. And when I said it was a big, I meant relatively, compared with dugouts. It was in fact small, and its dimensions had been still further reduced by the trebling of its walls. Our six campbeds exactly fitted into it, except for a foot or so at the door.

When we turned in at night, we walked or crawled over the intervening campbeds, unless ours was next the door. In that circumscribed area strange scenes were witnessed. That was before we lay down. The second-in-command was responsible for these. He went Peter-Pan when he got his clothes off. Uniformed and in his right mind, with his little calves bulging to the rear, and a huge bloated cap crowning his unusually large

141

head, he was a different man. He was quite an able officer and I had a fondness for him.

He was a small man, who was the living image of Lawrence of Arabia (as I have since discovered, for of course at that time the Arab lands had not yet met their deliverer). This battery 'Lawrence' was not quite so goodlooking, and he sported a Hapsburg lip. But otherwise he could have accompanied Allenby into Damascus (if he had kept his under lip in) and no one would have detected the difference.

This whimsical officer used to stand upon his bed in his underpants, a cane representing a rifle held in to his side, and drill us. It must have astonished the cook, when first this shouting voice came out of our nocturnal pillbox. He got used to it doubtless; but the first time he must have leapt to attention, for this little artillery captain had an excellent word-of-command.

Often there was a smell of gas, if the night shelling had already started. We had nothing but gas there. Then, taking this night-parade, our driller would break down in a fit of coughing, as the gas got into his throat.

'Jump to it, Boorfelt!' he clamoured, protruding his underlip, at attention upon his bed. 'Pree-*sent*. Umms!' He held his cane at the *present*, to the rather sourly-smiling Boorfelt—who felt the three pips ought to be on his shoulder, rather than on the little captain's. In the light of our small oil lamp he looked like a dishevelled schoolboy, he was so small and his eyes were so dreamy and twinkling, though he made them stare and frown to issue his commands.

Except for the O.C. we were like a small class of children, the shelled road outside of the importance of a noisy disregarded torrent. This bombproof, airless, sleeping cubicle was our nursery. We had to put up with a lot of grown-up nonsense from our nannie. Our seniors are such incorrigible children!

The second room was the officers' mess. The French had not taken so much trouble over that. But even so it had enough logs on top of it to build a tolerably large log-cabin.

The officers' 'toilet' was not far off; we had a lavatory, which was at a distance of about ten yards from the door of the mess.

142

Shelling of the battery—as distinct from the shelling of the road —began every evening about nine. As soon as we began to finish our tinned salmon and glass of Scotch, we kept our wristwatches under observation. Then began the visits to the lavatory, which we took in turn. The last one back was always apt to be caught, and would come jumping in out of the way of a gas-shell.

The gas-shells were small, came down with a soft sickly whistle, and struck the ground with a gentle *plock*. Their very sound was suggestive of *gas*. There was nothing to be afraid of unless they got a direct hit on your chest—except their gas. But in going to the lavatory they *were* liable to hit you. For some reason they fell, to start with, all round this place and on the pathway we had to take from the Mess.

In the morning the battery usually stank of sweet gas. Men were always going sick. A gunner who got down into a shell hole, where the gas clung for hours, was laid out. We kept them out of the holes if we could.

For weeks on end every man in the battery slept in his gas-mask. In lying down we fixed our gas-masks, with the tin teat just up against our lips. Before we were all asleep one of us —usually Boorfelt—would sit up, sniff, and say 'gas!' We would all sniff, and then said 'gas!' Then we stuck our tin teats in our mouths, and clipped the pincers upon our noses. So we would sleep for the rest of the night.

On rejoining my old battery friends, in this semi-coastal position (and I was glad to see them once more, for in the other battery I was an interloper) I found them finishing the concrete emplacements for the big naval guns. These concrete emplacements were in pits, below ground level. And the greatest care had been taken to conceal their presence from German airmen. This we successfully did, for it was only once in a way that we got any shelling and that not of a very determined sort.

We never fired these guns. We were waiting for the Attack which never came. Which illustrates my remarks regarding the gunner's life. Here we did not even retaliate. We were shelled but we did not shell in return. Yet, at the time, we were doubtless described as 'fighting' in France. Of course I do not mean to say we were not all very brave. It is merely that we were so very inactive.

Meanwhile the men did do a bit of superfluous concreting from time to time, picked the leaves off the gun barrel, and anything else they could find to do.—I could never find anything to do. I read Proudhon ('*la propriété c'est un vol*') my favourite political philosopher, and attempted to compute the cost of shells discharged daily on either side. I was not enough of an economist to fathom the depth of ruin this spelled for European society. But I did see that the merely military outcome was by this time meaningless. It was perfectly clear that we should all be ruined, and that some people meant us to be.

My gun, No. 4, was nearest the road. Every twenty seconds a shell fell on the road, with the regularity of clockwork. If I was near the gun—and I had to hang about in sight of it—I would stoop : the splinters from the shell usually passing at a height of about five feet from the ground. Or I propped up our sandbag-parapet with my shoulder, crossing my legs.

As on one occasion I stood chatting with the double of Colonel Lawrence I found that he was not bowing so politely as I was as the splinters came over. He was remaining officiously upright.

In my own territory, this would scarcely do. So the next time I refrained from making my bow. But a few minutes later a large viciously-hissing splinter passed at headlong speed immediately between our noses, which were about a foot apart.

I raised my eyebrows in discreet mockery, but my superior officer had raised his still more—his Hapsburg lip was within a quarter of an inch of this unceremonious missile, and his staring eyes observed it with amazement down the flanks of his nose, as it flew past—not as good a nose as that of Lawrence, but reminiscent, all the same.

I am reminded by this of another occasion when I happened to observe the expression on a man's face at a rather critical moment. This was later on. I was accompanying an officer whose business it was to select a battery-position. We had just settled upon one, which seemed in not too busy a spot, and otherwise desirable, when a shrapnel discharged itself immediately over our heads. As the shell was coming straight for us, we leapt as one man into a small shell hole, on either side of which we had been standing : our tin hats met with a crash, just as the shell exploded. The shrapnel rained about us, in a spray of bullets. I was looking up into his face, and as the shrapnel pelted down he screwed his face up in the grimace of the sufferer from constipation.—This was *not* the double of Colonel Lawrence, who was not a particularly nervous man. He was an educated man, which was unusual, among these officers, and capable of philosophic perception, which was even more so. He was even a prophet. He foretold my future—for a year or two, anyway.

Sixty per cent of the casualties on the Western Front were caused by shell-fire, forty per cent by bullets. (Bayonet wounds were so rare that they do not enter into the statistics.) Shell fire is an interesting subject, therefore, for the soldier. And there is nothing I do not know about shell-fire. As a matter of fact our position by the side of an important road was peculiarly adapted to making one an expert in that subject.

Each 'burst' produces its spawn of 'splinters', which proceed to whizz in all directions till they lose momentum, and drop, or flop, on the ground. They were flopping the whole time round us, as well as buzzing past our shoulders. The force with which they arrived depended, naturally, upon the nearness of the burst. I was often spanked with a spent one—like being hit with a stone not thrown very hard.

My sergeant was killed a few weeks after my arrival. One afternoon a staff officer came to the battery to recover a screwdriver (I think it was that, but it may have been a corkscrew or shoehorn). The bogus Colonel Lawrence suggested I should return with this officer to Group Headquarters, officially to liquidate this episode, and perhaps linger over a glass of navy rum. I thought I would do this, and we were almost out of sight of the battery when there was an unusually loud noise. Looking back we saw a black fountain of earth. It rose, and fell, out of the heart of the battery.

'Eleven inch,' said I.

'That's it,' said he. 'It looks as if it were your gun.'

145

I didn't think it was my gun. It looked as if it was back of the guns. All that would be happening at the battery position would be the usual exodus. The men would have had orders to leave it as rapidly as possible, and this they would carry out to the letter. They would be rushing out in the opposite direction to the road. This occasional shelling, with us, was always short-lived. Then everybody went back again. The holes were examined. That was the ordinary procedure.

I decided to deal with the screwdriver first. When over an hour later I got back to the battery position my gunpit (that of No. 4 gun) was like a small quarry. The sergeant and a half dozen men had been in it : it had been a direct hit, a few feet at the side of the gun. He and the six men were all killed or wounded. I wrote to the widow of my sergeant, saying what a popular man he was, and got a new N.C.O. for my gun and the necessary reinforcements. As this is written, so it happened. But that is obviously not how men's lives should be taken away from them, for nothing at all.

Had it not been for the screwdriver (or the shoehorn) I should probably at present be in a war-grave too. In our next battery position (in the Salient) the same thing, more or less, occurred. While I was off duty, back at our rest billets, there was an air attack. A bomb got a direct hit upon my gun. All my gun detachment were casualties. When I left France my subsection were all unfamiliar faces. Also 'Birdie', my colleague of No. 3 gun—my other section officer—was wounded in both lungs a few days before I left.

The hundred yards from Hellfire Corner to us was all Hell-fire. And the other side of the road there was a battery that, un-like us, had a good deal of lateral Hellfire, as well.

Our side of the road would normally have been a meadow. On the other side the coastal sand-dunes began. They were most substantial sand-hills, twenty or thirty feet high. A very high one rose just across the way from our concreted cottage. And it must have been composed by this time as much of lead and iron as of sand.

It was the dwelling place of a Field Artillery battery. They were mercilessly shelled, and they had brought to a fine art the technique of vanishing into their sand hill. At the first sign of danger the whole battery went into the sandhill.

Considering the length of our stay in this position, we were a rather sedentary lot. Except for occasional visits to Group Headquarters, immediately to the rear, we moved about little. None of our neighbours lived attractive lives. Though doubtless attractive people, they were not the sort of people you dropped in to visit. A 'Hellfire' tea-party presented little attraction to any of us. It was no great temptation to rush across the road, pursued by *five-nines,* and be immediately engulfed in the sandhill, in flight from guns of every calibre—with an excellent chance of being buried alive, for it seemed more than probable that one fine day the sandhill would cave in.

As to our neighbours upon our right, they were very much farther away. We could only see them as big specks, across intervening fields. They, too, were no doubt charming fellows; but we had formed the habit of watching them being shelled, by naval guns from somewhere near Ostend, and of dodging the débris flung far and wide by these huge projectiles. All *their* energy, however, was not taken up with darting in and out of a sandhill. Had they been a bit nearer we might have hailed them : but it seems that the life of war is conducive to a certain clannishness, if not exclusiveness, especially among the English.

For my part, I should not have stepped over in any case, in that direction, for the excellent reason that T. E. Hulme, I discovered, was there. And somehow reconciliations under these conditions did not appeal.

At the Naval Group Headquarters one day, hearing that some R.M.A. Batteries were in the neighbourhood, I asked the adjutant if he had ever come across a certain T. E. Hulme. Pointing out of the window, he said :

'He's over there. He's in the battery next to yours.' And he proceeded to express his lack of appreciation of the socratic method, when imported into the Mess. 'What a man !' he exclaimed. 'He'd argue a dog's hind leg off.' And I agreed that he was disputatious. I was sorry when I heard he'd been killed that I had not made my peace with him.

147

CHAPTER VII
Passchendaele

The centre of 'the Salient' was where my battery next found itself. The Salient was the bulge, of course, round the romantic ruin of the town of Ypres. No Norman Keep in ivy-clad decay was ever so romantic as Ypres, literally swarming with ghosts even at high noon (in the moonlight you could not tell which were the quick and which the dead) and looking as if Time, that does not hurry when making a ruin as a rule, had telescoped itself to make this one, Death having lent it a hand.

The famous Salient was a *stupid* bulge, but one of which the high command were inordinately proud; not because it was of any strategic importance, but because a great many men had been killed in its creation. It is obvious why a 'salient' is an unsatisfactory place for the men who are in it. They can be shelled from three sides, more or less, instead of one. But this Salient was sacrosanct. It was *the* Salient. It was as great as it was costly as a feat of arms, to hold it. So it was kept intact, as a monument of 'doggedness'. At the time I thought it was stupid to have a salient. Since I have found it was even more stupid than I had suspected.

Our forward position was up the Menin Road, to the east of it. It was not far from yet another 'Hellfire Corner', but we could not see this one as there was a rise in the ground that interrupted the view. All day long, however, we could observe the shambles on the Menin Road itself (the shouting for stretchers just reached us at our guns) which was chockablock at all times with A.S.C. and Anzac transport, ambulances and the rest of it.

The big Australian drivers, on their high seats, idly cracking their whips, moved up it at a leisurely pace, like characters of Callots—again incredibly romantic, grandiose and scarecrow figures from another age : or out of a contempoary print, depicting the prairie-wagons of indolent pioneers, pushing on lackadaisically into the Never-never, or the Back-of-Beyond. They displayed a superb indifference from the rushing deliveries of the mechanical war-god. For shell after shell pounded down without intermission upon this central artery of the battlefront. But these great sunburnt plainsmen refused to recognize the machine-age as in being—as any more than a thunderstorm, if as bad as that, for at least it was not *wet*. Its crashing shells were just particularly troublesome thunderbolts. They were in greater number, certainly, than were usually seen. That was all.—But for them the power involved was *nature*. These children of nature imparted an air of natural happening, of an elemental disturbance, to all the mechanical 'planning' of our latterday Clausewitzes upon the other side of the Line, and their understudies on our side of it.

But the Anzacs turned the field of battle itself into a less sinister locality, with their open-air habits and free and easy ways. I have seen them walking about after an attack in the empty space behind the Front Line, as unconcernedly as if they had been out duckshooting—potting the German airmen as they came over, contemptuous of the retaliatory barrage, while we, with more discretion, remained down in the captured trenches. They could not be prevented from doing that, although the relations between the officers and men was such that there was no question of interfering with this sport.

These colonial habits, however, invaded our dull battery, in the person of a spirited overseas officer. We had attached to us a lot of West Indian negroes, principally for purposes of shell-humping. In command of them came to us one Kamper, if I remember, from Jamaica. If Kamper was asleep in his dugout, his black servant had the strictest orders to wake him, at the first sign of a German plane. Out he would rush, revolver in hand, spring on top of his dugout and empty his weapon into the air, waggling it about in the hope that one bullet, at least would find its mark.

The great open spaces of Jamaica seemed to make him feel about these bogus birds much as it made his rugged colleagues from the Australian steppe. Fond as he was of his siesta—

however much he might be lapped in a Caribbean calm within his fleabag, he would not miss Richtofen for anything. For he was persuaded it was Richtofen he was settling accounts with when he came flying out of his musty, rat-infested lair, his red hair tumbling over his face.

Nestling at the side of Ypres itself was our place of rest and relaxation, for we had one here at last. It was then that I made my only attempt to live undangerously and to furnish a little.

I was alotted a sandbag dugout (6 feet by 4) by the side of a battered rivulet. My clay-room was upon its bank. My batman installed a shelf upon which I stood my dozen volumes in an orderly rank. All was set for a little picnic of the mind in this cell of a booted anchorite. 'The wilderness were paradise enow,' though I had no book of verses with me, but *Das Kapital* which was probably more suitable under the circumstances.

It was a smiling day when I moved in. But that night when I went to it I was promptly apprised as to what was to be the fly in this ointment. For making ready to follow Proudhon over into the pages of Karl Marx, his great opponent (and later, I found, mine) it became painfully apparent that the brook at night was stiff with pertinacious mosquitoes. My light had to be put out immediately; my sleep was intermittent and my disappointment knew no bounds.

With a few quiet bombs dropping in the ruins of Ypres, and an occasional shell in the dump at our back, I should have made a pretty picture, burning the midnight oil, above my battered rivulet. As it was I was bitten to pieces and Karl Marx had to wait. I preferred sleeping at the battery-position, though that was nightly plastered with high-explosive. I would infinitely rather have had my garden-coalcellar, allotted me in my first battery, where I got my trench-fever, but had no malarial insects.

The climax of the war was approaching. Or rather our high command were meditating the conversion of the Salient into something still more magnificent—a *real* bulge, namely, indefinitely elastic. The Germans of course could read their

150

thoughts like a book. And the Germans were explaining to them, as best they could, that this was *quite out of the question* They did their best to show them that it was quite difficult enough to stop where they were, and that it was wholly unfeasible to wade forward through the bog that lay between us and our enemies, and so on to Berlin.

The Front Line and a half-mile behind had become a first class quagmire. The irrigation which normally, in these Low Countries, drains off the water, had for a long time not been practised; and meanwhile every few yards shells had splashed down into the water, and mixed it and the earth into a sea of mud.

This great bog was traversed everywhere with duckboard-tracks—otherwise gangways of wood, for people to walk in Indian file. Off the duckboard-track, more often than not, conditions were frankly aquatic.

The preparations for Passchendaele were a poem in mud cum blood-and-thunder. The appetite of the Teuton for this odd game called war—in which a dum-dum bullet is a foul, but a gas-bomb is O.K.—and British 'doggedness' in the gentle art of 'muddling through', when other nations misunderstand British kindliness and get tough, made a perfect combination. If the Germans and the English had not been there, all the others would long before that have run away and the war been over.

These two contrasted but as it were complementary types of *idée fixe* found their most perfect expression on the battlefield, or battle-bog, of Passchendaele. The very name, with its suggestion of *splashiness* and of *passion* at once, was subtly appropriate. This nonsense could not have come to its full flower at any other place but at *Passchendaele*. It was pre-ordained. The moment I saw the name on the trench-map, intuitively I knew what was going to happen.

On the coast we had no O. Pip work, but now all the time one or other of us were going up to the front line with our parties of signallers. As I have said, I had not the slightest idea what was occurring, and since that time I have never cared to go back and investigate according to what logical system I was moved about upon this muddy board. There were 'zero hours', for which we waited with our eyes on our wristwatches, there were days of attack, or rehearsals for attack, practice barrages, sudden alarms and excursions, which died down ten minutes after the first flare up. I cannot tell you what any of these things were.

All that I know is that I moved hither and thither over this sea of mud and have since been told that it was a fool who was moving me. However, had it been the greatest Captain in the world it would have been all one to me. I am not interested in Great Captains. 'Everything bores me except the philosophic man.' There is for me no good war (*la bonne guerre*) and bad war. There is only *bad* war.

Ours, then, was an epic of mud. Mud was even one of our weapons—an alternative weapon. Once when two of the negroes had started a razor-fight it devolved upon me to stop it. So to start with I seized them respectively by the shirt-collar and opening my arms abruptly, as you open a pair of scissors, I flung them apart. One drooped to the right of me, one to the left of me : but only for a moment. I supposed I had ended hostilities : but then simultaneously each of them scooped up a handful of mud and discharged it across my face at his antagonist. And soon we were all three covered in liquid clay. Kamper appeared—revolver in hand—however, and as if by magic the two Blacks vanished and I found myself alone, straddling like a statue of clay, with only a razor at my feet to testify to the fact that I had not been dreaming!

I never got the right touch with the West Indian negro. At our Nieuport position one dark night the negroes were rolling shells up to the guns—very large ones, since the guns were out-size. This operation had to be effected without so much as a match struck, lest the German air-patrols should spot us. A negro sergeant I noticed was not only stationary, and peculiarly idle, but actually obstructing the work of the dusky rollers. I spoke to him. He neither looked at me nor answered. I could scarcely see him—it was very dark, and he was very dark. I ordered him to do a little rolling. This was *a word of command*. It elicited no response from the dark shape. Whereupon I gave him a violent push. This propelled him through space for a short distance, but he immediately returned to where he had stood before. I gave him a second push. As if made of india-rubber, he once more reintegrated the spot he had just left. After this I accepted him as part of the landscape, and the shells had to be rolled round, him, since they could not be rolled *through* him.

CHAPTER VIII

The 'O.Pip' on the Ridge

I have often referred to O.Pips, or observation posts. Here are a few typical experiences of that type of amusement.—When I had to go up to the observation post I had to be woken—no easy matter: that was the first step. Upon this occasion, as usual the signaller N.C.O. woke me. It was the early hours of the morning and I cursed him. I had been sleeping in a stretcher upon the ground; the stretcher was two inches under water, so I had been slumbering in a bath. My under side was submerged. I flung off the heaviest sleep I have ever been stupefied with, which is saying a lot, for I sleep like a log. It must have been the effort required to sleep half under water.—I rose dripping to my feet and put on my tin-hat. Then I drank a cup of tea and ate a biscuit.

It was an attack of sorts, infantry were moving up in the night, and it was important to do as much of the journey as possible before daybreak. We were late in starting. The O.Pip was a mile or two along the Line to our left. We crossed the Menin Road, and shortly afterwards, as the day was breaking, we found numbers of infantry held up beside the road we were to follow. A barrage had suddenly came down a short way ahead.

A couple of dozen yards from the road there were some empty dugouts, on a slight elevation, and I took my party there to wait. As I stood in the opening of a derelict Mess, my men inside, expecting nothing untoward, and still half-asleep, a shell whooped down at me. It was at *me* it undoubtedly had been aimed. It exploded two feet from my head, the top of the dugout wall was between my head and the burst. Without its crashing into your head, you could not be nearer to a shell than that, and I banged against the side of the opening and was then carried forward in a stampede of my trusty followers from within. We hastened away from this unfortunately chosen shelter, but the German battery meant business. We had to crouch as we ran, to allow the passage over our backs of the buzzing shell-splinters from the series of five-nines.

Having rejoined the infantry, more time went by, people coming back reporting the continuance of the barrage. Therefore we set out to see if we could not walk round it, or find a way through it farther down.

Upon a duckboard track as we tramped forward, we came upon two Scottish privates; one was beheaded, and the leg of another lay near him, and this one's arm was gone as well. They had been killed that morning—a direct hit I suppose: the Scottish battalion to which they belonged having lost a number of men, I later heard, on the way up.

As we approached them my party left the duckboards and passed round the flank of this almost sardonically complete tableau of violent death. Averting their heads, the men circled round. Their attitude was that of dogs when they are offered some food which they don't much like the look of. But a moment later when a shell passed over us, to burst a fairish distance away, my party bowed itself, as it advanced, as if to avoid a blow, though ordinarily such shelling would have been disregarded.

We encountered the barrage, but negotiated it without mishap. Everywhere the enemy was bustling and aggressive however, and the entire front was in an uproar. At length we came out upon the last stretch, the empty approaches to the Front Line, and there to our great indignation were machine-gunned by a low-flying plane.

It was the first time any of us had met with this particular type of aeronautical caddishness. I even didn't know they could do it. I was intensely surprised. Now, of course, airmen think nothing of picking off shoppers in the streets of a city, or whisking past a window and spraying a woman with bullets in her bath. It is recognized as one of the most triumphant assertions of man's mastery over his biped handicap. And we're all very proud to think that our airmen can retaliate and pick off bipeds of discordant nationality. But at the time we all felt it was an uncalled-for interloping to say the least of it, on the part of a particularly vindictive type of flying Bosche.

In spite of the unexpectedness of this occurrence, we saw at once that this low-flying plane was upon some ungentlemanly errand. Of course it was a Bosche—no English plane was ever so near the Line as this. We sank into a shell-hole with the rapidity of a well-drilled Music-hall troupe (dresses by Bairns-father). 'Don't show your faces!' said the corporal. I watched from under the peak of my cap the two men who were staring down at us as they approached, but we were not hit, only scan-dalized. With their staccato snapping superimposed on the roar of their engine, they went over our heads. But an infantry party going up the Line, the only other thing in sight, they successfully attacked, accounting for three of them, it seemed.

I forget the order of these events, but I believe this was the Broudsind Ridge period, preparatory to Passchendaele. Every-thing was perfectly vacant and quiet just here : it was the vacuum immediately behind the Line—a No Man's Land that had been left behind, and so was more No Man's Land than ever.

Upon the crest of the ridge ahead was our observation-post. We had no difficulty whatever in locating it. No one, in fact, could miss it. For it had a cluster of shell-bursts around it, rather as a mountain-peak is crowned or ringed with cloud.

We were not far off the ridge when I was considerably startled by the sudden emergence from a trench of a dramatic-ally perspiring Brigadier. He advanced toward me in some-what minatory fashion. Generals in such places as that were unusual. I saluted and he thrust out his finger, pointing at the crest of the ridge.

'You know the enemy is over there?' he asked me sternly.

'Yes sir,' I answered humbly.

'You know you are under machine-gun fire as soon as you get to the top?'

I answered that I did—that I had been here before.

To satisfy this general officer I got my party into a trench, and we circuitously approached the tumultuous spot which it

156

would be our task for the rest of the day to occupy. It was one thing to get to it, another matter to enter it. We were not a suicide club, I and my signallers (at least that was my attitude). And having got within hailing distance of it, we halted. When we got into it we should merely be wasting our time. So we might as well humour the Brigadier, and watch our step. I lighted my pipe, and discussed the incidence of the bursts with the corporal.

The danger from the machine-gun fire the Brigadier exaggerated. But that factor had to be taken into account in this last stage of the proceedings. The main thing, however, was to judge one's moment properly, with regard to the shell-fire. Most of the shells went slightly beyond, sometimes they would lengthen, and there were periods when they eased off, though they never stopped entirely.

We waited about ten minutes in a trench, then I gave the signal and we rushed at it heads down. I was last in and just yanked my tail into the funk-hole as a shell came down in the trench behind.

This observation-post was the regulation German 'pill-box'. There was room inside it for all of us. You may represent it to yourself as a monstrous Easter-egg, its shell of four foot thick concrete, sunk in the earth. Its domed top protruded slightly above the level of the parapet, covered with a thick coat of caked soil. It was entered from a trench; and as it had been a German pill box in the first instance, its entrance faced the enemy. It was from this trench at its mouth that the 'observing' had to be done, either by periscope or otherwise.

There were five of us, myself, the signaller corporal, and three signallers. We crowded down into it puffing and laughing. There was no floor, this was its only drawback; a miniature sheet of water was where that should have been. But this dark expanse of water—perhaps four feet across—had as it were a bank. It was on this shelf of clay that we sat or stood.

When we were not there our O.Pip was the home of a family of rats. They did not, however, leave it when we entered, but sensibly accepted our intrusion. They frequently were to be seen swimming in the water, and we would throw them pieces of cheese, when these rodents would indulge in a little fierce polo. The shells thudded upon the roof of this excellent concrete egg, and we, in our moments of relaxation, or when the shelling was so severe that it had driven us inside, fed the rats and smoked.

The German front-line trench was almost immediately beneath us—the two front lines were so close together here that we could almost look into it. It was very thinly held at this time. I sometimes thought there were no Germans there at all.

On another occasion I was in this observation-post when a great barrage was laid upon the German trenches. A Field Artillery officer was up there with me and we waited down in the trench for the barrage zero hour. We got up just before the storm broke. Then, to the second, there was the muffled crash of massed artillery, and over came the barrage—every type of projectile, groaning, panting, bumbling, whistling and wheezing overhead. Down they plunged upon the German trench, a chain of every type of burst, and a screen of smoke and earth defined, as far as one could see on either hand, the German Line.

As we stood watching—there was no occasion to consider exposing ourselves to enemy fire, with such a tornado as this absorbing all his attention—the other officer clutched my arm and pointed his finger. 'See that!' he said. I looked where he pointed, and saw something dark fly into the air, in the midst of the smoke. My companion said it was the leg of a Bosche, but I thought, though it looked rather like a boot and half a thigh, that it was in fact some less sensational object. It may all the same have been a German limb : and if so it was probably my strong feeling that there were no Germans there that made me incredulous.—Also I did not care whether it was a leg or not, there is always that.

It was from this observation-post that I 'registered' batteries upon the last vestiges of a village : and as I have said elsewhere, experienced a certain satisfaction at the thought that it was reputed to be empty. 'Registering' merely means that a conventional point is selected on the map, and one or more batteries begins firing at it. You, through your field glasses—up in your observation-post—observe the 'burst'. You telephone back to them (by field telephone) to 'shorten' or 'lengthen', according to whether the shell fell beyond, or short of, the object aimed at. (Same procedure, of course, if it is wireless instead of telephone.) This is called 'bracketting'. This conventional object, will be, of course, the *point d'appui* for their other calculations, once they have hit it a time or two.

On this particular day little observation work could be done because the wires were incessantly being cut by the enemy fire, which was very heavy. The attack had not materialized—if it was to have been an attack—but the enemy were in a very irritable mood. No sooner would I get through to the battery, than bang the line would go—no more messages would come through. It was then the very disagreeable task of the signallers to go and follow the line back and mend it where it was broken.

That evening we evacuated our pill-box under a perfect fusilade of shells. I lost my pipe as we went steeplechasing in and out of trenches. In the distance I turned to look back at this obnoxious death-trap, as one turns to look back at a mountain whose top one had just visited, once one is down below. The sunset had turned on its romantic dream-light and what had been romantic enough before was now absolutely operatic. A darkening ridge, above a drift of saharan steppe, gouged and tossed into a monotonous disorder, in a word the war-wilderness; not a flicker of life, not even a ration-party—not even a skeleton : and upon the ridge the congeries of 'bursts', to mark the spot where we had been. It was like the twitching of a chicken after its head had been chopped off. We turned away from this brainless bustle, going on all by itself, about an empty concrete easter-egg, in a stupid desert.

CHAPTER IX

Hunted with Howitzers

The most interesting observation post in my experience was one I never saw. This is how it happened. I offered to take another officer's O.Pip duty one day, because he'd been poisoned with some bottled prawns. I was instructed to, if possible, reach, and precariously occupy—for as long as possible—an observation post, but not to take it too seriously.

It was of the most evil report. It was a washout into the bargain. There was nothing to be seen from it, even if you had been allowed to look. Only one of us had been up to it. He was blown into it by a shell, and just after he left it another shell had frisked in by the front door. It was even doubtful if it was still there at all.

To say that I was eager to see this observation post would be an exaggeration. To do any *observing* from it was out of the question: all you could do was to hang on to it by the skin of your teeth; and, as soon as you decently could, shake the dust of it off your feet and turn your back on it—if it let you. However, I thought I'd look it over. I would observe *it*, even if *it* would not allow me to make use of it for observation. For quite certainly it itself was far more dangerous than any of the things I could observe *from* it. I was perfectly resolved if I noticed more than three shells abreast and at a time going in the front door, to squat down and invest it—rather than carry it by a frontal assault and occupy it. And my orders were, in any case, *de ne pas insister*. Not to insist: to have a certain regard for the lives of myself and my men. Our present O.C. was as much agreed as the rest of us that O.Pips were a snare and a delusion. If they had any use, except for 'registration', it was moral rather than technical.

Even in its position it was not like other observation posts.

160

It was, I was told, only to be approached by a route that itself was possibly even worse than the thing itself.

The road up—tracks as usual, though there was firmer ground on the successive ridges—had not been improved by tropical rains. There were no duckboard tracks along the roads themselves, and upon one of these the mud reached well over my knees on occasion. The cork-pulling exertion required for the extraction of each leg in order to progress at all was considerable. But at last we left behind that opaque river; and I suppose about half was terra firma, where the ground was higher.

But the way up was an epic of mud. We passed a row of gunners with their pants down sitting on a pole, and saw them chased off it by an inopportune shell-burst, like squibs in a lavatory, and then, in that condition, observed them become stuck like houseflies upon a section of flypaper, in a marshy patch. We observed several casualties, also transfixed in rufous mud, in a working party outside an Anzac telephone exchange —'Blightyones' but bleeding men are more grim to others than themselves: this was just as, for the last time, we had done the cork-pulling trick in the road that was a trough of mud. I went into the pill-box and had a talk with the Aussies who were as merry as grigs at their switchboards.

Now the ridge was in sight, where the O.Pip was situated, on top of the front-line. The signaller N.C.O. had been up before, he was our guide. Here again was the empty space behind the front line trenches, of considerable depth this time, a regular rolling waste, and we were crossing it diagonally.

It was then that I first became fully conscious of the German sausage-balloons. They seemed to be immediately over the ridge; surprisingly lowdown and shockingly far forward. For why on earth were they allowed to stop? They hung there with an impudent air of being *chez soi,* right over our front line.

As we approached they became more and more menacingly near. And it was now that I began to see why it was this particular observation-post was not like other observation-posts, but in a class by itself. The explanation was patent—and I remembered that the officer who had visited it before me had

161

talked a lot about sausage-balloons, but I had paid no attention to him.

What was the matter with this O.Pip was obviously that it was *itself* observed by another O.Pip—but one above it, suspended in the air. That was what was the matter with it. An expert Observer, vertically above him, was observing any Observer who might take it into his head to use this particular spot for his so-called 'observations'. The sausage-balloons generally had artillery officers in them as Observers, who sat up there with impunity 'observing' for all they were worth, of course, and possessing a godlike advantage over those upon the ground. Our balloons were nothing like so numerous nor so impudent, nor did artillery Observers use them so much. From the German sausage-balloons Observers could direct the fire of the batteries with which they were in touch upon any point they wished, and were apt to be right on top of our infantry. At the last observation-post I have spoken about there were none. It was just as it happened. And of course they were not usually right overhead.

And now, indeed, with this situation which I saw looming up in front of me, the futility of our O.Pipping reached its perfect climax. For it was a case of O.Pip versus O.Pip, but with our opponent given not only all the trumps but the whole pack of cards.

We did not have to wait till we reached our proposed observation-post to cross swords with the enemy-observer. He had doubtless been watching us for some time. He had seen us pulling our legs, with a sodden pop, out of the mud of the sunken road : he had seen me enter the Anzac telephone pill-box ; and he had remarked with a savage grin of glee, the signaller-corporal point to the famous O.Pip in the distance, as we started upon our last lap. 'Na na . . . So kommt doch! Kommt doch her, Ihr Soldatchen! Wir warten schon! Habt keine Angst, wir werden nicht roh sein. Also !'

We reached the final bog of bogs, which cut off the front line from the rest of the world. A hundred yards across or more it stretched along the near side of the ultimate ridge. It was spanned by a duckboard track.

We five would-be 'observers' stood upon the margin of this sea of mud. Nothing so far had happened. The sausage-balloon, startlingly near by this time, looked down on us like a strangely levitated black slug—a low form of life, in airy repose. Indeed, asleep. There was shelling behind us, out of sight, from where we had come, and there was a little shelling along the ridge where the front line was. Otherwise a peaceful autumn morning invited us to relax. Had there been no gas-bag floating there, I should have congratulated myself upon this auspicious calm. We filed out upon the duckboard track, I leading the party. I did not hurry. You must never suggest to a sausage-balloon that you are afraid of it.

The last of our party had left terra firma a few yards behind him when the first shell came down. It whooped out of the air and into the mud some yards to the side of us. I accelerated. The sausage had seen us! Shell number two a second later crashed behind us. They tended to go over! But this was followed by a shell twenty yards ahead. Still in the mud. But the *next* one settled it. For it got a direct hit upon the duckboard track immediately in front of me.

At this I turned and found that one of the hindmost signallers had already reached terra firma, and a second one was in the bog. I shouted out to get back and we returned to the 'shore' at the double. As we ran the shells continued to thump down and the splinters to whizz round us. It was obvious that it was our party that was the object of this shelling, and I thought the best thing to do was to get far enough away from this unpleasant pontoon to outdistance the over-personal attack. We then would see what was to be done next.

But as my party in this way beat a retreat, the shells followed us. There was no question at all that the shells were following us. They were not aimed at an area, or a track, or a movement of troops, but at five individuals. I looked back. The duckboard track was no longer molested. Clearly we were being chased. The accursed sausage-balloon was doing it. From its howdah, or gondola, we were being hunted. I felt more like a lion every minute—a lion who realizes that he cannot contend against creatures of another dimension. But forest-craft must be

163

brought into play! There was nothing for it but to take cover at once. This fusillade would continue so long as we offered ourselves as desirable targets. We must make ourselves small. A shell came rushing down ahead of us. I bent my tin-hat to the blast and jumped into a shell-hole. The N.C.O. who was on my heels came in at my back.

'We'll stop here till this is over,' said I. 'It's not too good.' 'It's not, you're right, sir,' said he. The next shell came very near indeed, with a furious wallop. It shook the earth at the side of us, in providing *our* shell-hole with a mate. I got under the lee of our little excavation, and my companion pressed up against me silently, all knees and elbows. No fellow human has ever impinged with so resolute a pressure upon my own flesh, as did the body of this N.C.O.

Fore and aft the shells came down—one short of us, the next one the other side. We knew well enough what that must mean.

'The bastards are bracketing!' muttered the N.C.O. upon my chest, as in this none-too-deep—this disgracefully shallow apology for a shell-crater, we made ourselves scarce, in almost an amorous embrace. 'That's what they're doing!' I said, in grim agreement.—'They've got us properly taped!' said he.— 'They seem to know we're here!' I answered. My voice was drowned in another explosion, and the corporal became still more affectionate.

For a quarter of an hour, it must have been, or it may have been ten minutes, the cannonade continued. I do not believe that unless you are about to meet your death you ever feel as if you were. My sensation was resignation to an ordeal, rather than expectation of extinction. The bitter taste of stupidity was in my mouth, rather than a fore-relish of death.

I should think you could count on the fingers of your hands the soldiers who have been fired at in this *personal* way by weapons of such dimensions—and a whole battery of them if it was the whole battery that was after us. For obviously for that to happen you have to have all the various factors that made it possible. First, a sausage-balloon sitting with impunity up in the air above you, upon a nice clear day : secondly the Observer in the balloon with plenty of time on his hands, and in the mood for a little sport : and thirdly, two men practically underneath it, in an empty landscape. Again, were it a larger collection of people, then it would no longer be *personal*.

What occurred was about on a par with having a man emptying a heavy pistol at you at a range that could not, seeing the weapon, ensure precision, but near enough so that the odds were, if he re-loaded and went on firing, he would get you in the end—if you stayed put, as perforce we did. It must be remembered that the Observer in the balloon overhead could see our eyelashes and the mole on the back of the corporal's hand, and the pip on my shoulder-strap, as he gazed down at us through his field-glasses. We were present to him in the most intimate way, as if we had been in his balloon with him. So, as he was probably an artillery-officer I think I am justified in surmising that nothing quite so personal as this happened to any artillery officer before as happened to me on this occasion. Whoever the fellow was up in the sausage-balloon, we came in considerably closer contact than theoretically it is possible for artillery officers on opposite sides to come with each other.

At last he stopped firing, though he still I expect was watching us. Not far off there was a dugout at the entrance of which I saw an Aussie standing. We left our shell hole and went over to the dugout, pursued by a shell or two. I indicated this rendez-vous to the remaining two signallers who were emerging from an adjacent shell-hole. The fifth was not a casualty but had just disappeared. The last time I saw this fifth member of our party was while I was getting into the shell-hole—I glanced round first to satisfy myself that the three signallers were all right. What he intended to do I could not imagine. Perhaps he had decided to go back to the battery I thought, like a homing pigeon or a lost dog, and I should find him there on our return. Or he might be wounded. At all events he was gone for good.

After a chat with the jolly Diggers—I forget what they were doing there all by themselves, but they had much that was disobliging to relate with respect to the lonely bog upon whose bank they lived—I went out again to essay the crossing. Before we got on to the wooden track the shelling started. But this gangway was no longer intact. It had been broken in two places. We should be bebogged among other things and with a murderous directness the fire was still bracketed on us. So I decided to retire once more in good order upon the Anzac refuge (which was much more amusing than the O.Pip would be and just as good) and wait for a more propitious moment, when my friend in the sausage-balloon had his hands full elsewhere.

This moment did not present itself. Further sallies were punctually met by a conscious directness of fire, and I thought their marksmanship got better instead of worse. The objective, I decided, namely the misbegotten O.Pip beyond the bog, was not worth the certainty of casualties. As it was it astonished me that none of us had been hit.

So I never saw that O.Pip. And after my report of what had happened to us, in conjunction with the report of my predecessor, another site was selected, further down the Line.—As night came on I withdrew, shaking my fist at the sausage balloon.

We had not got far when out of a deserted trench appeared the missing signaller, who fell in behind, without any comment, I on my side affecting not to notice his return. No doubt he had kept us under observation as closely as had the occupant of the sausage balloon.

The above is an exact account of a brush between one Observer and another Observer—not so wholly negative as it may at first sight seem, seeing that we occupied a 'five-nine' battery, plus an extremely competent Observer, *and* a balloon full of valuable gas (with necessary personnel) for an entire day.

Clearly the odds against us were prohibitive : we were unable ourselves to 'observe' anything, yes; but we successfully prevented an ideally placed Observer (who might have done untold damage elsewhere) from 'observing' anything else except us, so absorbing did he find us.

In conclusion let me reiterate the claim I have made above. Men have been hunted with rifles—for this was hunting not fighting, it must be remembered : they have been hunted with arrows, spears, lassoes and even harpoons. But what men before or since have been hunted by a howitzer? This is not a game at which two can play. The gunner, as I have said, is not a fighting man. But I have shown he can become a hunter if not a fighter, potting at solitary figures with no less a fowling piece than a howitzer.

CHAPTER X

Among the Brass Hats, and Sir William Orpen

My best friend in this battery was my partner, the officer of No. 3 gun. He had a great pal who was an artist, and so had become acclimatized to the artist's habits of mind. He felt less strange with me than the others did. It was like having a nice girl on the other gun—I do not mean this offensively, only that nature having endowed him with the gift of 'intuition' and given him a light touch, it was better than having somebody there who was regarding me as a rival cock who had to be crowed over and fought. The rank and file being the hens, of course : for they play the passive role. They stand round and watch the officers crow and fight.

My partner was so seriously wounded that we supposed he would pass out when he was taken away. He did not, as I heard from him after the War. I was broadcasting a story on the Radio and he wrote to me. A percussion shrapnel got a direct hit on a dugout and he was wounded in both lungs. This was a few days before I returned to England on leave.

The battery-position was no joke at all at night. It was heavily shelled from nightfall to daybreak. They were mainly high velocity shells. To look at, a high velocity shell is elegant compared with its more pedestrian fellows. It's what a Hock bottle is to a Burgundy bottle, beside the latter. Instead of the heavy arc of sound, reminiscent of a whoop, which gives you a fair warning, a high velocity shell just swishes over. They were swishing overhead all night at this place. When I was on duty at the guns, I would fall asleep in the duty-dugout with these things uninterruptedly skimming the roof at the speed of a comet. In the daytime I have had an H.V. dash into the ground a few yards away. We took no notice of them. They disappeared into the ground and were more unpleasant for the earthworms than for us.

A percussion shrapnel was another matter; and my poor partner got that. We were a good deal together. As officers, we moved about; and it was not only our habit to go forward (to O.Pips) we also went *back*, to back areas, long distances sometimes. For instance, if a part of one of our guns wanted mending, we would take it in the battery-car to the artillery workshops near Cassel.

Cassel was a very fashionable little health-resort, delightfully placed on a small hill. The more retiring and timid of the 'fighting' men from the Salient would have been a little shy of it, because of the red-tabs everywhere. My partner quivered at the sight of so much scarlet and gold. But I led him by the hand into the thick of the brass-hats, and once or twice we had dinner or lunch at the best hotel, with a beautiful view over the country.

We went still farther back, even, to St. Omer. This was not lousy with brasshats but a nice human spot. The town closed about eight o'clock at night. All the lights were put out, and the last of the inhabitants, with their mattresses on their backs, disappeared into the municipal cellars. The first bomb would drop as we left it. At this period the bombing of St. Omer was a nightly occurrence.

Cassel was not bombed. I may be wrong, but I do not believe it is considered good form for high-commands to bomb each other. Probably the Salamanca Junta and the Valencia Junta bomb each other because they are only 'Juntas', and neither admits the other is a 'high command'. Both are peculiarly *low* commands, in the view of their vis-à-vis.

One night I was dining and wining my gun-partner there still very nervous at the spectacle of so many 'high' officers—when I caught sight of a familiar face, under a brass-hat. This was no less an academic celebrity than the late Sir William Orpen. He came to our table and produced from his pocket a flask of whisky. 'Will y'have some?' he croaked in his quavering Dublin patter, which he had taken good care never to get rid of. 'It's good stuff—I know ut's good. It's from Haig's Mess I got-tut there this morning!'

I drank to the health of the High Command. I learnt that Orpen was doing watercolours and things of the War (I saw them afterwards—they were pallid and sentimental) attached to the G.H.Q. for the purpose. Upon hearing that I was with a battery in the Salient, he gazed in a half-mocking stare, twisting his eyebrows and smiling his wry Irish mockery at me.

'It's hell isn't it? It must be hell!' quickly he chattered under his breath.

I said it was Goya, it was Delacroix—all scooped out and very El Greco. But hell, no.

But he would have it hell. He'd doubtless called it 'hell' so often he wasn't going to drop the infernal cliché. Besides you couldn't say, in the ordinary way, 'It's Goya!'

'Ah yes, it must be hell!' he said. He pronounced hell, 'hail'.

'Hell sometimes for the infantry. But it's merely a stupid nightmare—it's not real.'

'Same thing!' said he.

I always wanted to be on the Staff. The glimpse frankly, that I got of this posh portraitist living on the fat of the land at Cassel made my mouth water. When with my first battery, the O.C. having learned a little bit the kind of customer that he had got into the Mess, said to me : 'I don't know, you know, what you're doing sitting on your bo-hind in this bloody battery. If I knew the *parlez-vous* as you do and was a first-rate sketcher, I should be on *the Staff*. That's where I should be!' And what's more he *would,* I'd have laid odds on that. He was the fellow who was hot-foot after the Military Cross. Nothing would have kept him off the Staff if he'd had half my excuses for being there. He'd have had all their D.S.O.'s and M.C.'s on him, a Croix-de-Guerre too, and anything else that was going.

But I never found my way about properly in that war, not in the way some people did. My natural modesty was one obstacle. If you don't *ask,* no one offers. I was a bad asker.

Of course, I read in the newspapers, of how our highbrow enemies—the Central Powers—'saved' their artists and important people like that. But it was, I suppose, a sort of compliment to me that no step was taken to 'save' me. Just as if I hadn't been an artist! I took it as a compliment, at all events. Eventually I 'saved' myself.

170

CHAPTER XI
The King of the Trenches

Why was the lieutenant pale? Why did he gaze so fixedly from beneath his new Gor'-Blimy? Because his mother came from Lima. That was also why his face was serious, and his nerves removed to a plane of reasonableness seldom reached by heat and shock. He had a certain gentle lisping breathlessness. Sandhurst had not curtailed his charm, which reached back to civilised Savannas.

He was astonished on the 4th May to see an unusual figure standing near him in the Trench. It was staring at his Flying Pig, and twirling a stick. It twirled and twirled the stick and looked at the Flying Pig. Then it gave the fascinating siege ordnance before it a blow and exclaimed 'Ha! *Ha!*'

That Ha! *Ha!* was a new note in Menzies' life of war. Lieutenant Donald Menzies (Lima, London and Linlithgow) absorbed the new sound that he recognized at once as belonging to this outlandish life, and temporarily placed it in what he supposed must be its proper position among the ejaculatory and explosive noises by which he was surrounded. That trench where they were had never heard of it as far as he knew. Perhaps it came from another trench? Or it might be that, except when uttered by that figure, it never occurred at all anywhere. He had never heard it before in any case. He noted and placed it with military tidinesss.

A breath of bald absurdity, a new comic gas, had entered Menzies' trench with that figure, however. Menzies looked at him again. Then with a delicate smile of recognition, he took in the situation. This figure must be his newly-posted commanding officer.

With politely sarcastic câlinerie he approached the new biped, with the new noise, dropped from some strange Christmas-tree into his trench.

171

'Good morning, sir.'

'Good morning. Good morning!'

The gentleman was whistling. —*'How-do-you-doodle oodle-oo. Oh fancy meeting you!'* was what he whistled. Meantime he lazily struck the gun with his stick.

'Captain Polderdick?'

'Polderdick! How did you know my name?' Polderdick's mouth grew round and slushy: the military moustache over it was a fierce camouflage hiding 'Ha! *Ha's!*' The ribbon of the D.C.M., the Military Medal, the usual South African medal and many others jostled each other, two deep, upon his advancing chest. A drawling, extremely circumspect and ponderous delivery, suggested that language was not without its pitfalls for him. The old ranker swelled with the officialdom and diaphragmatic pomp of all those promoted across that portentous gulf which separates officers from men when the change of worlds comes after a life-time of habit.

'How did you know my name?' he screwed his eyes up cunningly, his name, like his rank, was for him an object, a thing secured, perhaps by means of some stratagem, by this stranger.

'I supposed it was you, sir, who had been posted to us.'

'You were quite right my lad, quite right. It *was* me! Here I am! And there you are. And here *we* are! What next, my lad? Ha! *Ha!*' He twirled his stick round, imparting supple movements to it till it appeared to flex and waggle like a fencing sword. He prodded the Flying Pig, repeating his war-cry 'Ha! *Ha!*'

Then fiercely and quizzingly he wheeled round on Menzies, like a ruffled dog. With a fresh flourish of the stick, and a gutteral 'Ha! *Ha!*' he lunged, prodding Menzies in the stomach.

'Oh sir!' exclaimed the lieutenant, carrying his gloved hand to the region affected. After this initiation Polderdick wandered off, followed by his new subaltern, to inspect the rest of his stock.

'Handsome pieces of ordnance, my lad!' he exclaimed as they came upon one. 'Fine handsome pieces!' Then sinking

his chin down into his historic chest, with the object of fixing
his roaring mouth like a funnel over the lung where the deep
sound comes from, he began chanting, one hand over his ear
in the orthodox fashion.

> 'Won't you buy, oh won't you buy
> My sweet lavend-er-er,
> Fifteen branches one penny-y-y.'

'Burney' was known for leagues, all over the Line. Polderdick
was known as 'Burney'. He had a great name for intrepidity,
and as an able gunner. Menzies grew accustomed to the spectacle of his O.C. (arriving on the scene generally a little late)
coming down the trench whistling a few bars of 'Won't you
buy my sweet Lavender' or 'Goosie—Goosie—Gander', making
facetious passes with his stick. When he met an infantry soldier,
he would, to this Tommy's dismay, if it were his first meeting
with Polderdick, twirl his stick, with his 'Ha! *Ha!* my lad—
How's that? If you never get anything worse than that, my
lad, you can thank your stars. Nickwar? Pass on! To your
post!'

It was also his habit to poke his stick into all shelters and
dug-outs that he passed, blessing them or banning them with
his 'Ha! Ha!' He stirred up many a figure in some damp
black hole, who thought it was a visiting general being funny,
and cursed under his breath.

When Polderdick arrived the Line was quiet. A few days
afterwards the Trench was constantly shelled. Polderdick was
there. They began shelling with shrapnel. At the first patter of
the shrapnel Polderdick dived headlong into a dug-out, but his
tin-hat crashed with great force against the tin-hat of an infantry captain who was darting out at the moment. They both
disappeared, Polderdick's buttocks revolving as he fell inside.
Menzies crouched against the side of the Trench, which was
spouting earth a few yards higher up, from the last burst, and
was full of the momentary wasp-music of hurrying splinters.

'No, sir, I'm a flying pig!' Menzies heard his commanding
officer exclaiming. 'You got in the way, sir!'

'You silly bastard, you nearly broke my neck. Let me get out. What are you doing? Get off my leg!'

'Stop here, my lad, and keep me company. Outside all is war. Don't go looking for trouble, my lad. Gently does it.'

Two shells swooped and buried themselves like furies in the earth above Menzies' head, and a moment later two red fountains of earth poured down deluging him from head to foot. The infantry captain appeared and hurried past him down the trench. Polderdick's head peered out, looking to left and right. There was a considerable noise coming from every direction, and Polderdick shouted to Menzies:

'Keep those pigs barking. Give Fritz hell! Give him hell! Where's all this stuff coming from do you suppose?'

There were two cracks overhead, Menzies flattened himself against the side of the Trench, and the shrapnel spattered everywhere for a moment. Polderdick's head appeared again.

'My head's rotten!' he exclaimed. 'Did you hear just how I knocked it? It's rotten. I shall go to the rear. You "carry on, sergeant!" I'm off.'

'Have you hurt yourself?' asked Menzies.

'Rotten!' said Polderdick. He scrambled out, shook himself and stumbled quickly away, watched by the gunner corporal.

' "Burney's" got the wind up,' said the corporal.

'He banged his head,' said Menzies.

'Ah! so I saw!' said the corporal.

A stunt had been announced. It was the morning of the attack. There had been a good deal of shelling. Menzies, in coming up with the relief, met in the support lines a figure being borne upon a stretcher. It's eye, as he passed, appeared aware of him; the head remained facing the sky. A solemn eye swept over him, as they passed, in placid recognition, nothing more. Menzies felt it was his O.C., though he had not noticed the face as he passed him. He ran back.

'Are you hurt, sir?'

Polderdick's eye settled down in the corner of his head to observe his subaltern.

174

'My rheumatism's something cruel this morning. It's laid me out something proper. They're taking me back. —You carry on, my lad. Pass on! It's downed me this time properly.'

He spoke in the quiet voice of one in pain. Menzies got used, likewise, to this. Whenever a stunt was coming off, Polderdick disappeared, on a stretcher, if he could get one, to the rear, or he kept away till the worst was over.

Menzies and Marshall, the other subaltern of his section, talked over the situation. Marshall was resentful. He had been sent to Trench Mortars with death in his soul. A month of them had developed in him a hatred of everything in this inferno. Menzies did not entertain a severe view of Polderdick, however. He explained to the sullen Marshall the advantages, as he saw it, of the case. Also he excused him. He pointed out that Polderdick had been wounded in the temple. Before that— who could doubt, who had glanced casually at his left breast?— he had certainly been a very brave man. But also, of course (it was to be supposed) he had not then exclaimed 'Ha! Ha!' He had not prodded people in the stomach with his stick.—For Menzies there were two lives, where Polderdick was concerned. There had been one in which he had been a madly-brave soldier in the ranks (look at his ribbons, consider his record!). There he got his crosses, his nickname, his prestige. Then there was the other one in which he was just *mad*, without however being brave. He was charming, but no longer brave.

Much of his *madness,* Menzies proceeded to argue—as they sat at the tin-table of the café in Bailleul where they had gone in a lorry for the afternoon to get tobacco and condensed milk for the officer's mess—much of his peculiar wildness, had gone into, had been absorbed by, his physical daring, about that there was little doubt. It had had to go somewhere. It had gone into that. Then the wound in the temple stopped that up, brusquely. You see? (Marshall did not see: he cursed the metaphysical Scot, he yawned, he stamped, he lit cigarettes, he glared). The wound, for whatever reason, prevented his madness from any longer flowing into the moulds of physical heroism. It found other outlets. He became a different man. He did not forget his past bravery, however. His new incarnation was its distorted child. The 'Ha! *Ha!*' itself drew the gusto of its note from the cold, cruel, almost intellectual courage of the former Polderdick.

Physical strength remained with him. Could he not take one of the heaviest and least willing of his men in his arms, lift him kicking and howling until head and shoulders stuck up over the parapet? 'Ha! *Ha!* Look over there, my lad!' he would cry. (Menzies and Marshall had both witnessed this episode.) He still liked, in a sort of prolongation of himself, to look over the top through the eyes of a reluctant subordinate.— So Menzies discoursed, with his mild persuasive southern eyes wandering about the busy square. Marshall transferred all the feelings one by one that he had about Polderdick to Menzies. Menzies was mad! Menzies was balmy! He was madder than Polderdick. He had always disliked Menzies. He had been right. No one could help disliking a man who could talk such cock as that! Also he was evidently inclined to suck up to the O.C. He said nothing. He stood up and stretched.

'Well, shall we beat it? Come on, you bloody philosopher! There's a lorry, let's get that.' He started running.

Polderdick was not popular with his men. Like most ranker-officers, he was extremely exacting; it was his tendency to make them work if anything harder than he had worked so long himself.

At the point of the English Line where his battery was placed, a stream had once flowed and still took a little water across No Man's Land, bisecting the German front-line and the English. In the English Line (as in the German) a foot-bridge had been built inside the trench where this happened, with a parapet of sand-bags continuing the face of the Trench across the little gully. —On two occasions his men pushed 'Burney' off this bridge into the water, alleging accident, assuming dismay. The first time he clambered out. As a clown, his indignation was circumscribed. He protested and swore. But it happened again shortly afterwards. The second time he said nothing. But the men responsible for it had a good deal of work in the ensuing week. When in future he had occasion to approach the bridge he looked carefully round before crossing. If he was with men of his own he allowed them to pass first. He even would not cross when an infantryman was behind him.—His chief objection of falling into the water was that he believed a German sniper had his rifle trained on this spot. Menzies gathered this from his guarded inquiry: 'Many Tommies fall in there, my lad? It's a dangerous spot.' As the water did not make it dangerous, it must be that. And once, when a man was missing, he asserted that the man had fallen into the stream, been sniped, and had subsequently been borne down its waters to the rear. The corpse would turn up in the end, it seemed, beneath the windows of Corps Headquarters, which he appeared to conceive as situated on the brink of a pool, by this time practically full of men who had lost their lives in that manner.

He was not always beneath the shadow of this dream. Probably, as an outcome of his aquatic experiences, he one day said to Menzies:

'The British Army when I first joined was some Army! It was small, but it was a pukka army, second to none, my lad! There was initiative. Initiative is what you want. This is a ragtime army. Look at it!—It's a ragtime war, my lad, from what I can see of it. I should like to be in civvies again. No! straight I would, that's right!'—Menzies had a puzzled look. 'Burney' stared at him a moment: then he became more normal. 'A soldier should be on the lookout for opportunities. That's what a soldier should be. It breaks my heart to see chances lost, as I do every day.' He turned suddenly upon Menzies. 'Now, why don't you jump into the stream; swim up it, swim up it!'—He fixed Menzies violently with his left eye—'and bomb Fritz from the water? He wouldn't see where it came from.—You can swim, my lad, can't you?'

'Yes, sir. But there's not enough water to swim in. And the Boche has it under observation all the time.'

'Rot! That's rot what you're saying there, my lad! Don't tell me you couldn't.—No! But you're like me. You've lost interest in this ragtime war, is that it? No? Well you must be a B.F., if you haven't, that's all I can say!'

'I never have been interested, like you sir. You are a soldier.'

'Me! A soldier!? Get along with it! I'm not a soldier! I *was*!'

Menzies smiled affectionately at his chief.

But Polderdick, soldier or no soldier, grew depressed. This was really a necessary exploit, that the stream had been placed there to make possible. The consciousness of the things he no longer did weighed heavily on him. It was stupid to have to ask another man. He had never refused such occasions. How could they? *Yet he understood how they could,* that was the most depressing part of it. A world in which he was a major, surrounded by nothing but soldiers who were not soldiers, wholly given over to war that was not a war, was a ragtime world.

This restless spirit of haunting adventure would sometimes make him mischievous. He would come up from the billet into a quiet world, a local truce reigning throughout the stagey ditches and melodramatic crypts and holes of the landscape, of which he was a notable faun. A few lonely shells sang or creaked along overhead, bursting in the remote distance, like the noisy closing of very far-off doors. Butterflies drifted here and there. German and English, Fritz and Tom, read the newspaper, slept, wrote to Gretchen or the lovely Minnie.—Polderdick would gaze round at this idyllic scene with a dissatisfied and restless eye.

On one of these occasions Marshall was on duty. He was sunning himself on a stretch of wet mud. One gunner was asleep, another writing a letter. Polderdick appeared and fixed his eye upon Marshall. Blankly with sudden unction he declared.

'Ha! *Ha!* Mr. Marshall! An excellent opportunity for Trench Mortars! What do you think? Is that right?' He put up his periscope and peered into it. 'I see a Hun's back in what is evidently a post, an advanced post. They've got the cheek of the devil some of those Huns. The Fritzes in that sap to the left seem to have got it into their heads that this part of the line is a branch of the Millennium! Swelt my bob if I don't see two having a shave, the bastards, as large as life!'

As fast as they could be loaded, he sent his Flying Pig hurtling

178

in all directions. All the peaceable warriors in the trenches were filled with amazement, which rapidly turned to fury when they realised what was happening. A raucous murmur, a tenuous hubbub of alarm and inquiry, floated across No Man's Land. This was quickly succeeded by a fusillade of every description of missile and projectile on which the enemy could lay his hands quickly. A black cloud of anger surged along our trench. Infantry officers rushed up to Polderdick, shaking their fists in his face. But flourishing his stick mysteriously, he hastily retired down the communication trench, and was seen no more till the next day.

Meantime the *riposte* had come and a furious bombardment had fallen on the trench. In the rear the Field started, the Heavies joined in, layer behind layer, until the enormous guns right back on the old ramparts of Ypres were shattering the air with their discharge, and for a short time all was confusion. On both sides everyone stood by, expecting an attack. Marshall was wounded in the lung, two gunners were killed. Menzies was telephoned for from the trench by the breathless telephonist, and as he was hurrying up he met his O.C. retiring hastily along the duckboard track.

'Is it an attack?' he asked.

'An attack? No-o, attack be buggered! It's as quiet as Heaven up there!'

'Marshall's wounded. Didn't you know?'

'Marshall wounded? Who said so?'

'The telephonist. They're probably attacking. Look at all this coming over!'

There was a line of black stumps on a low ridge to their left, and every few seconds an immense impressive chocolate black burst rose up and spent splinters flapped in the mud on either side of the duckboard track.

'Yes, it's not over healthy here, I agree,' Polderdick said, starting anxiously forward, his eye on a line of burst on the road ahead, that he would soon have to cross. 'I'm going to get back. My rheumatism's something awful today. But it's quiet enough up in the Line. I came away because there was nothing doing. You can go up there if you want a nap.'

Menzies left him : by the time he reached the trench all again was as Polderdick had described it, very quiet, except for a few restless guns that still continued slamming on both sides. But there had been a number of casualties.

'Where's that son-of-a-bitch of an O.C. of yours? If he comes back here I'll put him under arrest! He ought to be shot! Is the man mad? Where is he?'

Informed at Battalion Headquarters of what had happened the O.C. Infantry was on the spot. Stretcher bearers were passing along the trench. The bodies of three gunners lay near the Flying Pig, the leg of one two yards away, and another beheaded. Marshall had been taken to the dressing-station.

'Burney' Polderdick prepared his story of this event. So well did he know his way about in the professional military mind, and so high was his military reputation, that his bluff soldierly view of what had occurred was accepted at Headquarters.— Shortly after this, his four Flying Pigs were moved to a neighbouring divisional front.

For anything below a General, as things stood, Polderdick had a sovereign contempt. In the new world in which Polderdicks were majors, this perhaps must of necessity ensue. His obsequiousness in the presence of a General-Officer was no doubt the complement of his wounding attitude to those below that rank. Lieut-Colonels, for instance, he looked upon frankly as so much dirt.

A feud instantly sprang up in the new position between a Company-Commander and himself (a company-commander under the Derby Scheme-*justescieux!*). It was to do with the site he had decided upon for the operations of his Flying Pigs. Secretly Polderdick obtained a written order from Brigade Headquarters to say that 'Captain H. H. Polderdick has permission to dispose his 9.45 Battery wherever he considers it will be most useful.' That morning he set about the installation of his guns in the position in the trench to which the Company-Commander particularly objected. A sergeant hurried up to say respectfully that 'Captain Nixon had given strict orders that Trench Mortar Battery was not to use that spot,' Polderdick came up and drove off the sergeant. Then Captain Nixon, cold leisureliness of an officer and gentleman, arrived. 'Burney' Polderdick stuck the written order under his nose. With the usual 'Ha *Ha!*' he followed up with the regulation lunge towards the belly with his circling stick. Nixon concertinaed, avoiding the exultant prod.

'Ha *Ha!* my lad! Pass on!'

Nixon passed on hurriedly, going for help. But now Polderdick's enemies gathered against him.

An unfortunate thing occurred in the rear, at his billet. His landlady or rest-billet-lady became restless and anxious. On one of those mornings when he woke up very much his new self, Polderdick asked her to come up to his room. When he had got her there, he locked the door behind them, and taking up his stick, twirling it, stamping his foot, he began prodding her in the stomach, with delighted 'Ha! *Ha's!*'—The woman escaped and complained to the A.P.M. She refused any longer to billet him.

The crowning peculiarity of the ex-sergeant was that he very rarely drank anything more than lime juice. A vine seemed to grow within his skull. No one would have believed that he was not intoxicated when, issuing from the Mess one dark night, and finding a Sunbeam not far from the door of the billet, he sprang in and expected it to go. Some A.S.C. men loitering there, who knew him, got behind and pushed it. When it was in the middle of the road, they peered round at him, and in the voice of Harry Tate's Eton-collared assistant, whined and bawled 'It will not *go,* Pa-paa! There is something wrong, Papa! It really will not go, Pa-paa!' He sat there snorting fiercely. It was the owner of the car, just then arriving, who refused to believe that he was not tight. He disarmed and confused this official by a deft stroke with his stick (which never left him) just below the region of the wind.

But his guns, although in position, and firmly cemented by written authority, were not so secure as they seemed. The infantry gathered for the attack. On a fine afternoon, when, in fact, Polderdick was on the point of exclaiming 'Ha! *Ha!* an excellent opportunity for Trench Mortars!' a suave, hirsute and old Colonel arrived on the scene, and made straight for the Flying Pigs. Polderdick, with a dramatic leap, intercepted him, stick in hand, twirling and feinting. He appeared to take it for granted that this interloper had designs upon his fat little ordnance.

'Are these your guns?' The intercepted Colonel fixed him severely with his veteran eye, that noted the Ranker's ribbons, and sought to quell the life-long 'common soldier' beneath the new Sam Browne. Polderdick, on his side, saw nothing but a Lieut-Colonel in this hostile person.

'Yes.—Yes: Yes. My guns. My pigs. My little pigs, sir.'

'I don't think that is a very good position for them.'

'No? No!'

'You must see that dug-out—'

'I see the dug-out. I've had my eye on it from the first. And if you know of a better hole, sir—well, you know what to do!'

'Yes, but that dug-out—'

'Yes sir, that dug-out—But you can't attack Fritz with a dug-out, sir. You fire nothing out of a dug-out, sir. You might fire Captain Nixon a hundred yards or so, with a big charge. But I'm accredited to these 9.45's, these "flying pigs" as they call them. I have no order, sir, as regards Captain Nixon—'

'Stop this tom-foolery please. Your guns are in the way where you have placed them. And they are not well-placed either—'

'I beg your pardon, sir?' Polderdick grew suddenly one harsh blotch of red, as though he had been slapped. 'Are you aware to whom you are speaking?' He drew himself up, and flung his chest out, the mad-soldier entering into him again for a moment following this direct affront to his professional pride. His voice too got its wild and shouting note. 'Do you know my name, sir? Captain Polderdick is my name, Polderdick. Burney Polderdick.'

He continued to glare at the Colonel for a moment; but his eye gradually filled with the peculiar light of the transformed 'Burney', though more wild even than usual.

'*I am the* King of the Trenches!' he shouted. 'Didn't you know who I was? Yes! I am Burney Polderdick, the King of the Trenches!—Ha! *Ha!*' He flourished his stick, twirled it lightly, lunged forward, and dug the Colonel in the middle of the stomach.

182

'Ha! *Ha!* The King of the Trenches!' he shouted in triumph, as the Colonel hastened away, his fingers convulsively grasping his stick, not venturing to give further utterance to his thoughts.

That afternoon Polderdick decided it was an 'excellent afternoon for trench mortars', and inaugurated this phase of his reign by a few unexpected salvoes. But the divisional commander in this new section was not the man for him. He took a disobliging view of the events reported to him.

Polderdick a few days after this was removed from the command. He was sent back to the Training Depot in England.

'I think, yes, we will have a bottle of wine!'

Burney Polderdick's last lunch with his subalterns was enlivened by this sudden decision. A bottle of Ordinary Wine was obtained. Menzies, who was Mess-secretary, was curious to see if Burney would pay for it. He supposed that he would not. But at the last moment the now exiled King of the terrible narrow Kingdom his madness had caused him to be expelled from, that he would probably now never see again, fumbled in his pocket, and produced the necessary ninepence. He had evidently meant to pay all along.

When the twirling stick receded, and passed the bend in the smashed and dilapidated street, although still, like a perfume, he could faintly hear the whistling of *Won't you buy my sweet lavender-er-er,* Menzies returned to the Mess with a regret at this personal loss.

CHAPTER XII

Political Education under Fire

I don't think artists are any more important than bricklayers or stockbrokers. But I dislike the 'hearty' artist (who pretends he isn't one but a stockbroker) more than the little aesthete. I felt less inclined to immolate myself in defence of Mayfair and the 'stately homes of Old England', the more I pondered over it. I was only concerned at the idea of deserting my companions in misfortune.

When I had first attested, I was talking to Ford Madox Hueffer about Gaudier's death. I'd said it was too bad. Why should Gaudier die, and a 'Bloomsbury' live? I meant that *fate* ought to have seen to it that that didn't happen. It was absurd.

It was absurd, Ford agreed. But there it was, he seemed to think. He seemed to think *fate* was absurd. I am not sure he did not think Gaudier was absurd.

The 'Bloomsburies' were all doing war-work of 'National importance', down in some downy English county, under the wings of powerful pacifist friends; pruning trees, planting gooseberry bushes, and haymaking, doubtless in large sunbonnets. One at least of them, I will not name him, was disgustingly robust. All were of military age. All would have looked well in uniform.

One of course 'exempted' himself, and made history by his witty handling of the tribunals. That was Lytton Strachey. He went round to the tribunal with an aircushion, which, upon arrival, he blew up, and sat down on, amid the scandalized silence of the queue of palpitating petitioners. His spidery stature was reared up bravely, but his dank beard drooped, when his name was called; and he made his famous retort. 'What,' sternly asked one of the judges, 'would you do Mr.

Wyndham Lewis. 1920.
portrait of Ezra Pound.

portrait of Rebecca West.

Wyndham Lewis. 1921.
Self-portrait.

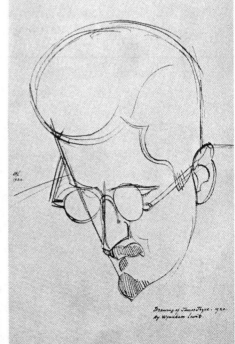

W.L.
1920.

Drawing of James Joyce. 1920.
by Wyndham Lewis.

Douglas Jerrold

Wyndham Lewis 1931

portrait of
T.S. Eliot.

Wyndham Lewis.

Nancy Cunard

Wyndham Lewis 1922

Wyndham Lewis 1922.
Head of Noel Coward

Strachey, if you discovered a German preparing to outrage your sister?' and Strachey without hesitation replied : 'I—would—place—myself—*between*—them!'

But the 'bloomsburies' all exempted themselves, in one way or another. Yet they had money and we hadn't; ultimately it was to keep them fat and prosperous—or thin and prosperous, which is even worse—that other people were to risk their skins. Then there were the tales of how a certain famous artist, of military age and militant bearing, would sit in the Café Royal and addressing an admiring group back from the Front, would exclaim : '*We* are the civilization for which you are fighting!'

But Ford Madox Hueffer looked at me with his watery-wise old elephant eyes—a little too crystal-gazing and claptrap, but he knew his stuff—and instructed me upon the very temporary nature of this hysteria. I was too credulous! I *believe* that he tipped me the wink. He was imparting to me I believe a counsel of commonsense.

'When this War's over,' he said, 'nobody is going to worry, six months afterwards, what you did or didn't do in the course of it. One month after it's ended, it will be forgotten. Everybody will want to forget it—it will be bad form to mention it. Within a year disbanded 'heroes' will be selling matches in the gutter. No one likes the ex-soldier—if you've lost a leg, more fool you!'

'Do you think that?' I said, for he almost made my leg feel sorry for itself.

'Of course,' he answered. 'It's always been the same. After all the wars that's what's happened.'

This worldly forecast was verified to the letter. There is no better propaganda against war, I think, than to broadcast such information as this (though that was not Ford's intention : he was very keen on the War). The callousness of men and women, once the fit of hysteria is over, has to be seen to be believed—if you are prone to give humanity the benefit of the doubt, and expect some 'decency' where you won't find it. They regard as positive enemies those whom a war has left broken and penniless. The 'saviours' and 'heroes' get short shrift, upon the Peace Front. No prisoners are taken there! Why, in such a

185

'patriot' country as France, men have, since the War, been promoted to the highest offices of State, who had been convicted of treason and 'traffic with the enemy'. Sir Roger Casement would be an O.B.E. if not a Knight of the Garter, had he not been of a romantic and suicidal turn and got himself shot.

It has been my firm intention to talk no politics in this book. I will not refer to what went on in my own mind as a result of these experiences, more than an indication, just here and there. I have spoken nowhere of the men, while I was in France. It is impossible to say anything about that. If one is not to talk politics, one has to keep one's mouth shut. All the fancy-dress nonsense of 'officers' and 'men', under the snobbish English system, is a subject distinct from war, and yet very much involved with it.

As an officer it was my unwelcome task to read great numbers of private letters. Naturally the officers would among themselves discuss with smiles the burning endearments, or the secrets of his poor little domestic economy, revealed by his letters, of this man or that. These rough and halting communings, of the most private sort, were passsing through our hands every day. Yet most of the censors were as literary artists, of not a very different clay to those who had to submit to this humiliating censorship.

My own thoughts I kept strictly to myself. I preserved my *anonymity,* in the sense in which I have already explained that principle. When I am dressed up in a military uniform I look like other people, though at other times I very easily depart from the canon, I find. One or two of my mess-mates sniffed at me suspiciously. But on the whole I was a masterpiece of conformity.—I am physically very robust. It is easy for me to go to sleep. And conformity is of course *a sleep*.

I started the war a different man to what I ended it. More than anything, it was a *political* education. I am slow to learn but quick to understand. As day by day I sidestepped and dodged the missiles that were hurled at me, and watched other people doing so, I became a politician. I was not then the accomplished politician I am to-day. But the seeds were there.

I had no sentimental aversion to war. A violent person, who

likes the taste of blood, as another does the taste of wine, likes war. I was indifferent. But this organized breakdown in our civilized manners must have a rationale, in a civilized age. You must supply the civilized man with *a reason,* much as he has to have his cocktail, flytox, and ice-water.

I, along with millions of others, was standing up to be killed. Very well: but *who* in fact was it, who was proposing to kill or maim me? I developed a certain inquisitiveness upon that point. I saw clearly that it was not my German opposite number. He, like myself, was an instrument. That we were all on a fool's errand had become plain to many of us, for, beyond a certain point, victory becomes at the best a Pyrrhic victory, and that point had been reached before Passchendaele started.

The scapegoat-on-the-spot did not appeal to me. So I had not even the consolation of 'blaming the Staff', after the manner of Mr. Sassoon—of cursing the poor little general-officers.

> *'Good morning, good morning,' the General said,*
> *As we passed him one day as we went up the line.*
> *But the lads that he spoke to are most of them dead*
> *And we're cursing his staff for incompetent swine.*
> *'He's a cheery old sport!' muttered Harry to Jack.*
> *But he's done for them both with his plan of attack.*

That was too easy and obvious. It amazes me that so many people should accept that as satisfactory. The incompetent general was clearly such a very secondary thing compared with the incompetent, or unscrupulous, politician, that this conventional 'grouse' against the imperfect strategy of the military gentleman directing operations in the field seemed not only unintelligent but dangerously misleading. 'Harry and Jack' were killed, not by the General, but by the people, whoever they were, responsible for the war.

Nor could I obtain much from cursing my mother and father, grandmother and grandfather, as Mr. Aldington or the Sitwells did. For it was not quite certain that we were not just as big fools as our not very farsighted forebears. There was not much sense in blaming the ancestors of the community to which I belonged for the murderous nonsense in which I found myself, up to the neck, it seemed to me.

On the other hand, as it was not war *per se* that I objected to, I was not forgetful of the fact that most wars had been stupid, and had only benefited a handful of people. No one objects to being killed, if the society to which he belongs, and its institutions, are threatened, we can assume. But any intelligent man objects to being killed (or bankrupted) for *nothing*. That is insulting.

Where was I then? If you have a little politics you will say, perhaps, is *any* society worth being killed, or ruined, for? Is the Sovereign State to be taken seriously? Are any merely national institutions so valuable, so morally or intellectually valid, that we should lay down our lives for them, as a matter of course?

I could not answer that question by a mere yes or no. Naturally I can image a State that it would be your duty to die for. There are many principles also, which *might* find themselves incarnated in a State, which I personally consider matters of life and death. But whether the machine-age has left any State intact in such a way as to put men under a moral or emotional compulsion to die for it, is a matter I am unable to discuss. That would 'take us too far', as the valuable cliché has it.

And too far I am not going upon those tortuous roads. This is a plain tale of mere surface events. I am not out to do more than limn the action. I am keeping out the pale cast of thought as far as possible.

CHAPTER XIII

Kamper makes Whoopee

The officer who had replaced on No. 3 my wounded gun-partner looked round as I took him up to the guns and pronounced himself as agreeably surprised. He dropped into an easy patch. Three days, later, however, we had the worst shelling we had experienced. Our Mess was subterranean. Several of us were there doing some work on trench-maps. After the disturbance one by one we went out to the urinal. I was always the last in these processions—a question not of valour but superior sphincters or perhaps a cast-iron kidney.

The atmosphere still somewhat electric, a telegram was brought down. It was to the effect that my mother was dangerously ill. It was her second attack of pneumonia since the outbreak of war and therefore more liable to have fatal consequences. I hurried back to England, on special leave, the War entirely banished from my consciousness by this threatened personal loss.

She did not die then. She died from yet a third attack, in the great pneumonia epidemic which immediately followed the War, and which was undoubtedly the result of it. Consequently she was as well and truly killed by the military upheaval as if it had been shellfire and not pneumococci that did the trick. She was fifty years old and an extremely vigorous woman. And as far as my private feelings about war and all its works were concerned, this death affected me more than anything else. Parents who have lost the apples of their eyes in wars and who mourn them extremely, are apt to experience a hostile feeling thenceforth for the members of the nation which they hold responsible for their death : 'The Germans killed my son', they are liable, for instance, to observe : or 'the English'. I, sustaining a loss the other way round, had not the consolation of feeling a slight coldness for the Kaiser. Mine was, momentarily, a more abstract vendetta.

The oxygen cylinders were still there when I reached England. But the danger-period was over. My leave was for this special pupose and the moment arrived to return to my battery. 'Why return to your battery?' It was Guy Baker who put this leading question. 'Listen. It's quite unnecessary.' I pricked up my ears. 'Why not paint a picture instead?' The old devil grinned invitingly at me. A poor joke, it seemed to me—but Baker had a big idea. 'All young artists have got cushy jobs,' he said 'except you, painting pictures of the war.' I had not heard of this. And he then unfolded to me the all-important facts, which led eventually to my entering the charmed circle of the Staff; not as a brasshat, but with a palette on my thumb.

England's artists were being 'saved', by Canada of all countries, and by Lord Beaverbrook of all people. I mean of course that we do not associate the land of the 'Mounties' and of Montcalm with the fine arts, and Lord Beaverbrook I imagined fully occupied making and unmaking Governments and and Cabinets.

I said that I 'saved' myself, a few pages back, but it was Guy Baker who called the taxi, forced me into it, drove me to the entrance of the Albany, Piccadilly, and insisted on my visiting P. K. Konody, the art-critic. Konody it was who was charged with the selection of the artists, or advised Lord Beaverbrook in the matter. I was reluctant to take this step at first. Konody had wanted to call a paper 'the Vortex', and I had forbidden this and told him it was only over my dead body he would employ the word 'Vortex', of which I considered I had a monopoly.

Konody received me, almost literally, with open arms. When I asked him if he had among his artists an artillery-artist, to paint howitzers, he shouted NO! When I said I knew all about howitzers—how would it be for me to paint one—he screamed OF COURSE! ! ! With his dramatic miteuropean accent he gave this suggestion such a rich Austrian welcome as no suggestion ever had before or since. Two days later I found myself in the presence of Lord Beaverbrook, in an office off Regent Street.

And in his very much quieter way this genial Press Baron welcomed the idea too. And so it came about that I returned to the Front, this time to Vimy Ridge, as a painter-soldier, attached to the Corps-headquarter Staff of the Canadian Army.

I have always considered Lord Beaverbrook the brightest of the Press Barons and he must have a very remarkable instinct for affairs, to have got rich so young, to have pushed politicians about just as he wanted to, and to have created far and away the best cruiserweight newspaper in England, the *Evening Standard*.

Three feats; not the least of which is to run an original paper in England and to make it pay. He always showed towards me an extreme courtesy. On one occasion, during this period, he placed me upon his righthandside at luncheon at the Hyde Park Hotel, where he was being officially fêted, so that I was sort of fêted too. I suppose as I was the only person in Khaki that I was being the Unknown Soldier for the moment, but it was very jolly. He asked me I remember whether I would rather go round the world with Augustus John or with Orpen. We both agreed that the former experience would be more full of incident. He was very natural and amusing. We both seemed to have the same quiet tastes.

So I got my Staff job, was seconded from the English Army and attached to Canadian War Records—an office created by Lord Beaverbrook for supplying the Dominion of Canada with a complete picture gallery of the War. But now came the *longueurs* of the War Office. Everything was settled except the seconding.

In the War Office, where next I had to present myself, I saw a fierce little dugout Major who bounced and bristled when I mentioned pictures.—'To paint a picture!' he exclaimed. 'I've never heard of such a thing! Is that the way to win the war?' His bluster meant nothing. I refrained from pointing out that his own occupation was hardly calculated to put the Germans to flight.

Through the good offices of Lady Cunard, who was a great friend of the Quartermaster General—one of the three highest officers in the British Army—I obtained four successive extensions of leave while awaiting transfer. Why it could not be done quicker I have not the faintest idea. I suppose if there were less red tape there'd be fewer jobs in the War Office.

For six weeks, or maybe more, I was in the society of Lady Cunard continuously and it was here that I had an opportunity of observing at first hand the less seamy side of the war—though of course by that time all England was one vast Heartbreak House. The saturnalia that accompanies such fevered conditions was there too. But Lady Cunard, as a great 'political hostess', whose roll call of guests was never complete without at least half a dozen Cabinet Ministers, provided the more *responsible* picture, of the England engaged in 'winning the war'. The saturnalian picture I obtained glimpses of elsewhere.

There must have been people in England who understood what was happening. Lord Lansdowne was one of them no doubt. But I met none, and day after day I was amongst politicians and members of the official class who were 'winning the war', on the 'Home Front'. Examining in retrospect the attitude of mind that was common to all those people, I can detect no consciousness of the national calamity that the War had, by that time, come to be. They were 'seeing it through', in what they regarded as the traditional English fashion.

Anybody, however, who has taken the trouble to observe fairly closely the attitude of these same classes of people—the clubman, the man of the so-called 'ruling class'—during the last few years (say 1933-37), will be in no way surprised at this strange obtuseness. For today they are busy committing themselves, and their country, all over again to the same unprofitable adventure. So much short-sightedness, so little ability to learn from even the most bitter experience, has to be seen to be believed.

The major war that is at present in preparation (Great War No. 2) will finish what the last one began. The class that will be directly responsible for it cannot survive it : nor can the State—as a 'sovereign state', that is. With their eyes open, but rather dreamily and as if bewitched, they sign their own death-warrant. But they were the same then as they are now.

Do you want me to say whether I think it will be a good thing or a bad thing, if all this society is swept away, in a second and even vaster conflagration? But really that is a thing that each man must decide for himself. What do you think? A stupid society, like a stupid man, is not of much good to itself or anybody else. There is always that. But here it is as an observer only that I am writing. All I can say is that the *last* time they didn't know what was happening to them, or to England. They were keeping a stiff upper lip, on the Home Front, and living very much for the moment and whatever consolations it might bring.

As to the saturnalia, Kamper, the officer in command of our Jamaican Blacks, supplied me with a good deal of that. For he turned up in London too, on leave from the battery. And though the sphere of his activities was far removed from the worldly splendours of Mayfair, they resounded with the vital principle to such an extent, as sometimes to blot out, in memory, some polished happenings entirely. The piratic silhouette of Kamper jostles with those of Vice-regents and Ministers of State. I see him with great distinctness, a svelte Laocoon, in the toils of a conquest he had made, at the top of the basement stairs of an eating-house. It was his last night in London—the leave-train in the morning was to bear him away.

'Don't make things too difficult, darling!' I heard Kamper breathe out in a maudlin undertone. Next moment there was a violet spasm—he had untied the lover's knot: the white snakes, by which his neck had been constricted, writhed in the air, and the woman abruptly disappeared into the basement.

I have another vignette of this enjoyable colonial on the roof of the hotel in the small hours of the morning. Midway through his leave we had a Zeppelin raid. The sirens woke us.

Standing at the foot of the stairs, I looked up at the sky and there were the searchlights converging upon a bright silver fish, which dropped egg after egg upon London, as one could hear from the big roaring bangs. But then came a deafening explosion. It was Kamper coming into action. Still bearing up beneath the White Man's burden—for one of the hotel domestics clung to him in delighted terror—his Norseman's head thrown up, his arm outstretched, he was taking aim at the Zeppelin. Up among the roofs the crashing reports reverberated quite dwarfing the anti-aircraft guns, the bombs and all the rest of the surrounding uproar. It was an unspeakably noisy weapon, which I am persuaded Kamper must have chosen for its bark rather than for its bite.

Finally my seconding was an accomplished fact—all but one ceremony. I had to return to my battery, to report to my O.C. and be personally seconded by him. A postcard would have done just as well. But no; at the time of Malplaquet that was how it was done, and so this pointless displacement had to be gone through with. Once more I found myself in the officers' club at Poperinghe, and in due course back in my dank dugout.

This episode was not without its grimness. The sensation of a desertion came back to me with redoubled force, more as regards the men than the officers. Each of my fellow officers naturally asked himself why in God's name he hadn't been taught to paint pictures. 'Some people have all the luck!' was the general attitude.

Then too, the shelling did not stop. Obviously it should have stopped, to enable me to get peaceably through my ceremony of secondization. Destiny, I felt, might regard it as a joke in excellent taste to blow my head off, just as I was receiving my formal Godspeed from my O.C.

I am never sure that there is not an Observer up above us, like the Observer in the sausage-balloon, but yet more advantageously placed : one who is quite capable of setting a battery on to one, and in a word, causing the fire to be more *personal* than otherwise it would be.

If that is the case, and if he was watching me, he did not on that occasion molest me. The O.C. seconded me. How he knew how to do it I cannot imagine, as in civilian life he was probably a bank manager. But he said the magic words, and I saluted him for the last time. I turned my back with a sigh, half relief, half regret, upon the English Army. The squalid, insanitary, little rat-hole where I slept, beside the battered rivulet—with just a quiet bomb or two, no more, in the misty night, dropping sullenly in the ruins of Ypres—what is the claim that such places, such conditions, have upon one's desires, that no Ritz suite or castle-palace can compete with?

Perhaps I am *half* a romantic. Half my mind was elated at the congenial prospect of twirling my brush once more and bringing to life upon the canvas a painted battery. But half my mind was forlorn as I said good-bye to my untidy little batman. I was like the heartless young squire bidding a last farewell to the simple village maid he has betrayed, beside the cottage gate. But my batman I am afraid would let the image down badly, if we pressed it too far, even if I could to some extent have sustained it.

Once more upon the shores of England a little more *seconding* went on, and then I was finally dispatched to Canadian Corps Headquarters, upon the Vimy Ridge.—It was a very different ridge to the ridges I had been used to in the Salient.

CHAPTER XIV

The Booze Artist

The Canadian Corps Headquarter Mess, and the Chateau
where the war-artists were lodged, would be a book in itself
and an extremely entertaining book too. All I can relate is the
mere outline of the sort of thing it was.

When I reported for duty, or put in an appearance—for
formality was conspicuous by its absence—the Staff were not
themselves. There was great tension. Everybody had a stern
look, for something of extreme gravity had happend. There had
been a leakage of whisky. What was far more serious, one of the
most influential Mess servants was implicated.

After lunch a council of war was held. I was present, as an
onlooker. No one wanted to act, and yet Action was called for
and that of a rather radical order. For the leakage had amounted to bucketsful. Nearly half the headquarter's stock had
vanished. Much as these men-of-action disliked Action, it was
incumbent on them to be up and doing. So it was brusquely
decided to call in the man to whom everything pointed as the
culprit.

'Send in Sergeant Shotspur!' ordered the senior officer.

But Sergeant Shotspur was not far off and he forestalled this
command by opening the door and stepping into the room.
He had had his ear to the keyhole all along, that was quite
clear. And from the expression on his face it was evident that
Sergeant Shotspur was in no mood to be trifled with.

Sergeant Shotspur took two paces forward, clicked his heels,
saluted and glared at the assembled company. He glared not
as a soldier glares, but as a lawyer glares : and one who is pretty
sure of his case—whose brief-case is stuffed with cast-iron alibis.

'You asked for me?' said Sergeant Shotspur. To say that the
Headquarter Mess looked confused would be a fulsome under-

statement. They looked so uncomfortable that I felt sorry for them.

These men were the best of fellows, a most likeable lot. But they were very awkwardly placed. And they had not the dourness of the Australians. The fact was that they were officers, but they were not 'gentlemen'—at least no more so than the sergeants and the Mess servants, and they had no ambition to be imitation toffs, as the English had. They held commissioned rank; but it was on such a rigid understanding that they should not throw their weight about, they enjoyed it under such awful democratic safeguards, that the only advantage it took with it was that they had the equivalent of much more *money* than their subordinates, not much more *rank*. Also they had a Sam Browne belt and the others hadn't.

Often I have felt sorry for an English King, groaning under the weight of all the 'constitutional' safeguards that accompany his paradoxical rank—caged in by all the spectacular lack of power that doth hedge a King in England. For what's the use of being a King if you can't say *bo* to a goose without being put on the carpet by any jumped-up minister? But an officer in an Anglo-Saxon colonial army is in a not much better case.

After a lot of clearing of throats, *whisky*—the fatal word— was mentioned. No sooner was it out of the mouth of the officer who had had the temerity to mention it, than Sergeant Shotspur cut him short with a clearing of the throat that boded no good for anybody. He stiffened, his eye took on a steely glare, and he apostrophized them as follows :

'I'm no booze artist!' he thundered. 'I'm no booze artist, gentlemen, and I'd have you know it! I've been teetotal from birth! I was reared on milk and milk is still my drink. If a man wants a drop of Scotch, okay. I'm not a bigot. But you won't catch *me* sniffing round it. A principle's a principle, gentlemen—them are mine and I'll stand by them so help me God! It's not to a booze artist you're speaking. Whisky says nothing to me.'

There was a dead silence in the Mess. With drawn faces we cast guilty looks at each other. Then one of the bolder spirits ventured a remark.

'We had no intention *at all* Sergeant of suggesting you were fond of the bottle. You've missed the point of this. All we were suggesting was that not only the bottles but whole cases *disappear*. They vanish! '

'Vanish! I don't get you sir. The stuff disappears because it is *swallowed*!'

The outspoken officer gently shook his head.

'We know, sergeant,' he said, 'that *some* of the whisky disappears that way. We drink some of it ourselves.'

'Yes sir,' the unbending Shotspur answered shortly.

'That we fully realize, sergeant,' the officer went on very soothingly. 'But there is far more of this whisky that disappears without our getting a chance of swallowing it. That's what we're complaining about. We hoped, sergeant, that you might be able to account for that.'

With such circumlocution, it was at last made perfectly clear that there was more than one way of getting rid of a bottle of whisky. There were *other* artists, besides 'booze-artists'. There were financial wizards, for instance. These latter might have other uses for a bottle of whisky than the vulgar one of pouring it down the throat.

The Sergeant's face slowly cleared.

'I get your meaning sir,' he said. 'The whisky might have been *sold*!'

Everybody nodded his head brightly, with an air of the most intense relief.

'You got it, sergeant!' they responded in eager chorus.

They beamed assent at the sergeant, and the sergeant—his honour safe, prepared now to relax—beamed back at them.

'Of course—I do see that, gentlemen. That might quite well have occurred,' he agreed. 'I never thought of that.'

'You can't suggest how this leakage might have come about, sergeant,' someone diffidently enquired.

The sergeant shook his head.

'No sir,' he said. 'There I can't help you. I can't understand how they can be short. I think they *are*. I thought myself there was a few missing.' He frowned. It evidently had given him a little cause for uneasy thought. 'I can't figure out who would *take* any of them. There aren't any *thieves* in this Mess, gentlemen. Not among *us.*'

He paused, and eyed the company, in a way none too flattering to the company.

'We've got clean hands!' he said, his voice rising a little.

'Of course, of course, sergeant,' hastily remarked the senior officer present. 'Thank you, sergeant. We just thought we'd ask you. I guess that will do, sergeant!'

Sergeant Shotspur saluted, stamped menacingly, about-turned, and marched out of the room. The Mess looked at each other in silence for some moments. Then it burst out laughing, slapping its thighs and bucking about on its chairs.

'Well, well, well!' cried a big booted major, standing up and pulling down his belt. 'I guess we'll have to call that enquiry closed!'

'Yes—I don't think any more will disappear just yet!' said the senior officer grimly.

'What has been happening to the whisky?' I asked my neighbour.

'Happening to it? He's been selling cases of it at a time. He got three bucks a bottle!'

'He must be tolerably well off.'

'You've said it!' my neighbour laughed. 'It had to be stopped. One day last week he ran out of it—we had to have lime juice.'

CHAPTER XV

King John

Augustus John arrived at Canadian Corps Headquarters a few days later. He had been made a major in the Canadian Army. He was the only officer in the British Army, except the King, who wore a beard. In consequence he was a constant source of anxiety and terror wherever he went. Catching sight of him coming down a road any ordinary private would display every sign of the liveliest consternation. He would start saluting a mile off. Augustus John—every inch a King George—would solemnly touch his hat and pass on.

We lived in a large château. Our life there was uneventful—quiet, dignified, and aloof. The contrast to the squalid mud hovels of the Front was a little startling. And we had a staff car at our disposal which reported for duty every morning.

I ran down to my battery in the car—to my new Canadian battery. It was a '6 inch How' battery. I had nothing to do with it, of course, except to paint it. It stood by itself, in the great open spaces of Vimy Ridge. There was nothing near it.

This battery seldom fired. Everything was different in this part of the Line—so different that to start with I could scarcely believe my eyes, or ears.

Nobody ever fired on the Vimy Front, at the time I was there. Nobody thought of war. I was told that for months nothing had happened there. Complete peace had reigned on both sides of the Line. By mutual consent the Hun and the Canuck abstained from hostilities, except for a shot or two now and then. Nothing was to be gained by fighting in this sector. So why fight? Away in the distance, over in the ruins of Lens, a shell would fall occasionally. That was all; like a big door banging far away in the distance. After my recent experiences this peace was almost uncanny. They always say that it is impossible to start a war again after an armistice. This local peace must have been very enervating for the troops, I should think. I did not like to ask them about this as I thought they might interpret it as swank, as if I were saying I'd just come from a very hot part of the Line.

I made the acquaintance of the officers and men of the battery. I was my own master, of course. Next day I went down again with my sketchbook, took up my position and began to make a few drawings of the guns. It was a fine sunny winter's day, there was no battery or anything at all in sight. Just a rolling expanse of old battlefields, gradually softening into an effect like a rather untidy looking common.

I took up my pencil and was just about to make a mark on the paper, when immediately overhead a great angry shrapnel burst occurred, spraying the ground all round and, in this idyllic scene, causing such an uproar that all the birds in the neighbourhood began dashing about—the officers came flying up out of the Mess dugout, shouting in amazement, 'What's that?' and as to the gunners, pottering about the guns, they just vanished to right and left as if they'd been shot.

I know this will scarcely sound credible. But it is exactly what happened. It was just as if the Germans had got wind of my activities, and had said, 'Ha! We will put a little shell-fire into this picture!'

I felt in some way guilty for this outrage. But of course I could offer no explanation for it. On their side, the officers, when they had recovered from their stupefaction, seemed to feel the need of an apology too. They assured me that nothing of the sort had happened for longer than they could remember. But I assured them that I held them in no way responsible for this event. It was, in fact, the sort of thing that might happen *anywhere,* during a war. And I, for my part, did not even hold *the Germans* responsible. The gun probably went off by mistake while they were cleaning it.

There was nothing further of this kind, I am glad to say. It was the first and last shell I saw fired in anger on the Vimy Ridge (if it *had* been fired in anger, which I very much doubt). I made the necessary sketches. The unnecessary sketches, I should perhaps say, as I could draw a gun with my eyes shut of course. I completed my group of designs—at my leisure needless to say. For frankly, I liked the life.

Augustus John was working very hard, on his side, though not neglecting the social side of life. No artist who neglects the social side of life is an artist—he is a square peg in a round hole. One day we decided to go in search of Ian Strang, who was a Camouflage Officer (a divine job) in another beautiful château not too far away. It was not far from Arminteers, I think.

I believe this half-ruined city was Arminteers, where the famous young lady came from, but I can't be certain. It looked as though it might be.

We got to this town anyhow, and discovered an excellent hotel to lunch at. In its courtyard upon a trestle table was the most surprising collection of English pornographic literature I have ever encountered. (It must have been Arminteers.) All the Anglo-Saxon pornography of the Paris quays and the Palais Royal transported to the Front, for dugout-reading, and the *dolce par niente* of rest billets.

The lunch was good. This was war, and my superior officer and myself did ourselves proud. We should have done so if it hadn't been war, but that made no difference. I have an extremely strong head. It is that one of my many manly virtues which perhaps becomes me most. What is more I am civil when I'm drunk, which is more than can be said for some people.

Time is not a dimension that I hold in very great esteem as you would know if you knew me better, but I drew my friend's attention to the manner in which it was slipping away (that's one of the things I don't like about it) and we returned to our car. Augustus John (looking very like the late King, only after an awfully good lunch, and petrifying all troops within sight) commanded the chauffeur to drive to 'the Camouflage Section'. That was admittedly a bit vague but I was in no mood to insist upon a precision of outline which was alien to the large sweep of our purely excursionist plans. John waved his hand over to the left and said 'You know where it is, don't you? It's somewhere over there. Not far!' and got into the car.

We started off and bowled along a high road at a pretty smart pace. John and I were discussing one thing and another and the time slipped away, in its usual sly way. The chauffeur stopped and I leant out of the window.

'Aren't you sure of the route?' I asked.

'No, sir,' he said in his curt Canadian fashion.

'Not think we're on the right road? Of course it's the right road!' shouted John. 'Go straight ahead. We'll be there presently.'

We proceeded, and again John and I spoke of this thing and that. Time slipped away—after its customary underhand fashion. Suddenly I thought I noticed a shell-burst, of all peculiar things, in a harmless-looking field we were passing, though otherwise the landscape looked normal enough for anything. I decided I must have been mistaken. A cow must have been kicking the earth up as a change from chewing the cud. Then at the next cross-roads I remarked that the sentry was crouching in his dugout and had his tin-hat pulled down over his eyes. At the same moment I noticed, not far away to our left, the tower of a church, and this time it was unmistakeable. The tops of not one burst but two or three at least were plainly visible.

Stopping the car, I got out and approached the sentry.

'Where does this road lead?' I asked him.

'To the Front Line, sir,' he answered.

'To the Front Line?' I asked him, sternly.

'Yes, sir!' His voice trembled, he cowered a little, for he saw the King, he thought, in the car at my back. 'It's just up the road there a short way, sir.'

He stared at me tongue-tied after that, for he had a vision of the King of England being driven right into the Front Line and possibly over it into the German Line.

I ordered the Canadian chauffeur to take us down the road to the left—presumably parallel to the Front Line and not far behind it. In a couple of minutes we entered a village street. There were two howitzer batteries firing away for all they were worth on the side of the road, the gunners crouching close up to the guns. Shells were whooping down every few seconds in front of the batteries and in the neighbourhood of the Church. I told the chauffeur to stop at a dressing station, and got out.

The Camouflage Officer I learnt was to be found about a mile or two behind the village; and as speedily as possible with the able collaboration of the chauffeur, I got us out of this incredibly warlike hamlet. The troops of course all thought it was the King—but whether they considered I was abducting him or that he had insisted on looking into the war at first-hand I do not know.

As we left Augustus John peered out of the celluloid window at the back of our heads, to gaze, I suppose, at these hideous happenings that we were leaving behind. But he caught sight of something else which arrested his attention.

'Look!' he said pointing upwards.

I peered out of the little window, too, up in the sky. There were half-a-dozen aeroplanes whirling round each other, obviously with some sinister intention. Augustus John screwed up his eyes and nose with his Romany craftiness, and grinned with mischievous satisfaction.

'Well,' he drawled, 'no once can say we haven't been *under fire,* can they, what!' And he gave a gruff little laugh to himself, at the funny things that happen to a man—in the most unlikely places, too.

PART IV
Adam and Eve

CHAPTER 1

Captain Guy Baker—In Memoriam

The War ended, I was of course in the 'post-war', and you know what I think of that. That period was just what you would have expected after the morass of mud, uplift, Tipperary, easy money, heartbreak house—in a word, the squalid serio-comedy the Great War was.

The War went on for far too long, or too long for a 'totalitarian' war, as it would now be called. It was too vast for its meaning, like a giant with the brain of a midge. Its epic proportions were grotesquely out of scale, seeing what it was fought to settle. It was far too indecisive. It settled nothing, as it meant nothing. Indeed, it was impossible to escape the feeling that it was not *meant* to settle anything—that could have any meaning, or be of any advantage, to the general run of men.

Meanwhile the War had demoralized the world, in accustoming it to purposeless and incessant violence. And the terrible futility of the 'Welsh Wizard's' phrases did the rest. It was they, more than anything else, that drove the iron into the soul of an overtaxed humanity. They provoked a bitter laugh, where it would have been better to keep laughter out of it.

Without Mr. Lloyd George's labelling, the War might have sunk out of sight, an almost *anonymous* horror. They gave it as it were a name, a satiric identity. It was 'the War to end War'. It was 'the War to make the world safe for democracy'. It was 'the War to make England a place fit for heroes to live in'.

What a terrible felicity of expression to convey, with a merciless blatancy, all that things are *not*! If only Mr. Lloyd George had kept his little lawyer's mouth shut, things would have been easier.

These slogans were like insults. It was adding insult to injury to utter them.

The 'Post-war' started under the shadow of this verbiage. Quite at its opening a fearful plague overwhelmed the world in which more people were wiped out than in all the war put together. I was in a military hospital with double pneumonia; enormous Anzacs, the flower of colonial England, were dying like flies, having escaped all the hazards of war. Our hospital was full of them. When I came out of my delirium I found I had made a notable recovery. My poor friend Guy Baker, on the other hand, not so strong as I was, succumbed—resourceful to the last, and attempting to persuade Frederick Etchells, the artist, who had come to visit him, to put him into his kit-bag which was beneath the hospital bed and smuggle him out. I believe Etchells should have done it. If he had not found Baker dead in the kitbag at the end of the bus-journey, he might have recovered, and we should still to-day be assisting at his orgasms of overpowering mirth. For he was a man who could get drunk on a bottle of ginger beer (as Augustus John once said of him). Such a man we could not afford to lose.

When the War started Captain Guy Baker was I suppose about forty. He had left the Army some years before, owing to ill-health. I never knew what was the matter with him, but he was pretty sick most of the time, both before and after his brief war service. He hobbled round and attested, nevertheless. They did not make him a colonel as I think he had expected. Actually he went to France as a captain in the infantry.

Before that he had sprained his shoulder. He was a very conscientious soldier and one extremely alive to what was due to military rank. One day at Aldershot he was about to enter a hut when suddenly a General emerged and took him unawares. He was determined to be wanting in nothing where a respectful and soldierly smartness was concerned; he swung up his right arm in a spectacular arc to the salute, his hand convulsively waggling an inch from the peak of his cap. He showed me (as best he could, poor fellow) how he did it. He put all his soul into that salute. But he nearly broke his arm. For weeks he wore it in a sling

When he got to France something of the same sort happened. He went 'over the top' with his battalion. But with his customary zeal, he literally leapt over the top; with the result—wracked as he was with rheumatism—that might have been expected. His leg cracked under him. He rose and hobbled after his battalion, which by this time was snugly installed in shell-holes fifty yards ahead. In the most leisurely way—it was the only way that was open to him—under a withering fire, he followed his men. He was dragged down into a shellhole, everybody marvelling at his gallantry, so he told me. After a short stay there, he returned, with the survivors, to the trench. By this time he was suffering the agonies of the damned. And when he returned to England he was for over a year on crutches —in addition to the fact that his arm never recovered entirely from the effects of the terrific salute.

How this man ever managed to do what he did was a matter of astonishment to me. He had some chronic skin disease that made him break out in unsightly rashes, and he seemed eaten up with rheumatic affections as well. But he clowned through his little military act with the most indomitable devotion to duty. He told me that it 'broke his heart' to serve in such a subaltern capacity. But he was not fit even for a staff job.

Baker had a small collection of my pictures which he bequeathed to the South Kensington Museum at his death. The Regular Army produces a few such freakish intelligences as his, and when it does it is a most attractive hybrid that you get, of which I suppose 'The Bengal Lancer' (Major Yeats-Brown) is the archetype. But Guy Baker is my favourite professional soldier.

His brother (who was a football international) had a charming house near Bristol. In going round the stables there with me the incorrigible 'captain', in showing off a horse a little flashily, nearly received a kick which would have forestalled all his martial contretemps. His familiarity with the horse all but cost him dearer than his deference to the General officer.

I started the War with an indecent amount of hair on my head. I had enough for three men. I started the 'post-war' with barely enough for one. After the pneumonia this happened. The fever had uprooted it and I was within an ace of going bald. An awfully intelligent skin-specialist advised vibro-massage. When I had about three hairs left, I called a halt to this massacre of the follicles.

So at the commencement of the 'post-war' the mere outward man tended to be more polite and well trimmed. I was still so exotic however that Russian refugees would come up to me in hotels and address me in the palaver of Rasputin.

I was rather in favour of the Russian revolution at first. Later on so many powerful people began muscling in at this end that I thought there must be something fishy about it. Mr. Gollancz alone is enough to put off any moderately sensitive man. I've always been a great supporter of the underdog. Bolshevism soon got to have such a top-dog look about it that I became a bit doubtful.

Just before I contracted pneumonia my personal appearance was professionally reviewed by Ezra Pound and Ben Hecht. I was dining at Pagani's Restaurant in Great Portland Street with Hecht and Pound, and from the impresario angle they surveyed me from head to foot. Hecht is now a film magnate in America, but at the time he was a journalist, and one of the enterprising minority of 'new' writers. He and Pound went over me with a fine comb—they pulled my hair, my nose, my stature, even my taste-in-socks, to pieces. My hair, Ezra assured Ben, looked quite different when I wasn't being the military man. Ben Hecht thought that the face really went with the haircut and the Sam Browne belt. He said that to put me across in America they'd better forgo all attempt to make me a type of high romance. My features were too regular and agreed too well with the uniform I was wearing ever to be susceptible of 'artistic' disfigurement or bohemian make-up. He said he thought I was what an American would think an English officer looked like. It was better to start from that basis, for the purposes of mass advertisement. I laughed, for I knew how wrong he was, and within a year or two my appearance would have satisfied the most pernicketty romantic canon.

It was at dinner, I remember, that the news of my father's death reached me. He was twenty years or more older than my mother. Pound and Hecht were surprised to hear that he

210

died in Philadelphia, in their own country. How he got there is unimportant—except in so far as I was cheated of my patrimony. My mother's death from a third attack of pneumonia followed close on his at the tail end of the Great Epidemic that immediately succeeded the Great War. I had had it. I was in Military Hospital near the Euston Road with double pneumonia for weeks. My mother came there to see me, nodding her head, with her poor tragic face and brought me books. Six months later she was dead. I was distracted at the time by this, the reader may believe me, and that event, for my mother was not an old woman, gave me a peculiar feeling about the Great War which I have not noticed in most War Books, because it had worn her down and killed her : and I swore a vendetta against these abominations.

Ben Hecht I have always found a very pleasant fellow. About six or seven years since, I had dinner with him and his wife in New York, on his roof-garden, or roof-arbour. Vines grew all over a dusty trellis, the grapes of which his wife cut.

MacArthur was there, with his handsome olive face and soft blue eyes, who has since become Ben Hecht's business partner. MacArthur was in the famous Rainbow Division in France and at the time I met him was very natural and gentle : he was always fighting, according to Ben. That morning he'd knocked out a muscular drayman, who had been rude, he thought, and who wanted a fight too. Ben said MacArthur always knew when a man wanted a fight. That's a thing I've never for my part been able to tell : but that's probably because I've never been on the look-out for that sort of thing. But for MacArthur himself (as he was then), I will swear *no* man could tell of him that he wanted a fight. For a gentler, more discreet, more noiseless creature I never encountered, the soul of a sort of beautiful natural chivalry.

Looking over New York as the sun was setting, Ben Hecht said to me : 'I always call that a Jewish sunset. I call it that because all the smoke you see, which makes the body of the sunset, comes out of chimneys owned by Jews. So I call it a Jewish sunset.' And it had indeed a Jewish look : a sort of fulminating Old Testament heaviness, and brooding beauty.

211

CHAPTER II

I go Underground

After I'd grown my hair again, I was demobilized. Round this time some of my old *Blast* associates wanted to start things up, and begin the 'post-war' with a bang.

There was William Roberts, who was a Field Artillery gunner during the War: Edward Wadsworth who had done naval clerking in a Mudros office and had got a rather rolling nautical gait as a consequence; there was Turnbull who had been a Flying Corps officer in France and done some excellent pictures of air-battles; there was Frank Dobson, the sculptor, who had been blown up by a mine in France, and looked as if he had, what's more, but who, as all sculptors have to be, was very industrious, and whose stones were worth showing (Baker had known him in Cornwall before the War and had introduced him): lastly Frederich Etchells was there too, probably the most promising of my colleagues but already beginning to abandon painting for architecture. There were others, all interesting artists.

Not all of these people were dying to exhibit (Etchells loathed the idea) but some were very anxious indeed that we should do a bit of 'blasting' again. They pressed me, as a born leader in such affairs, to up and 'blast' a way for them through the bourgeois barrage. And at length I thought I would. I founded 'X Group'. After a short while I left this Group and it fell to pieces. Roberts said this when he reviewed this book.

One of 'X Group's' most prominent members was MacKnight Kauffeur, who became the Underground poster-king: he disappeared as it were belowground, and the tunnels of the 'Tube' became thenceforth his subterranean picture galleries.

I went underground too, as I have said at the opening of this book, but in another way it would be far too technical an excursion to explain to you why I went underground. You'd have to know a great deal about painting, and writing too, to follow it. It will be sufficient to say that I still had to learn a lot of things in my two professions. This I preferred to do in secrecy. So I withdrew into a place called Adam and Eve Mews. There I did my first satisfactory paintings. Before that time I had accomplished nothing—all I had done had a promise, or was at the most a spirited sketch, or plan (like 'the Plan of War', in *Blast* No. 1).

The War, of course, had robbed me of four years, at the moment when, almost overnight, I had achieved the necessary notoriety to establish myself in London as a painter. It also caught me before I was quite through with my training. And although in the 'post-war' I was not starting from nothing, I had to some extent to begin all over again.

For those not of military age, the War had been in some cases a godsend. The 'post-war' was dominated by people who, like Bennett and Shaw in letters, were already old men. They thrived on it. Those who were schoolboys during the war did not benefit. They seemed to suffer from a kind of reflected shell-shock, an emotional paralysis.

The War, as it has turned out, was not for me either bad or good, because if it had not occurred I should certainly have wasted my time in a hundred ways: and the obligation to make a new start—and the decision I took to make a *really* new start while I was about it—was in the long run beneficial. I might never have submitted myself to the disciplines I did, if I had not been thrown back on myself. In a rather silly way, I had been too successful. So in the long run the War helped my career; but it was a long run all right.

It is important to understand what an odd place England is to be an artist in, especially a painter. The English experience little response to artistic stimulus. In their bones, they *are* the 'Philistines' Matthew Arnold said they were. They have heard that they are 'civilized' and that civilized people are fond of art. So they make the necessary arrangements for the unavoidable presence of the fine arts in their midst. All 'pictures', when they come into the world, are to be sent immediately to a concentration camp, called Burlington House. And once a year the British Public will go and look at them. After that they will forget all about art until the same time next year.

Any art outside of the place set aside for such things is not *art*. Else it would be inside. What it *is* is not quite clear to Englishman. Usually it is a joke. It may have a certain nuisance-value or joke-value. But it really has no business to be there. And it has not of course any money value.

Now in Mayfair there have always been a number of people who are wise to the fact that no serious art can ever be *inside* the Royal Academy, and therefore if there is any good art it must be outside. But they also know that as a result of this extremely uncongenial atmosphere for art, there are very few good pictures *anywhere* in England, by living artists. And as they are not expert in these matters, and usually not prone to like pictures, they are not going to dash off in search of that rare flower in these foggy islands, a good picture.

These conditions result in a great deal of lunching, and dining and cocktailing for artists, but very little work, as I have explained elsewhere. So the fact of the matter was I was none too keen, if I had to start all over again, to repeat my time-wasting and rather silly experiences. *Blast!* urged my colleagues —some of them blessed with incomes. But once more to go through all that comedy appealed to me less than it did to them. I had found from bitter experience that an artist in England is compelled to sacrifice so much time explaining *why* he is an artist at all, that the necessary time for the donkey-work, to do the stuff, is not available.

For a few years after the War I had *some* money. So I resolved, in making this fresh start, to go about it in a very different way. My solitary 'X Group' reversion to type was undertaken against my better judgement.

These years spent in underground work were exceedingly useful. If I went underground, I was still visible from time to time. Even I would make occasional sorties of a few weeks at a stretch into Mayfair. At Mrs. Bengie Guinness's house in Carlton House Terrace, and at Sunningdale, for instance, I would taste expensive food and enjoy the conversation of people prominent in such circles—by far the wittiest of whom was Sir Denison Ross. I even started—at Sunningdale—a portrait of Mrs. Bengie Guinness, who was a particularly handsome woman, like a powdered eagle. But I dropped this, a little brusquely, I am afraid, in a fit of impatience with all such modes of breadwinning. I am sure had I finished it it would have been a fine portrait, and would have put money in my pocket. But I got what almost amounted to a complex about Mayfair.

My old friend Harry Melville (who, to give him an identity at this time of day, was an heir of some sort to the famous Lord Ribblesdale) used to deliver me lectures in Adam and Eve. 'For the sake of your car-*reer*!' he would boom impressively at me, 'you *must*—*four* times a *week*—make up your mind to put on *a boiled* shirt!' But the boiled shirt game did not seem to me worth the candle.

Adam and Eve was not my first stop after War, but was my longest. My semi-retirement had now lasted two or three years : work had been continually going on from the nude, from still-life, and much 'out of my head', with the object of creating a system of signs whereby I could more adequately express myself. A hurried Show at the Leicester Galleries had disgusted me, and I knew that a stiff spell of work was what was demanded of me. I got through an unspeakable amount of work : some of this I sold privately, most I destroyed. Then, at the end of my money, I made a sortie into the portrait-world.

Except for a big oil-portrait of Miss Edith Sitwell, I confined myself to portrait-heads in pencil or aquarelle. The reason for this is as follows. If it is your purpose to do a *good* portrait—I mean one not too indecently pretty, or merely photographic, you will almost invariably have a free fight with your sitter (or her husband or his wife) at the end of it. Unless you are a jolly good businessman you will have the portrait on your hands. Under these circumstances it is obviously better not to undertake an oil-portrait which is going to eat up a good deal of your time. If it is a pencil head, which has only occupied two or three afternoons, that doesn't matter so much.

When you get better-known some of these difficulties are smoothed out. But I was not so well known then as I am now (and being well-known as a writer is just as good as being well-known as a painter, though celebrity as a *chef* would not help you as a dress-designer). The 'sitter-complex' was a very serious matter.

Sitters are apt to be very nice right up to the final sitting. They are hoping that at the last minute something will happen to the picture which will transform an extremely interesting-looking young woman into a raving 'society-beauty', out of whose face every vestige of meaning has been extracted, the proof of your superlative craftsmanship. When this doesn't happen, the storm breaks. The cheque that is to pay your studio-rent (which is already overdue) is not forthcoming. And, although *as a portrait* it's fine, no one wants a portrait of somebody else. So there you are.

This, I am bound to admit did not happen to me more than once. But once was enough, and other artists told me it was *always* happening to them. So I thought I'd take the cash I could get for the small stuff and let the credit go. I pot-boiled to some purpose—but always on a modest scale, like a cautious punter—about that time. In spite of it all, in the end, I had to do a moonlight flit—flitting with Miss Sitwell's portrait down the Mews at the dead of night, and setting up my easel elsewhere.

Miss Edith Sitwell's portrait was sold last year (1936) to the Fifty Shilling Tailor—or one of them—for a good price. This, it is true, was because it had never been exhibited before. So the scores of sittings spent in recording this picturesque enemy of mine had to wait fourteen years for its Fifty Shilling tailor.

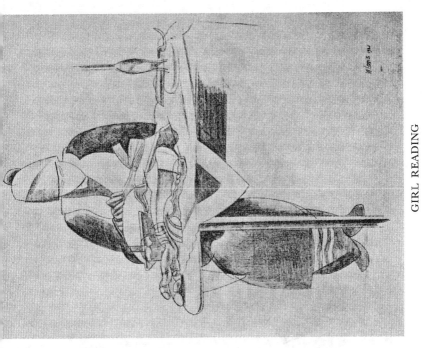

GIRL READING

CONTEMPLATOR

THE THREE SISTERS

DAWN IN EREWHON

CHAPTER III

The High Wall at Adam and Eve

There was a brick wall with a locked gate in it. This protected my garden-studio, at Adam and Eve. Over seven foot, it was an obstacle to all but sixfooters, and sixfooters are not usually dangerous. It's the little men you have to keep out.

In my absence this wall was often scaled. A wall's no use really. And the smallest of men would go over it as readily as the biggest. I once found my garden full of little men, who turned out to be a deputation from a small dago country, who had heard that I led a painting-gang called 'X', and wanted my gang for some dealer's racket.

Going underground, or locking myself in, was all very well. But no one of course was going to believe that an artist really wanted to be let alone and to get on with his work. They took it to be deeply-meditated coyness.

One of the smallest men who ever stormed my wall was Colonel Lawrence—'Lawrence of Arabia'. It presented no obstacles, naturally, to *him*. He left no message. Later he told me of his exploit.

A sixfooter who went over it and camped in my garden was Kit Wood, the young painter who subsequently killed himself by throwing himself under an express train at Winchester.

Kit Wood was the only 'post-war' English painter of outstanding merit. He and Henry Moore, the sculptor, are the two English artists, more or less in their cradles when the war began, who are of more than local interest. Moore has brought to the abstract shaping of stone artistic intelligence of a very high order. Wood had not so fine a mind. But his romantic nature was able to organize itself sufficiently to get something out of paint. His pictures have imaginative beauty which is as easy as a reverie and it does not put you under duress like a nightmare. It is the gentle dream of a dairymaid. But it is a pukka dream.

He was a big healthy blond : the teutonic kind of Englishman, tall and good-looking. But, alas! his great social attractiveness brought him into bad, rich, opium-eating company. He trod De Quincey's path; only there was a rushing locomotive at the end of it, instead of a vision of a Roman Consul— a locomotive to which he gave himself screaming, in answer to the shriek of its throttle. And doubtless it was kinder than those to whom he gave his young friendship.

He used to try and persuade me to 'have a pipe' with him as he called it. I asked him if he got imposing dreams, like that of the 'Consul Romanus' of De Quincey. He answered no. There were no dreams at all. His consciousness did not leave the everyday plane at all. It merely was able to sun itself in a placid animal well-being, apparently. He felt perfectly normal—as he would like to feel but didn't at ordinary times.

'So you take it to feel normal?' I asked in some astonishment. For it had never occurred to me that this abnormal stimulus was resorted to in order to make men feel like other men. Yes, he answered : that was it. And it had never occurred to him, it seemed, that this vicious circle of 'vice' constituted an odd way of arriving at where ideally you began.

Of course I told him that all he felt under the influence of opium for an hour or two I felt all the time : that all I could hope to achieve by recourse to this drug was to reach the abnormal condition from which *he* so desired to escape. He assured me that there were very few people in London with whom he would desire to 'smoke a pipe', and that I was the one he would first select. But though agreeably flattered, I was compelled to say that I was sorry, but I saw no purpose in feeling sick next morning for nothing—unless he could promise me a vision. And even then I had some pretty hefty visions of my own, without a narcotic. I must have morphia laid on at my nerve-centres, I said.

I have a most undeveloped moral sense. But the fearful death of this charming and talented young painter made me sort of indignant. The people who had so maltreated him could have selected something less unusual than a good artist for their purpose—though of course it was because they had detected something rare within this big blond envelope that they had coveted it. Ah, well! The fact of the matter is that Nature should not consign any really important message she has to send us to a big blond envelope.

The late Charles Rutherston, the art collector, was always a welcome visitor at my studio. For him I left the gate ajar. This was not only because one naturally likes people who come 'collecting' the works of one's hands, but because he was one of the pleasantest and least affected people of my acquaintance. He thought nothing of buying two or three dozen designs at a time, the best of which are now in the Manchester Museum, and are sent out to tour the country for the instruction of art-masters.

His brother, Sir William Rothenstein, came too: always welcome because so witty. I gave him one of my best drawings of that time. This is how it happened. He came in one day just before his brother turned up and made me very conceited by the generous praise he bestowed upon all he saw. One thing—a drawing in ink—the best small thing I had, he asked me to put aside. He must *possess* that, he said, if he could, and at once I put it aside. That was for *him*. After a few weeks I sent it round to his house. Meeting him in Church Street one day he bore down upon me all brilliantly lighted up, his eyes shining, uttering an apology six yards away about this drawing which brought a blush to my cheek. If one artist could not give a drawing to another! I exclaimed—for, of course, I had *given* him that. He should have understood. And peering brightly up into my face he thanked me as only he is able to thank: 'There is a saying,' he said, 'in the bible, *Blessed is he who gives and blessed is he who receives!* So I will accept it without hesitation.'

Those Old Testament guys certainly did provide a formula for every occasion! On the way back to my studio I bought a bible and hunted up a few handy saws on the spot.

Sir William Rothenstein was until last year principal of the

South Kensington Schools and in that capacity irradiated his intelligence over the back areas of England, and many a poor fellow now can draw a cow—or, to be more accurate, teach another fellow how to draw a cow—who otherwise would have remained completely unresponsive to the presence of that quadruped. What it was possible for a man to do, Rothenstein did. You can't make a silk purse out of a sow's ear, and the times are not propitious for folk-art. But he did more than Roger Fry in the way of popularizing artistic sensibility.

Rothenstein's brilliant services as an educationalist have rather over-shadowed his achievement as a painter and draughtsman. This great wit, for he is the last of the wits, is quite a different man when he paints. No sign there of the flashing intelligence. He becomes a humble workman, fumbling almost in his grim sincerity.

Noel Coward sat for me, to mention one or two of my sitters, and Senator Marconi. The former came from Swiss Sports with a rush and a swing, of course, all suntan and Mayfair magic : the latter crept in with one eye and a very stern expression. The live-wire of the English Stage and the wireless wizard both had fine heads. I have done Coward again quite lately but he then had become a Red Indian—still fine, but a bit Choctaw.

I found that my women sitters were apt to dislike Coward. Of course he saw through them, and his actor's charm was too like their own. I believe in the end that Coward's career will rival, for sheer success, that of Sir James Barrie. He can no more help becoming a knight than I can help speaking Spanish when I want to speak German. He has not invented Peter Pan, that is true. But perhaps he has done better than that. He has *been* Peter Pan. That takes more doing.

CHAPTER IV

The Wedding of Roy Campbell

Roy Campbell, who is at Toledo with his wife, got married while I was in Adam and Eve, and I went to the wedding. It was in the Old 'Harlequin' night-café in Beak Street.

I heard from Campbell this morning (June 26, 1937) and learnt with some surprise that he was at Toledo. The Government Army is only five miles away and that must be rather close quarters; and his house, too, was destroyed by shell-fire last year. I don't know what he's doing there. I supposed he was in Portugal, where he had a job as a supercargo. But the plains of the Tagus drew him back I imagine : he had become almost a Spaniard. I cannot see him as a Portuguese.

Campbell has not any regulation political bias, I think. He may incline to Franco because he is a catholic, and to the Old Spain rather than the New Spain because he likes bull-fights and all the romantic things. But of politics he has none, unless they are such as go with a great antipathy for the English 'gentleman' in all his clubmanesque varieties; a great attachment to the back-Veldt of his native South Africa; and a constant desire to identify himself with the roughest and simplest of his fellow-creatures in pub, farm, and bullring. Such politics as go with those predilections and antipathies he has, but it would be difficult to give them a name. He certainly is neither a communist nor a fascist.

He married the very beautiful Miss Garman. Her brother is a well-known English communist, who in his turn married a Guggenheim, a member of the millionaire family—also, I suppose, a communist. He, too, was surprisingly good-looking when he was young.

The marriage-feast was a distinguished gathering, if you are prepared to admit distinction to the Bohemian, for it was almost

221

gipsy in its freedom from the conventional restraints. It occurred in a room upstairs. In the middle of it Campbell and his bride retired. The guests then became quarrelsome.

Jacob Kramer and Augustus John were neighbours at table and I noticed that they were bickering. Kramer was a gigantic Polish Jew (and still is, I believe) and he was showing John his left bicep. It was between John and himself. It expanded convulsively under his coat sleeve, and he kept drawing John's attention to this fact.

John did not seem interested. But Kramer would not be put off or have his bicep high-hatted like that. It went on moving about under his sleeve in an alarming fashion, and Kramer looked at it as if irresistibly attracted. It was such a funny thing to have in your sleeve, a sort of symbol, he seemed to feel, of Power. He tapped it as a prosperous person taps his pocket.

'I'm just as strong as you are John!' he kept vociferating, screwing his neck round till his nose stuck in John's face.

'You've said that before,' John answered gruffly.

'Why should I put up with your rudeness, John—*why!* Tell me that, John! You're a clever man. Why should I?'

John shrugged his shoulders, and looked down rather huffily at his spoons. He sought to indicate to his neighbour that philosophically interesting as the question might be, it was no time to discuss it, when we were convivially assembled to celebrate the marriage of a mutual friend.

At this moment Roy Campbell entered in his pyjamas. There was a horrid hush. Someone had slipped out to acquaint Campbell with the fact of this threat to the peace. In a dead silence the bridegroom, with catlike steps, approached the back of Kramer's chair. That gentleman screwed round, his bicep still held up for exhibition and metaphysical examination. He was a very supple giant, and by this time he was sitting one way but facing another, having as it were followed the bicep round behind himself.

'What's this, Kramer?' barked Roy, fierce and thick, in his best back-veldt. 'What are you doing, Kramer!' Roy Campbell pointed his hand at his guest and began wagging it about

222

in a suggestive way as if he might box his ears or chop him on the neck with it.

'Nothing, Roy! I'm not doing anything, Roy!' the guest answered, in a tone of surprise and injured innocence.

'Well you let John alone, Kramer! Do you hear!'

'I'm doing nothing to John, Roy, I was talking about painting,' Kramer said.

'Never mind painting, Jacob. Is that how you talk about painting, Jacob?'

'Yes, Roy,' said Kramer, in an eager and concilliatory voice. 'I get worked up when I talk about painting, Roy.'

'Look. Could I throw you out of that window if I wanted to Jacob?'

'I know you could, Roy.' Kramer nodded his head, his eyes screwed up.

'Well then let my guests alone, Jacob. You let my guests alone. Don't let me hear you've interfered with John again. Mind I'm only just upstairs, Jacob. I'll come down to you!'

A strangled protest and assent at once came from Kramer; and stiffly and slowly, his shoulders drawn up, his head thrust out, in apache bellicosity, Campbell withdrew, all of us completely silent. When the door had closed, Kramer got up, came round the table and sat down at my side. He'd put his biceps away. He continued with me the conversation about painting which had taken such a personal turn on the other side of the marriage board.

This was a typical 'Post-war' scene: this is how, in the 'post-war', you married and were given in marriage. The 'Post-war' produced its types. Occasionally I meet them now and can tell them immediately. Still 'post-warring' away, getting old, drowning Time in drink, and completely impervious to the changes in the world around them. They are not my favourite type by a long way.

The 'post-war' in a sense was a recrudescence of 'the Nineties'. The realities that had begun to peep out in 1914 in England were submerged for a decade. Roy Campbell was never 'post-war'—he struggled in the toils rather amusingly. I remember coming upon him in the Eiffel Tower Hotel in Percy Street on one occasion, delivering emphatic thumps upon the table at which he was sitting.

'I won't be a Nineties man!' he was vociferating. 'I won't be a Nineties man. I w-w-w-w-won't be a Nineties man!' He was glaring at somebody—for this was a personal defiance: and I think it must have been Ronald Firbank—who was the very *genius loci* of the 'post-war', and the reincarnation of all the Nineties—Oscar Wilde, Pater, Beardsley, Dawson all rolled into one, and served up with *sauce créole*.

CHAPTER V

Sitters

It was almost impossible to do a portrait of Ronald Firbank, he was so interested in what I was doing. He wanted to look over my shoulder while I was drawing him. I pointed out that this was impossible.

We started off by my getting him up on the model's throne, an operation demanding a certain tact. He was afraid he might fall off. He fluttered at the thought of so much self-exposure. But I got him up. I stood in front of him for a little, to see he stayed put. I knew him well. I did not expect it to be easy.

He rolled his eyes and frothed at the mouth. He said that I ought to see him the first thing in the morning. I said I wished I could. The young day, he told me, gave him, fresh from sleep, a new face. It only lasted an hour or two. Breakfast was apparently the last straw. It was breakfast that started the débacle. To put the matter shortly—*Bacon and eggs!* Having soiled himself irretrievably with breakfast, he got through the rest of the day as best he could. *Until the night came.* With the night, things began to look up again—that is his face did. His beauty returned to him, the artificial light helping things out. But it was never quite the same as the first hour of the young morning. That was *really* the time to see him!

I am, myself, a late riser. I told him he must have confidence in me; that I should never see him as I *should* see him—that I should hate him anyway if I had to rise so early to look at him. But that I could well imagine what it was like and would endeavour to get into what I was about to do something of this immaculate daybreak beauty. Then I sat down and began work.

He writhed about on his chair, clasped and unclasped his hands. But I was not unaccustomed to hitting moving targets

225

in the sitter line. I selected a position to which I noticed he always returned, however much he twisted and tossed. I disregarded the other positions he successively took up.

I fixed my eye upon his mouth. He gasped, as he saw me do this. Firbank was what is called 'toothy' and he foamed rather easily. A lather would collect upon his prominent muzzle. He leapt off the throne all of a sudden and rushed over to my side and looked down at the paper on which I was drawing.

'I *had* to look!' he exclaimed.

'Well?'

'Oh, I don't know! You are *cruel,*' he gasped.

'Don't you like it?'

'Oh, I don't know! It's lovely!' he stood writhing at my side.

I stood up.

'Return at once to that throne,' I said sternly. 'Or I shall probably beat you with that mahlstick.'

Shuddering and screaming he rushed back, barked a knee upon the edge of the throne, and reoccupied the chair.

But he got worse and worse. His stomach began rumbling and he flushed so much at this and then went so pale, I was afraid he might faint. At last he bounded off again and came gibbering round behind me.

'I *had* to see what you were doing. I couldn't bear it any longer. I just had to have a look!' he panted in my ear, clawing at his arms and knees.

I got him back but it became quite impossible after that. He jumped on and off the throne every second minute. Also he had remarked how I had selected a certain position out of all those he presented me with, and he avoided it deliberately.

Again I stood up. I had to get a head of him done—it was for some publication and I was being paid for it. I dragged a table near my easel and I made him sit upon the corner of it, within reach of my foot. To say that he now remained quiet would be untrue. But he seemed more able to keep still this way than in a chair. And I was able to correct him from time to time with a warning kick.

I got my head, *tant bien que mal.* I consider it the best head

226

that was ever done of him. Augustus John was as usual a little too flourishing and juicily skilful. For you can suggest too much juice with a pencil just as much as you can with a brush. Mr. David Low the caricaturist does that, for instance. He has a juicy line very like a John line. How I managed it I don't quite know—some process of deduction rather than of mere sight. But I got him, and he even seemed to like it himself, after it was all over.

Firbank is buried in Rome next to the grave of John Keats. I shouldn't like to have a grave next to his. If there's one place where one may, I suppose, expect a little rest it is in the grave. And Firbank in his winding-sheet upon a moonlit night would be a problem for the least fussy of corpses in the same part of the cemetery, 'Thou still unravished bride of quietness!' I can imagine him hissing at Keats, 'come forth and let us seek out the tomb of Heliogabalus together shall us!' If there were only a Keats Society, I'd get up an agitation to have his grave moved.

From this you must not gather that I objected to Firbank. On the contrary. He seemed to me a pretty good clown—of the 'impersonator' type. Facially, he closely resembled Nellie Wallace. He seemed to like me—I had such relations with him as one might have with a talking gazelle, afflicted with some nervous disorder.

In Stulik's one night I had dinner with him and a young American 'college-boy' who was stopping at the Eiffel Tower Hotel. The presence of the fawning and attentive Firbank put the little American out of countenance. He called the waiter.

'I guess I'll have something *t'eat*!' he announced aggressively.

'What will you have, sir?' asked the waiter.

'I guess I'll have—oh—a *rump-steak*.'

He pored over the menu : it was evident he felt that a rump-steak would disinfect the atmosphere.

'Yessur.'

'Carrots,' he rasped out defiantly.

'Yessir. Carrots, sir.'

'Boiled pertaters.'

'Yessir.'

227

'What? Oh and er . . .'

But with gushing insinuation Firbank burst excitedly in at this point.

'Oh and *vi-o-lets!*' he frothed obsequiously.

Reacting darkly to the smiles of the onlookers the college-boy exclaimed, but without looking at his cringing 'fan'—

'There seems to be a lot of *fairies* round here!'

And he sniffed the air as if he could detect the impalpable aroma of an elf.

About this time I did a set of drawings for the weekly *Sketch*. The Lady Tredegar of to-day, then Miss Lois Sturt, sat to me for one of them, as also Viscountess Rothermere, Mrs. Dick Guinness and her daughters. I thought Lois Sturt was the most beautiful of all the debutantes: that rarest of all things in England, a dark plump beauty. And Lady Diana Manners was the despair of my pencil. I was amazed to find that upon a model's throne and facing a raging north-light, at twelve in the morning, she was far more beautiful than any photograph had led one to believe.

During the War I became acquainted with one of the most extraordinary women of the circle to which Diana Manners belonged, Sybil Hart-Davies: before her marriage her name was Duff-Cooper and she was the sister of the recent War Minister. She was a woman with a great taste for learning. Her proficiency in Greek was such as to dumbfound Lord Oxford, who was doubtless unaccustomed to hear Greek from the mouths of the aristocratic amazons of England.

On one occasion I was lunching with Sybil Hart-Davies in the Criterion Restaurant during the War, and her brother and Diana Manners were discovered in the distance, the former in uniform. She told me there was a romance. But it was a romance that culminated on the battlefield, when this somewhat diminutive figure behaved like a paladin. Unsusceptible as I am to the chivalrous impulses, my artist's eyes enlightened me, as I was tracing on the paper this pure, historically-English, profile: I understood as I drew, how these things come about; another factor in war, which until then had eluded me. Once I painted a woman who was subsequently murdered. I had the same clairvoyance then. I swear that the brush, and especially the pencil, is like a *planchette* set.

A certain Bob MacAlmon I got to know about that time. He was a young American model and poet, who married Sir John Ellerman's daughter. I got, through him, when I went in his company to the black-bearded Sir John Ellerman's, a glimpse of the household of the richest of the rich. This shipping magnate seemed a very nervous man : for all the herds of Highland Cattle browsing above his staircases, no placidity was discernible in the atmosphere of that interior.

Sir John Ellerman's fellow-magnate, Workman, on the other hand, whose house round the corner, with its windows in Park Lane, I often visited, was quite different. In that house, too, there were Highland Cattle. But a slumbrous calm obtained. With three liveried menservants at lunch incessantly pouring out champagne, from the most sedative caledonian intonations that have ever massaged my ears, one obtained all the advantages of an all-too-brief Lochside holiday. And yet in this mansion there were more exciting things than Highland Cattle, for Mrs. Workman (of whom I did an excellent portrait) was one of the only people in England to understand French painting, of which she had some remarkably fine specimens.

It was no doubt the greater cultivation that was productive of the superior calm. The moral is I think that there is no short cut, by way of Highland Cattle. The more exciting type of art has the more sedative effect—combined with a scottish accent. A Renoir or two and a Picasso secure poise. But not your faith in potboiling bucolics.

CHAPTER VI

'Death to Mussolini'

A man hurried into my workshop sat down, wrenched from his pocket a portentous cheque book a foot long, unrolled it, flung it open, produced a fountainpen and cried :

'What shall I make this out for Mr. Lewis?'

His name was either Boni, or Liveright—or perhaps both. He was a New York publisher.

I was taken aback, so I said, 'What for?'

'Have you anything to sell?' he asked peremptorily.

I said there was much that I should be prepared to sell, indeed, very few things that I wouldn't, but the question was, what did he want to buy?

'Have you a book to sell?' he shouted.

I shook my head.

'A book, no.' I said.

'That's too bad,' he remarked, pitching his voice back into the key of everyday at once and with some difficulty getting the cheque-book back into his pocket.

You may have been wondering when or how I wrote my books. With this plethora of small portraits this can have been none too easy, one would say. My pen had not, however, been idle. Actually at the moment I *had* books, or the manuscript of them, within a few feet of where I stood. But they were not for sale.

It was not my wish at this time to either publish or exhibit. If my money had lasted, I should have done no portraits. I should probably have gone nowhere and seen no one. But it is difficult to remain underground, unless you are a mole, without any money.

What I had in my drawer was a book called *Hoadipip*. And I had parts of another called *Joint!* Neither saw the light, but these were the first approaches to yet another composition, of a later date, called *The Childermass. Half* of that has been published.

This 'post-war' was full of work for me, for which I had not much to show. But until 1926, when my career proper began as a writer, my life was a private one. What I have undertaken to write here has no concern with an existence that was so private that only two or three people ever saw what was done in it, or knew in fact how I spent my time.

My next public appearance that I can call to mind was at Venice. The malodorous lagoons and *rios* of that aquatic ruin was filling up with the *Septembrini,* as the Venetians used to call them—herds of lipsticked Nancyish nobodies, who put in an appearance at the commencement of September.

The date of this visit is easy to check, because it was a few weeks before Mussolini's March on Rome. The hoardings lavatories, and railway stations had everywhere chalked slogans —'Death to Mussolini!' and counter-claptrap. But pickets and posses of militant blackshirts, fascist bands, with clubs and knives, clattered about on all hands. They were the modern equivalents of the 'prentices of London': cobblers, barbers, watchmakers and young watermen.

These portents meant nothing to me. I would have drawn them, if they had stopped still, but I did not eye them as an alert historian. They interested me no more than the first batches of *Septembrini,* if as much.

When I found myself in Berlin, a long time after that—a year before Hitler came into power—I was determined not to be caught napping a second time. To the crack of revolver shots, and to the thunder of the charge of Gryzinski's bottle-green police, clubbing the Nazi crowds, I lent an attentive ear. I set down my impressions—as a spectator, not as a partisan. But everybody in England at that time was determined to lend a deaf ear to those momentous sounds nearer home. I was laughed at and told I was dreaming. Had I ridiculed what I saw, assured the public that Hitlerism would be as dead as the Dodo within six months, I should have been complimented on my penetration and sense of reality.—A pity we should always

231

want to hear what corresponds to our wishes and prejudices!

So had I in Venice been able to foresee that some day I should be reading, in common with the whole of Europe, of the exploits of the 'Black Arrow' brigade at Bilbao, the Italian fascist legion, I should have paid far more attention to these excited bands of fanfaronading youths. I shared to some extent the anglo-saxon attitude of my companions, that these were political amusements of the dagolands, as tiresome as our football and cricket. Yet I was very observant and I cannot understand how I can have missed the meaning of all this.

Even when, a year later, people in London used to discuss Mussolini and dismiss him as 'the Kerensky of the Italian Revolution', and say that he would only be there a few months longer, when the communists would take his place, I had no opinion to offer one way or the other.

The sort of politician the War had made me was a straight 'leftwinger', as it would now be called. There were no *complications,* if you understand me. There were the Rich and the Poor, and the former massacred the latter in wars, to fill their pockets. That I was far too humane to accept as proper behaviour. Of course I knew that the term 'the Rich' was analysible in various ways. I had *some* understanding of the complexities. But I had not advanced far enough in those investigations to make head or tail of such an elaborate piece of political mechanism as Mussolini.

This ex-communist blacksmith, whom Lenin described as the ablest of all Italian communists, who was about to establish what we now know as 'fascism', was entirely over my head. Had I known then of his theory of *checks*—namely that it was undesirable that *any* class should be in a position of ascendancy—I should have known better where I was. For English political philosophy is full of these compromise gadgets, of the golden mean. But neither I nor any one else had at that time heard of those theories.

So I found myself on the spot, in the first stages of the Fascist Revolution in Italy, without the least suspicion of anything unusual being afoot.

CHAPTER VII

A Duel of Draughtsmanship in post-war Venice

'He's the boy who's got Clouds!'

A very tall figure was sauntering off (this is still in Venice) a man with a dimpled chin and fine brown eyes, which were a little those of a big child which looked out upon a nice but annoying world. He had just been standing over us, talking to Hugo Rumbold, who had been stammering away and convulsing our café-party. Hugo was a private clown who was literally worth his weight in gold. When we asked him who it was, that was Hugo's answer: 'Oh, he's the boy who's got Clouds.'

The others seemed mildly surprised that he should have got Clouds, although Nancy Cunard said—'Of course! I ought to have known!' By this she apparently meant that he was the sort of boy who gets Clouds and that *she,* with her extensive experience of such boys, ought to have spotted him as a Cloud-boy at first sight.

Richard, or more familiarly 'Dick' Wyndham, was *with* Hugo, it was later discovered. What I liked about Dick Wyndham was the attractive candour and absence of vulgarity which made him seem almost like a nice workman among all these 'clever' people. He was the nephew of the distinguished late-Victorian dilettante, George Wyndham—and so a descendant, but with a bar sinister, of the famous Lord Egremont, who was the patron of Turner, and a great name in the world of painting. Hence 'Clouds': it is a house, and he'd just been left it by George Wyndham.

At that time Dick was the simple soldier rather. I taught him how to sketch Venetian palaces—the fingers of one hand grasping the pencil and the fingers of the other grasping the nose, as all the best palaces are washed by cesspools. From this little seed has flowered the Richard Wyndham of to-day, whose pictorial achievements require no introduction from me.

Osbert and Sacheverell Sitwell were both there, the pleasant corpulence of the former vibrating to the impact of his own and Hugo's pleasantries; Sacheverell with the look of sedate alarm which at that period was characteristic of him. We would meet in the café every day. Eventually Bob MacAlmon turned up too.

An impromptu combat was arranged in the café one night, when an Italian painter challenged me to a match of draughtsmanship. Egged on by the Sitwells, I took him on. William Walton—now the premier composer of Britain—was the object chosen for the exercise of our skill. Walton sat with his head on the plush back of the seat and we drew him.

I won this match hands down. The Italian was crestfallen, but he had to admit defeat. And had I been living in Rome in the time of Caravaggio I should have been knifed that night as I went home, for a certainty, for muscling in on a pitch where I didn't belong. My antagonist was called Pietro di Cortina, quite in the old style. A rather romantic episode.

I had gone to Venice at the invitation of Nancy Cunard, the daughter of Lady Cunard, to do her portrait, and was stopping in her palace. (Palace sounds very grand, but any big house is a palace practically.) Nancy Cunard I had first met when she was a débutante before the War, in the house of the Countess of Drogheda off Belgrave Square. She was very American and attractive after the manner of the new World, rather than the Old. She is still all this, and has been on the Aragon Front helping the Catalans to repel the attack of the 'Rebels', whether successfully or not it is impossible to say at present.

Venice was very 'post-war'. It was typical of the time that anyone so sensitive to the trembling of the political veil as myself should have been able to remain mesmerized by Hugh Rumbold's intoxicating stammer, in an orgy of laughter, while Rome was burning (or rather being seized for Fascism). The communists and the fascists were already spitting and fighting all round us. How was it I was so hard of hearing? I will tell you. My political education, begun in the War, was not yet complete. I do not think that until the General Strike (1926) I finally discarded my anglo-saxon aversion for these plebian problems.

Another 'Post-war' excursion of mine was a notable visit to Paris in the company of Charles Rutherston and Frank Dobson, the sculptor. My days were spent with Rutherston and Dobson, visiting collections of Chinese art, my nights with James Joyce; an exquisitely balanced arrangement. 'The Dante of Dublin', as Mr. Gogarty calls him, cast a dreamy spell over Paris-by-night, and Sung and Ming weighed in, in the day-time, with their more subtle spell.

Sometimes, however, there was no day for me at all: only night. Once I had been up all night, for about the third time in succession, and I became entranced. Rutherston came into my darkened bedchamber to fetch me as usual about lunch time, and found me stretched out upon my back apparently dead, my hands together on my chest like a crusader. He gave a passable imitation of the last trump, he told me, but I did not move a muscle. I was deadly pale he said, and entirely like a statue or a corpse. So he left me. This alcoholic trance endured until the following morning. All this was bad for Joyce's rheumatic eyes, and Mrs. Joyce objected to my presence in Paris then. She thought I led the 'Dante of Dublin' astray. But we made our peace later on.

The 'post-war', as I lived it, would be incomplete without Garsington, where I made a public appearance. Garsington was where Lady Ottoline Morrell lived, not far from Oxford. At week-ends forty or fifty undergraduates would come over for an all-day party, and week-end guests of Lady Ottoline would encounter this horde of the 'academic youth' of England. I met Forster there as a fellow guest, the 'Bloomsbury novelist'. A quiet little chap, of whom no one could be jealous, so he hit it off with the 'Bloomsburies', and was appointed male opposite number to Virginia Woolfe. Since then he has written nothing. But the less you write, in a ticklish position of that sort, the better.

I may include a photograph of myself on the lawn where they played interminable croquet, in conversation with Lord David Cecil and other undergraduates—a post-war vignette. Lady Ottoline herself in the 'post-war' shared with Miss Sitwell the distinction of being the only woman not to succumb to the short-skirt fashion : both stalked about in sweeping trains, to the astonishment of a world which had gone strip-tease. Also the majestic splendour of their personal ornaments added to the general confusion in their neighbourhood.

CHAPTER VIII
'Lawrence of Arabia'

After Adam and Eve I had a studio in Holland Park. This I rented from George Robey's daughter. Or rather George Robey let it to me, he having rented it for his daughter who was a painter. She was quite unlike her didactic parent—a slight, fair, intelligent face, and quite pretty. (This last is no reflection upon George's personal appearance.)

One night I was sitting in this studio—a little gloomily for things were not going any too well. I had spent the last of my money and had not yet got the hang of the art-game and such humble money-spinnings as my simple wants prescribe. Outside the wind blew the leaves of Holland Park up and down the street, and within I sat before a fire, giving a companion the benefit of my opinion of sundry aspects of life as lived by the 'creeping Saxon', and wondering whether I should not throw in my lot with Léonce Rosenburg, the Paris dealer. That enlightened Parisian had seen some pictures of mine, and had said to me when I was in Paris : 'Lewis, these things of yours are the only things being done in England to-day which would interest Paris. Give me some of these, as many as you like, and I will sell them for you.' I agreed with my old friend Nina Hamnett that if you have to starve, it's much better to do so in Paris than in London. And I was feeling a certain nostalgia for the quays of the Seine.

I have never been overburdened with the obvious forms of diffidence and I could at the time have barged my way into Paris. There under the wing of the great Léonce, I might have set the Seine on fire. I should have been the only Anglo-saxon painter who ever set the Seine on fire. Furthermore I should have been free to do what I liked, a thing no artist can do unless he is a *rentier* in London : Léonce would have egged

237

me on to be more and more diabolically daring and devilishly inventive. Paris would have gasped. At present I should be living in a villa just outside Paris with a Japanese cook and a Zulu butler, with three highyaller kids getting ready to go to Eton. But Fate decided otherwise. Colonel Lawrence the 'uncrowned king of Arabia' broke into this promising dream.

A knock came at the door. The wind howled, and blew the blowsy leaves of Holland Park against the studio window. My companion and I looked at each other. There was a second knock—a timid knock. I went to the door, half opened it, and went outside on to the steps. These led down to a locked gate. There was a small figure at the bottom of the steps. There was only one way he could have got there and that was over the wall.

This clearly must be a dun, I thought. That at eight o'clock at night a tradesman's bully should scale my wall and present his bill seemed to me to be pressing too far the privilege of the creditor.

'Who might you be?' I enquired, not without a note of sarcasm.

No reply came from the foot of the steps.

I descended the steps, a little truculently perhaps, and stood beside the small and unobstrusive figure in a raincoat—hatless and it seemed to me furtive and at the same time odd.

'Well,' said I. 'I await your explanation. Was it you who knocked upon my door?'

'Yes,' muttered the stranger.

'I should like to draw your attention to the fact that I rent these premises, that my gate is *locked*—which signified that I do not desire visitors—and that you are trespassing.'

'I know,' said this enigmatical person, in a low and gentle voice, turning his head slightly to one side, as if the victim of a slight embarrassment—which did him credit and put me in a better humour.

'Well,' said I. 'Who are you, anyway?'

'I am Lawrence,' said he.

Now for some moments I had been thinking that for a dun he was on the quiet side. And no dun says, 'I am Lawrence,'

238

like that, when you ask him who he is. I had heard, also, that Col. Lawrence wanted to see me. Slowly it dawned on me who my visitor was.

We were silent for a moment—while none-too-quickly, I was substituting the person of a political martyr for that of an economic thug. Then I took his hand, and apologized for my mistake. He did not come in then : but I saw him the next day and during the next few years I saw a good deal of Lawrence, at odd times. When he came up on leave from the camp where he worked as an aircraftsman, he would call on me, and we would have lunch in a neighbouring tea room.

At the start I asked him why he was doing what he was doing. He said, what else could he do—he had no money? I suggested some sinecure, of a minor administrative order, that would leave him free to occupy himself as he wished. But he said he could not do that. He said he could not be a don— he 'knew no latin or greek'; at least not enough to be a don— only the usual amount. He had no income. He had to live. He preferred to remain in the Army. I asked why he could not become an officer, instead of being 'Aircraftsman Shaw'. He said shortly that he was too old.

The spectacle of this stupid waste of so much ability always depressed me. As he would turn up in his aircraftsman's uniform, having ridden at breakneck speed from Plymouth, or some East Coast Camp, I always felt distressed. It was a sort of hari-kiri that he was indulging in, and this self immolation disturbed me.

You know his story doubtless : it was a simple one. On behalf of the British Government he had promised the Arabs their freedom, if they would fight for it. They did so, and the Turks, with their help, were defeated. Then when he entered Damascus with Allenby and observed the way things were going, Lawrence saw that many of the Arabs to whom he had pledged himself were about to be tricked. Thereupon he threw in his hand. He resigned and withdrew. A little later he decided that his name, which had been dishonoured, should be no more borne by him. So he shut his eyes, opened a telephone book, and put his finger on a name upon the page. Opening his eyes again, he found that his finger was resting upon the name 'Shaw'. And (apologizing, as he told me, to George Bernard Shaw for having made so free with his patronymic) he became Shaw and enlisted as such in the Air Force.

At a party once W. B. Yeats asked if we had heard what Lawrence had said about what he had done. He then delivered himself of what Lawrence had said, regarding this great affair, as it affected him personally. Lawrence was supposed to have said—in the grandiose brogue in which Yeat's obiter-dicta are so pleasantly if pontifically clothed :

'I was an Irish nobody.' (Pause.) 'I did something.' (Pause.) 'It was a failure.' (Pause.) 'And I became an Irish nobody again.'

This has to be rolled out, in slow-time, if you want to get the full savour of it, as it stands in the repertory of a great raconteur. Something of the sort Lawrence may have uttered certainly. But a less grandiloquent person never stepped. And, being an 'Irish nobody', he had no brogue, only a modest little Oxford accent.

I remember after the War the wife of a fashionable draughtsman saying to me, when Colonel Lawrence was mentioned, 'Lewis, I have heard that he is—well,' she lowered her voice, 'a traitor.' From this I assume that at the time his action was greatly resented by some people, who even went so far as to attribute to this 'Irish nobody' the traditional Irish rôle of traitor.

For my part, he seems to have acted very nobly in refusing to participate in a political fraud. For 'if you promise them ought, you should keep your pro-*mise*,' whether they be Arabs, Englishmen, or whatnot. Had Lawrence been a 'traitor', on the other hand, he would have made much more fuss than he did about this betrayal, by the government he served, and whose instrument he had been. I am sure he should not have done so, seeing how much he liked the Arabs.

A man who knew him very well remarked to me that 'Lawrence did not know what he wanted'. I should amend that, and say that he did not want anything *clearly*. He was 'a failure' because he was wanting in the qualities that make the man of action. The society he had served so brilliantly betrayed *him* too, in a sense. Then, as a 'man-of-action', he should have called it to account. Not languished enigmatically in one of its camps as an 'aircraftsman', imperfectly incognito, as it were publicly neglected. I say he *should* have done this to sustain the part of the man-of-action since he had chosen it.

He had told me that Rudyard Kipling did not like what he had written, because he considered 'he had let the man-of-action down'. I should say that *after* his Arabian exploits he 'let down the man-of-action' far more than during them. For my own part I do not at all mind seeing the man-of-action let down. *Je constate,* that is all.

As to the Arabian exploits themselves it is quite clear what Kipling meant, and, according to his lights, Kipling was right. There was the episode, in his *Seven Pillars of Wisdom,* of the Arab boys who had to be executed, and none of the Arabs would do it. So Lawrence has to do it himself. He takes them up on to a sandhill (it is a long time since I read this, and I have not the book with me now), and shoots them with a revolver. Only *he turns his head away* to do it. There is a school-girlish touch in that, I think, which would hardly appeal to the author of Barrack Room Ballads. If you accept the rôle of executioner, you should at least *look* at your victims.

On one occasion Lawrence told me that his friend Lord Allenby wanted him to be Governor of Egypt : he wanted to propose this, and for Lawrence to agree to accept, if the governorship were offered him. I said, 'Well, are you going to do it?' He shook his head.

I asked him why he would not be Governor of Egypt. He answered that if he had to sit in judgement on another man, he would always feel that he should be where the accused man was, and the accused be in the judgement seat instead of him. For a man-of-action this was an unpromising attitude of mind, to say the least of it. And I could not help asking myself how he ever brought himself to blow up the Turkish troop train in the desert. But that was in the course of a war of liberation. That was the answer, possibly.

It is not necessary for me to say that *The Seven Pillars of*

Wisdom is not a great work of literary art. But it is a historic monument to the most distinguished of those engaged in 'the great adventure', as the World War was always referred to in the Press. It is a record of the doings of a very interesting man, of great ambitions paradoxically associated with great idealism. The ideals were English, the ambitions Irish. There was a further confusion of a more intimate sort, which disturbed the symmetry of his extrovert existence.

There seems no good reason, except accidental ones, why Arabia should have been the scene of Lawrence's activities. He had asked Doughty, you will recall, this same question which rises in the mind apropos of his Arabianism just as it does apropos of Doughty's. The latter said he went to 'the desert Arabia' in order to rescue English Prose from the slough into which it had fallen. The Arabs didn't really come into it. It was a matter of English prose-style. In Doughty's case this was probably true. Iceland (to which he originally intended to go) would have done just as well, and would have been nearer to the Sagas and the chronicles of seamen upon which Doughty founded his archaic but delightful jargon. But for Lawrence, would another race have done as well as the Arabs? The South African negroes, or the *peones* of the New World? Myself, I should say that they would. For abstract *freedom* was the essential thing, rather than the identity of the people who were to be made free.

The one-time Governor of Jerusalem, Sir Ronald Storrs, told me a lot about the period when Lawrence was in process of becoming 'Lawrence of Arabia'. Storrs was one of those associated with Lawrence at the outset of the War who reached himself some eminence in the course of it. He liked Lawrence. But others who started level with Lawrence, and at whose expense he took the lead and pushed himself into the position of a glamorous white-hooded paladin, did not like him quite so well.

This Irish adventurer, with the disarming urbanity of an Oxford intellectual, did not stand on ceremony with his duller colleagues. He must have stolen more than one march on them. Obviously he outmanoeuvred his colleagues before he outmanoeuvred the Turks.

There were more things than one about him, to cause him to play a lone hand. There is no egotism like the Irish. It shuts the Irishman up in the world of his own to a surprising extent. I know of no exception to this rule—it may be the secret of the political ineffectiveness of Ireland. It may be why the Irish have 'always betrayed their leaders'. They cannot tolerate a leader, unless it be themselves.

Yeats, Joyce, all, in one way or another, illustrate this. They all have the soul of the petty chieftain, jealous and superb. It even breaks through the cosmopolitan veneer of the late George Moore.

In discussing with me once the nationality of the hero of *Ulysses,* Joyce expressed surprise that many Jewish friends of his should have objected to him choosing a Jew for such an unheroic rôle as that of Leopold Bloom. He said that, for his part, he considered the destiny of Ireland not unlike that of Israel. But in fact there is all the difference in the world. For Jewish success is a triumph of organization, the subordination of the individual to the race. Whereas the unsuccess of Ireland can probably be traced, as I have said, to a total absence of this strange solidarity.

The Irishman is capable, however, of organizing *himself*. Very readily he becomes his own personal 'racket'. And if his 'racket' is successful, then he will become *entirely* inaccessible.

Lawrence had his full share of this egotism. And, apart from that, one of the little touches of nature that make the whole world kin, namely the sexual appetite, was wanting in him. That would tend to isolate him, too.

Over his competitors, in the field of Arabian adventure, he would stand as one apart, and able to act without considerations of trammelling *esprit de corps*. All this suited the country, so to speak—or the isolations of the desert suited him, it would be better to say. Also as an Irishman—the national egotism apart, that makes them all little theoretic chieftains—he would not be overburdened with deference for the stately Government he was serving. He would even be inclined to think how this Government could be made to serve *him*. And it is quite certain that he would have far more respect for a Bedouin chief than he would have for Whitehall or the F.O. He in a sense would feel that he was stealing this bloated power to put it at the service of his friends of the Desert.—And *then,* at the end, this Power that he did not respect got the better of him, and his Arab friends suffered at the same time a disillusion—if they ever had any illusions which I think open to doubt.

As a companion he was delightful. For him I was 'the author of *Tarr*', and I did a set of drawings for his book—not so quickly as I should, and all of a sudden I heard it had appeared to my great disappointment. This group of designs I propose however shortly to publish, making the necessary arrangements with his executors to include some explanatory fragments of the text. When I was in the Atlas Mountains, among all those Arabian scenes which are the backgrounds of his great military exploits, I altered some of them. For there I was seeing at first hand what originally I had only drawn from the pages of his book or of *Arabia Deserta.* I was surprised to learn from him that 'kitchen arabic' was all he knew : but he certainly obtained a remarkable insight into the Arab nature, which, on the spot, the experience of the eye confirmed.

The 'uncrowned king of Arabia' eschewed, with an almost pathological intensity, all vulgar pomp. The traditional *shyness* of the Englishman was incarnated in him—in this small and shrinking figure. A great deal has been said about Lawrence's 'magnetism' : how if he went into a camp of rough Bedouins as soon as they caught sight of him they would rush towards him and kiss his hand, or press their lips upon his cloak. As a matter of fact this was, I imagine, rather a tribute to his rank and renown and the power of the British Raj, than to himself. Very few people indeed possess magnetism of the order attributed to Lawrence. And Lawrence was not among them.

Moving about with a Berber guide, in the High Atlas, who was conducting me to a secluded Kasbah, we entered a field where a young sheikh was standing, supervising the operations of the harvest on his domain. My guide went up to him, dropped upon one knee, kissed his hand, and afterwards carried his hand to his forehead, with an air of religious abasement. He would doubtless have done the same thing to Lawrence, who, for him, would merely be a great British sheikh.

In conclusion, there is the persistent notion of a bogus demise: that Lawrence did not die as was reported in the newspapers. When I was in Germany recently I was asked more than once 'if Lawrence was alive'. Why should he not be dead? I asked. The idea seemed to be that he was back in Arabia once more, working underground as an agent of the British Government. To what ends? No answer. All I could say was that I did not believe Lawrence would consent, at any price, to engage once more in Arabian politics. I may be wrong. If so, I quite misunderstood him.

PART V

A Tale of an Old Pair of Shoes

CHAPTER 1

War and Post War

In this, the last compartment of my book, I am going to deal mainly with three figures; Eliot, Pound and Joyce. These three people are important, each in his own way : the three most important people I was associated with in the period I have chosen for this narrative.

If I were a politician, a doctor, a biologist or an engineer, then the people I have selected for this privileged treatment would be politicians, doctors, biologists, or engineers. But for me *a book* is more important than a party-cry, or a serum, or a theory of evolution, or an aeroplane-engine.

All books are obviously not important. Indeed most are not. But because so many are not, that does not alter the fact that a book can be just as important as anything else. So no one need be ashamed of talking about books, rather than poison gas, which wipes people out, or vaccines which may save them from death.

Plato's *Republic* for instance is important, so is *Hamlet,* so are the collected works of Molière. In every period a very few books are important. Contemporaries are never agreed as to which these are. I may not have a trio of Platos or Shakespeares to show you, but I've got as near that as I can, and I am quite certain no one can come any nearer than I have in the period in question. I've got a sort of Browning in my friend Ezra, the 'Dante of Dublin' in James Joyce, and Eliot is the highbrow hero of England and America still (though he has been joined now, in England, by Auden).

We were all in the post-war, but that period produced nothing but a lot of sub-Sitwells and sheep in Woolfe's clothing, and we were not of it. I call us here 'the Men of 1914'. Nothing occurred in England, the highbrow line to put up a challenge for the supreme highbrow laurel until Auden came along. He and his school (which was mixed up at first with T. S. Eliot's school) were the key men of the Depression, just as we were the literary big noises of the War and the 'waste' it left in its wake.

Nearly ten years ago, before Auden left Oxford, he came to see me in Ossington Street, and I got to know Stephen Spender at the same time. Spender, who is half a Schuster, and combines great practical ability with great liberal charm, showed me a lot of jolly poems, mostly about Auden—he said modestly, a much better poet than himself. And then Auden came himself. He was very crafty and solemn : I felt I was being interviewed by an emissary of some highly civilized power—perhaps over-civilized—who had considered that something had to be done about me and so one of its most able negotiators had been sent along to sound me. The author of *The Dog Beneath the Skin* is, I understand, Icelandic in origin. This causes him to be absurdly fair—or he was then, those blondes darken quickly : I always think of him as a rather *psychic* phenomenon. I should not be surprised if he were 'fey'.

For forty years Shaw and Wells had been Fabians first and literary artists afterwards. Even Wilde had been a great outcast first, and was never more than a minor poet. What I think history will say about the 'Men of 1914' is that they represent an attempt to get away from romantic art into classical art, away from political propaganda back into the detachment of true literature : just as in painting Picasso has represented a desire to terminate the Nineteenth Century alliance of painting and natural science. And what has happened—slowly—as a result of the War, is that artistic expression has slipped back again into political propaganda and romance, which go together. When you get one you get the other. The attempt at objectivity has failed. The subjectivity of the majority is back again, as a result of that great defeat, the Great War, and all that has ensued upon it. And as there are more Wars—bigger and better Wars—to come, that is that, I believe we must regretfully conclude.

All the same, we *are* out of the 'post-war', thank God. Nothing to-day stands much chance of settling down into a snug and unchallenged success, and this applies to the second-rate as much as to the first-rate. In a world where what is sauce for the gander is sauce for the goose there is always hope. And to-day that is eminently so. Therefore for the present we are all right. Nothing is going to *set* anyway, again—not for a century or two. But let us get back to the beginning of things, to the opening years of the present epoch, 1914–1926 namely.

CHAPTER II
The Period of 'Ulysses', 'Blast', 'The Wasteland'

The men of 1914 were a 'haughty and proud generation', I quote Mr. Ford Madox Ford: the Joyces, the Pounds, the Eliots, my particular companions. Nineteen fourteen is the year I have selected for the commencement of this history, and as observed by Mr. Madox Ford, who has seen the generation of James, Conrad, and Hudson this new 'generation' was remarkable for its 'pride'.

If Mr. Ford was correct, what was the origin of this arrogance? We were of course a youth racket—oh yes! among other things. This may have contributed to that impression of 'haughtiness', experienced at contact with us by the middle-aged observer.

It was scarcely our fault that we were a youth racket. It was Ezra who in the first place organized us willy nilly into that. For he was never satisfied until everything was *organized*. And it was he who made us into a youth racket—that was his method of organization. He had a streak of Baden Powell in him, had Ezra, perhaps more than a streak. With Disraeli, he thought in terms of 'Young England'. He never got us under canvas it is true—we were not the most promising material for Ezra's boyscoutery. But he did succeed in giving a handful of disparate and unassimilable people the appearance of a *Bewegung*.

It was Pound who invented the word 'vorticist': it was Pound who introduced Joyce to Miss Harriet Weaver—indeed thrust him down her throat—and thereby made a great many things possible which would not otherwise have been so: it was Pound who tirelessly schooled and scolded Eliot (as the latter is the first to recognize) and his blue pencil is all over *The Waste*

Land. Ezra was at once a poet and an impresario, at that time an unexpected combination.

Benjamin Disraeli was of course the first 'Youth' racketeer to make his appearance in England. But that was a political racket. It was named by him 'Young England', and he used it as an emotional lever to oust Peel, and to hoist himself into power. When Peel fell, Disraeli said that it was Young England that had done it, though in fact it was his own cunning old fingers and resourceful tongue that had done the trick. But Ezra was not a politician *de métier,* and his racket was merely an art-racket.

All politics to-day, and all the 'Youth-racket' element in politics, are put across by means of men-of-letters, journalists, *philosophes,* or the propaganda of intellectualist sects, groups and phalansteries, rather than via the Clubs or the floor of the House of Commons. And as I have already indicated, earlier in this book, there was a tidy bit of political contraband tucked away in our technical militancy. But I was not the responsible party.

However, the fact that we were a Youth-racket it is not amiss to remember : not the first in England, that was Disraeli's, and perhaps Rossetti ran another one, but still we were the first one in this century. And although there have been hundreds since—there is a new one every month or so—ours was much the most important.

But it was not that that made us 'proud'—as, of course, it is nothing to be proud of. But since people saw us somewhat as Ezra presented us—and as *he* of course, was *very proud* of us! —it may be that the adjectives of Mr. Madox Ford which I have quoted have after all something to do with this circumstance.

I have said 'the men of 1914'. But we were not the only people with something to be proud about at that time. Europe was full of titanic stirrings and snortings—a new art coming to flower to celebrate or to announce a 'new age'.

In retrospect already one experiences a mild surprise. In future this surprise will increase, year by year. What will become of those stern and grandly plastic glimpses of a novel universe, which first saw the light in the Western capitals immediately before the war, it is impossible to say. Some of it has been taken up into everyday life. Though one Kauffer does not make an Underground summer, poster art is somewhat more alive than it was, and a few shop-fronts, here and there, give a 'modern' flavour. One thing however is certain. Apart from the gallant rear-guard actions spasmodically undertaken in the British Isles by literary sharpshooters steeped in the heroic 'abstract' tradition, usually still termed 'avant-garde' for want of a more appropriate word; and save possibly for the rather untidy sunset, for a few years yet, in the 'new' American Fiction, by the end of this century the movement to which, historically, I belong will be as remote as predynastic Egyptian statuary.

To the English eye—and I am of course speaking here of how these things are seen from London—the period of *Blast*, of *Ulysses,* of *The Waste Land* will appear an island of incomprehensible bliss, dwelt in by strange shapes labelled 'Pound', 'Joyce', 'Weaver', 'Hulme'. With an egoistic piety I have made it my business to preserve in these pages something of the first-hand reality. My reporting may, who knows, serve to trip up one or two of the Ludwigs and Stracheys of a future time. I have even gone so far as to put down a barrage of gossip about Joyce's little beard, and Eliot's great toe, to make things less easy for these distant scribblers.

Yes Mr. Joyce, Mr. Pound, Mr. Eliot—and, for I said that my piety was egoistic, the Enemy, as well—the Chiricos and Picassos, and in music their equivalents—will be the exotic flowers of a culture that has passed. As people look back at them, out of a very humdrum, cautious, disillusioned society (I am assuming here that the worst will have happened and the world bled itself white; so that the Europe of that time has become like modern China, culturally extinct), the critics of that future day will rub their eyes. They will look, to them, so hopelessly *avant-garde!* so almost madly up-and-coming!

What energy!—what impossibly Spartan standards men will exclaim! So heroically these 'pioneers' will stand out like monosyllabic monoliths—Pound, Joyce, Lewis. They will acquire the strange aspects of 'empire-builders', as seen by a well-levelled and efficiently flattened out Proletariat, with all its million tails well down between its shuffling legs!

Even, people may ask themselves if such creatures ever in fact existed, or did not rather belong to the family of the phoenix, or if dragon-blood did not flow in their veins. How otherwise could they find it worthwhile to make these efforts, or to believe so bravely in the future of the world, which by then every schoolboy will know is a bughouse and leave it at that. But 'biographies' will still be written. Whatever happens, there will be plenty of biographies. So let me step in at once, and make it as difficult as possible for the distant biographer to do his usual uncannily inaccurate work.

I will fix for an alien posterity some of the main features of this movement. No one is better fitted than I am to do so, in all humility I may asseverate. I was at its heart. In some instances I was *it*.

However, I may seem to sweep on too fast and far, and to speak as if Mr. Eliot were not there, alive although no longer kicking, to write a morality next year, to be played in the Chapter of some venerable Close; or his melancholy ex-lieutenant Mr. Read, to write yet another dashing but dull rear-guard book, about the 'abstract' arts; or Mr. Henry Moore to polish a whole necklace of fine abstract stones. Of course I have not forgotten that. And I do not mean to say that all the masterpieces of this school have yet been penned, painted, or planned. But what I do say is that whatever happens in the world during the next century or so, there will be no society present upon the globe to think, live, and speculate in a manner conducive to the production of such works as *Bouvard and Pecuchet, Ulysses, The Hollow Men, The Ambassadors, The Portrait of Carlyle*, to name a few of the sort of productions that I mean, and to mix my times and arts a little too. The last society likely to do anything of that sort vanished with the War. It is a case of goodbye to all that, and for good. And one has to be no great prophet to foresee that whichever of the forces confronted upon the political stage to-day may get the upper hand, the Red or the Black, any detached artistic effort, on the grand scale, will be quasi-impossible. There will not be present the will, the psychological incentive, the time, or *the peace,* that are requisite for that. This applies to Germany as much as to Russia, to America as much as to Japan. Martial law conditions have come to stop. The gentler things of life are at an end.

We are not only 'the last men of an epoch' (as Mr. Edmund Wilson and others have said) : we are more than that, or we are that in a different way to what is most often asserted. *We are the first men of a Future that has not materialized.* We belong to a 'great age' that has not 'come off'. We moved too quickly for the world. We set too sharp a pace. And, more and more exhausted by War, Slump, and Revolution, the world has *fallen back.* Its ambition has withered : it has declined into a listless compromise—half 'modern', half Cavalcade!

The rear-guard presses forward, it is true. The doughty Hervert (he of 'Unit One') advances towards 1914, for all that is 'advanced' moves backwards, now, towards that impossible goal, of the pre-war dawn. At his back struggles a thin militia—except for one giant, the last of the Mohicans, Mr. Moore, the sculptor. But it is in vain. We are all taking in each other's washing. Soon as a society we shall none of us have any money to pay the laundry bill, that is the fact of the matter.

The above statement, unsupported by data and by argument, might appear at first sight a mere outbreak of irresponsible pessimism. So let us see how one can arrive at such a discouraging estimate of the chances of the arts at the present time; and why it is quite reasonable, with all proper detachment, to believe that they have not the chance of the proverbial Chinaman in the 'new' age of which they were so naïf as to allow themselves to appear the clamorous harbingers.

256

CHAPTER III

Towards an Art-less Society

The Arts with their great capital A's are, considered as plants, decidedly unrobust. They are the sport, at the best, of political chance: parasitically dependent upon the good health of the social body.

The most robust *looking* art by a long way is sculpture. Yet it is just snuffed out by a change of wind—or to pursue the parasitic image, by a brusque change of position on the part of the human dreamer. The frailest looking of the visual arts, drawing, possesses far greater endurance. Mere scraps of paper that it is, in this respect it has more vitality than basalt.

This book and especially this section of it is mainly concerned with the art of writing. There is always a lot of writing, of sorts, going on at any period. If quantity meant anything, to-day would be a golden age for the art of writing. You cannot snuff out penmanship by upsetting a régime. The crash of a great religion does not diminish the output of the written word. But writing as an *art* is very susceptible to shock. That gets upset by almost anything. And to-day it is as an art in as great a decline as its sisters.

A few arts were born in the happy lull before the world-storm. In 1914 a ferment of the artistic intelligence occurred in the west of Europe. And it looked to many people as if a great historic 'school' was in process of formation. Expressionism, Post-impressionism, Vorticism, Cubism, Futurism were some of the characteristic nicknames bestowed upon these manifestations, where they found their intensest expression in the pictorial field. In every case the structural and philosophic rudiments of life were sought out. On all hands a return to first principles was witnessed.

Such a school as was then foreshadowed would have been of

far more significance than the schools based on a scientific naturalism à l'outrance which filled the galleries and mansions of the Nineteenth Century, and would have had equally little in common with the elegancies of the Eighteenth. And in literature a purgative almost equally radical was undertaken.

The natural sciences which had been responsible for the Industrial Age had acquired maturity, it seemed, and the human mind was to indulge, once more, its imagination. Scientific still, essentially, it was to go over from the techniques of the sciences into the field of art. There it was to create a novel world, free from the shoppiness of the impressionist.

These arts were not entirely misnamed 'new' arts. They were arts especially intended to be the delight of this *particular* world. Indeed, they were the heralds of great social changes. Then down came the lid—the day was lost, for art, at Sarajevo. World-politics stepped in, and a war was started which has not ended yet: a 'war to end war'. But it merely ended art. It did not end war.

Before the 'great War' of 1914–18 was over it altered the face of our civilization. It left the European nations impoverished, shell-shocked, discouraged and unsettled. By the time President Wilson had drawn up his famous Fourteen Points the *will to play* had been extinguished to all intents and purposes forever in our cowed and bankrupt democracies.

The great social changes necessitated by the altered conditions of life were not to come about, after all, rationally and peacefully. They were to come about 'catastrophically' instead (that is to say, after the Marxian prescription). And the great social changes which with such uncouth and wasteful violence started to get themselves born, in that tragical atmosphere, extinguished the arts which were to be their expression, and which had been their heralds.

No one, it is true, ever supposed that some bigoted theorist of the mass-life, or some Brasshat, either—much less the 'Financial Wizard' who controlled the Brasshat and subsidized the bigot—would ever feel drawn towards *an art*. That would be the last thing he would favour. No one imagined that such figures would give a row of pins, under any circumstances, for

258

the sort of question in which the artist, or philosopher, is interested. But then, although he had in a sense announced, the artist did not foresee, these interminable convulsions of War, Revolution, Economic Nationalism and Slump.

That the artist of 1914 was no seer is of little general importance, since it would have made no difference if he had been. Yet the artist is, in any society, by no means its least valuable citizen. Without him the world ceases to see itself and to reflect. It forgets all its finer manners. For art is only manner, it is only style. That is, in the end, what 'art' means. At its simplest, art is a reflection : a far more mannered reflection than that supplied by the camera.

Deprived of art, the healthy intellectual discipline of wellbeing is lost. Life instantly becomes so brutalized as to be mechanical and devoid of interest. Further, there is a worse thing than no art at all (no manner, no style)—the saccharine travesty of art, namely, of the kind supplied by the Hollywood magnate.

In considering art here I am not complicating the matter by going on to consider how life also is brutal and empty without the heightening it acquires through the metaphysical or religious values. We need go no farther than art ; and for the purpose of this discussion art can be isolated, conventionally, from those values. For it is possible to have life with a minimum of metaphysics : the age of Lord Shaftesbury and Pope is there to prove it, though I do not say it is the best life. But *without art*—then life is utterly impossible. And there is unquestionably less and less *art* in life at the present time—and less and less in what passes as art, too.

The activities of the artist of 1914 did foreshadow all that has come to pass in the meanwhile. But those events obviously could, by a kinder fate, have been arranged differently, so that they would have been productive of less unpleasant and stultifying results. Great changes *could* have been achieved—indeed greater changes—with less destructive haste. Passchendaele and the 'Thirty days that shook the world', that was not the *only* way to adapt ourselves to the novelties of the Power House and the internal combustion engine and consummate the revolution that the Luddite Riots began.

In the event what has looked like a speeding up, brought about by the very violence of the methods employed, has at the same time involved a remarkable retrogression. To match the mechanical advance, there has been a backsliding of the intellect throughout the civilized world. And this backsliding is glaringly demonstrated in the continued impoverishment of artistic expression, not in one art, but in every art.

In seeking to establish the reasons for this great decay, we have of course to marshal in our minds all that nexus of disastrous events of which the Great War was the first, and of which Great War No. 2, now in preparation, will be the next. But causes that had led European society into the violent and destructive courses which we know, had done their work already, in part, before Mons, or before that sinister expression 'Entente Cordiale', had ever been heard of.

If you, in 1937, fix your attention upon any art—upon the art of prose narrative ('fiction'), upon the Stage, upon Opera, upon orchestral music—you will be forced to the conclusion that in every instance 'commercialism', as we say, is most efficiently destroying it or has already destroyed it.

Organization (magical word, and magical fact—nationalization transforming capitalism, in other words) in the business of the publishing and selling of books, imposes every day a greater handicap upon the book that is a work of art rather than a business commodity. The Stage in England, again, has never compared favourably with the great standards of acting found on the European continent. Germany is still the best place to see Shakespeare reasonably well played. But poor as English acting has always been, it is to-day at its nadir. A natural immaturity, awkwardness, a philosophical ineptitude, in the modern Englishman is powerfully assisted by the capital interests which control the Box-Office. These insist upon cheaper and cheaper goods for quicker and quicker returns. So in the land of the Tudor Dramatists the Stage is a standing scandal. And the few good players we have can do nothing about it. They are compelled to blunt their talents in play after play of a staggering ineptitude.

If we turn to Opera, we are told that 'Wagner is still the big box-office noise'. (I quote from the *Star*, 6 May, 1936.) No one supposes any longer that a 'great' opera will ever be written again. As far as Opera is concerned, and for what that form of art is worth, the best Operas date from the last century. There will be no more Wagner, much less Mozart. And as to the supreme orchestral compositions, they all seem to have been written, too. There are no more Bachs or Beethovens just as there were no more Leonardos and Michelangelos after the Renaissance, only hasty reminders of what artists once excelled in doing, or despairing jokes, or jazzed-up echoes of perfection.

These are not lost arts—much music is still written and very intelligent music, and the dying struggle of the visual arts is often impressive. But something has occurred in the world that has long ago caused the greatest creations to stop being born. No more will come.

Literature, or rather language, is a hardier material. But that it will shortly be quite impossible to imagine a book of a very high order of excellence being written any more—and we may soon have reached that stage—is no more inconceivable, than it is inconceivable to anticipate the appearance at any moment of a new Beethoven.

And it is here that I can perhaps best make you see what I mean. We are already prepared to feel that maybe great literature is a thing of the past, just as we have grown accustomed for a long time now to think of great music as a thing of of the past. I doubt if the toughest master of words can really stand up against the massed attack of the syndicated 'Book-world'—of Big Business ('collectivized', one could quite properly term it, because if 'Big Business' only becomes big *enough* it then approximates to one simple body).

As to Painting and Sculpture, there it is the same story. The traffic in 'Old Masters' shows no sign of diminishing. Larger sums than ever are 'fetched' by the works of any famous painter of the past. And the artist who is an outsider, who may with luck survive, cannot command big prices, and must struggle for survival in an increasingly unenterprising world.

As to the Royal Academy and Paris Salon type of art, that is ruined, luckily, entirely, by this new shrewdness of the New Rich.

So, although it is still possible to write a good book, to paint a good picture, and not to perish, it is more than problematical whether that will be the case to-morrow. An artist starting his career to-day does so under the most enormous handicap. And to-day we are only halfway to full collectivism, to the consummation of the capitalist materialism.

You may say that it is not the business of the literary critic, or of the art critic, to play the prophet. But in everything we do we have to be directed, to a greater or lesser extent, by what we assume will be the conditions—climatic, political, business, or what not—this time next year. Indeed, it is very much our business, if we set out to discuss the condition, flourishing or otherwise, of an art to arrive at some conclusion regarding what promise it has of continued life. Or the society on which it depends is sick: well then, it is our business to consider how sick, and what course its illness is likely to take. So I need not apologize for, in a mild way, playing the social prophet.

In any estimate of the immediate future of the arts in Europe, in any prognostication, the political factor must be the key-pin of your prophecy. And there, I am afraid, the artist can take very little comfort.

What do we see, when we gaze out upon the political scene? We see two hostile ideologies contending for the mastery of the world—Communism and Fascism. Both advance their policies (they cannot do otherwise) in a paralysing atmosphere of martial law. And the constraints, the pseudo-religious intensity, of these systems, do not lend themselves to the relaxations of the senses, nor to the detached delights of the intellect, whatever else may be claimed for them.

Chirico, the 'official' painter of Fascist Italy, is a better type of painter than those encouraged in Communist Russia. In return for a pastel of a gladiator, once a month, it is probable that the Blackshirt Emperor would allow you great latitude in your choice of subject.

262

But neither the imperialism of the Soviets, nor the Spartan programmes of Germany or Italy, leave much room for any thought but that of *action*. And Action, as a religion, is apt to set up a climate as unsuitable for artistic pursuits as the most narrow of thoecratic régimes. If we were called upon to fight a new Ice Age, there would be no place for civilization among the encroaching icefields. We should be absorbed in problems of frostbite, scurvy, and circulation.

And human nature—not Nature this time—has brought us to Ice Age conditions. The mass stupidity and helplessness of men, with all the power of machines to back it, threatens us with a new 'scourge of god', and we certainly shall have to put aside our books and pictures. And every time this happens, in the history of our race, we take them up again, when the dark age is over, with less assurance and with less genius.

As to what has happened to pictorial art in contemporary Russia, the exhaustive book of illustrations recently produced by *The Studio* is qualified to enlighten us. Page after page we see picture after picture of the most inconceivable dullness. Eighty per cent of the illustrations are of works which might have been exhibited forty years ago or more in any of the semi-advanced ('Secession') exhibitions in Northern Europe, and which we encounter in great quantities in all the principal continental and American museums. It is as if England had become a communist republic, and twenty years after the happy event the London exhibitions were full of Friths, Clausens, Herkomers, and Jaggers, with a left-wing comprising a few C. R. W. Nevinsons and a few bucolic posters by Mr. Paul Nash.

The fact of the matter is that a militant bureaucratic oligarchy, whether of Left or Right, is exceedingly 'bourgeois'. If there must be 'art', let it be a propagandist photograph, they seem to say, or a picture of a pretty girl—for the Commissar and the Stockbrokers are brothers under their skin. That is *life*! All the rest is literature—or 'intellectualism'. As to criticism—a 'criticism of life', or any other sort of criticism—that is the last thing they want and of course one does not blame them.

So all the so-called 'revolutionary' artists—who have been regarded by the Royal Academician as the 'Reds' of the painting world—as 'bolsheviks' of art—turn out to be anything but *persona grata* with the highpriests of Social Revolution. They are 'anarchists', merely. And if there is one thing any good communist dislikes more than another it is an anarchist.

But the immediate future must more and more be controlled by these two antagonistic political principles. And looked at purely from the standpoint of the artist, neither promises the requisite conditions for an improvement in the position of the arts.

Beyond this epoch of political upheaval, what is in store for men? We need not urge our prophetic souls any further than the limit of these struggles—that bourne is quite sufficiently far off. As far as it is possible to compute, it is unlikely the arts will again enjoy such a period of favourable calm as was experienced by those artists who came upon the scene between the French Revolution and the 'Great War' (of 1914–18). That is the gist of the matter.

Now that we have got our bearings in time and space a little co-ordinated, we can return to the period of Adam and Eve, before I flitted down the Mews with Miss Sitwell under my arm. That is when I went to Paris with Eliot, where the three principal members of the Pound Circus came together.

CHAPTER IV

First Meeting with James Joyce

James Joyce had come to Paris from Zürich. In the summer of 1920 I went there with Thomas Stearns Eliot. We went there on our way to the Bay of Quiberon for a summer holiday, which his wife said would do him good. We descended at a small hotel, upon the left bank of the River Seine. It was there I met, in his company, James Joyce for the first time. And it was the first time that Eliot had seen him, too. Joyce was the last of my prominent friends to be encountered; last but not least.

It had been agreed before we left London that we should contrive to see Joyce in Paris. And Eliot had been entrusted with a parcel by Ezra Pound (as a more responsible person than myself), which he was to hand to Joyce when he got there. We did not know at all what it contained. It was rather a heavy parcel and Eliot had carried it under his arm, upon his lap, as it was too big to go in a suitcase.

At that time I knew very little indeed about Joyce. He 'conveyed nothing' to me, I was in the same position as the white-coated doctor I mentioned in my introductory remarks—except that I did not, in my person, resemble James Joyce in any way, whereas certainly the doctor did, and yet had not even heard of his double.

Beyond what Ezra Pound had told me, which was mostly apologetic (the good Ezra assuming that I should laugh at him for his over-literary respects and genuflexions) I knew nothing. That was the situation. It was in consequence of this that in our subsequent intercourse Joyce and myself were often talking at cross-purposes.

I had not read *The Portrait of the Artist* nor *Dubliners*.

265

Exiles and *Chamber Music* I had never heard of, *Ulysses* had not, of course, yet made its appearance. But Joyce, on the other hand, had, I am persuaded, read everything I had ever written. He pretended however not to have done so.

In very marked contrast with Joyce I was indifferent as to whether he had followed the fortunes of Tarr and Kreisler or not. There was no arrogance at all in my indifference. But, as it is easy to suppose, since their author assumed I had read all his books (*Ulysses* included although it had not been published) but was pretending like himself to have forgotten, things were at first very involved. Bad jams occurred in the dialogue, in both directions.

It does not follow that a couple of authors, when they come face to face need meet as 'authors'. But aside from everything else, James Joyce was in a superlative degree the writer of books, the champion Penman, and breathed, thought and felt as such. We had been starred together on many occasions. He saw me as a Penman, too, and as a champion—one I expect he thought he could easily 'put-to-sleep'. It was quite impossible, under these circumstances, to encounter Joyce otherwise than as one of a pair of figures in the biography of a big Penman— I, of course being the interloper. For the biography would be one devoted to *him,* not to me. And finally why I on my side was indifferent was of course because I had no feeling for history. I was in fact a chronological idiot. A burlesque situation!

But this light comedy was sufficiently curious for it to be worth while to go into yet more detail. *Some* pages of the 'Portrait' I had read, when it first appeared as a serial in the *Egoist,* a paper edited by Miss Harriet Weaver. But I took very little interest. At that time, it was of far too tenuous an elegance for my taste. Its flavour was altogether too literary. And as to its emotional content, that I condemned at once as sentimental-Irish. Even now, for that matter, I feel much the same about *The Portrait of the Artist,* with the important difference that I have obliged myself to read a great many more books, in the meanwhile, many of which suffer from the same shortcomings, as I see it. So I do recognize the *Portrait of the Artist as a Young*

Man to be one only of a large class, and of its kind a very excellent example.

On my side my first meeting with James Joyce was (at first) devoid of any particular interest. I found an oddity, in patent-leather shoes, large powerful spectacles, and a small gingerbread beard; speaking half in voluble Italian to a scowling schoolboy: playing the Irishman a little overmuch perhaps, but in amusingly mannered technique. Soon I was prepared to be interested in Joyce for his own sake. I took a great fancy to him for his wit, for the agreeable humanity of which he possessed such stores, for his unaffected love of alcohol, and all good things to eat and drink.

What should have been a momentous encounter, then, turned out to be as matter-of-fact a social clash as the coming together of two navvies, or the brusque *how do you do* of a couple of dogs out for a walk. The reason: just my inveterate obtuseness where all that is historic and chronological is concerned. It is because I cannot see things as *biography*. I have not got the Barretts of Wimpole Street mind. My insensitiveness in this respect is to blame if all this part of my narrative is literally *flat,* like a Chinese or a Japanese picture.

I have gone ahead like this, outrunning the physical, to take all surprise out of these happenings, as a preliminary disinfection. Also I have hoped to drive home the fact that I have nothing up my sleeve, in these harmless exercises.

Returning, however, to my narrative of the physical encounter. T. S. Eliot—need I say the premier poet of Anglo-Saxony? —T. S. Eliot and myself descended at a small hotel. The Eliot fan will appreciate this way of putting it. He will see I know my Eliot. The hotel was nearer to the quays of the Seine than to the central artery of the Saint Germain quarter. It was the rue des Saints Pères, or it may be the rue Bonaparte: no matter, they are all the same. Our rooms were the sort of lofty, dirtily parquetted, frowsily-curtained, faded apartments that the swarms of small hotels in Paris provide, upon their floors of honour. These small hotels still abound.

T. S. Eliot ringing for the chasseur, dispatched a *petit bleu* to James Joyce. He suggested that Joyce should come to the hotel, because he had a parcel, entrusted to him by Ezra Pound, and which that gentleman had particularly enjoined upon him to deliver personally to the addressee; but that it would likewise be a great pleasure to meet him. This was accompanied by an invitation to dinner.

An invitation to dinner! I laugh as I write this. But at the time I did not know the empty nature of this hospitable message, seeing to whom it was directed!

The parcel was then placed in the middle of a large Second Empire marble table, standing upon gilt eagles' claws in the centre of the apartment. About six in the evening James Joyce arrived, and the Punch and Judy show began.

Joyce was accompanied by a tallish youth, whom he introduced to Eliot as his son. Eliot then introduced me to Joyce. We stood collected about the shoddily-ornamented french table, in the décor of the cheap dignity of the red-curtained apartment, as if we had been people out of a scene in an 1870 gazette, resuscitated by Max Ernst, to amuse the tired intelligentsia— bowing in a cosmopolitan manner to each other across Ezra's prize-packet, which was the proximate cause of this solemn occasion.

When Joyce heard my name he started in a very flattering fashion. Politely he was galvanized by his historic scene, and then collapsed. It was as if he had been gently pricked with the ghost of a hat-pin of a corsetted demirep out of the Police Gazette, and had given a highly well-bred exhibition of *stimulus-response*. Suppose this exhibition to have been undertaken for a lecture (with demonstrations) on 'Behaviour', and you have the whole picture. He raised his eyebrows to denote surprise and satisfaction at the auspicious occasion; he said *Ah! Wyndham Lewis* civilly under his breath, and I bowed again in acknowledgement, at the repetition of my name. He then with a courteous haste looked around for his son, who was heavily scowling in the background, and effected an introduction. His son stiffened, and, still scowling, bowed towards me with ceremony. Bringing my heels together, unintentionally with a noticeable report, I returned the salute. We all then sat down. But only for a moment.

Joyce lay back in the stiff chair he had taken from behind him, crossed his leg, the lifted leg laid out horizontally upon the one in support like an artificial limb, an arm flung back over the summit of the sumptuous chair. He dangled negligently his straw hat, a regulation 'boater'. We were on either side of the table, the visitors and ourselves, upon which stood the enigmatical parcel.

Eliot now rose to his feet. He approached the table, and with one eyebrow drawn up, and a finger pointing, announced to James Joyce that *this* was that parcel, to which he had referred in his wire, and which had been given into his care, and he formally delivered it, thus acquitting himself of his commission.

'Ah! Is this the parcel you mentioned in your note?' enquired Joyce, overcoming the elegant reluctance of a certain undisguised fatigue in his person. And Eliot admitted that it was, and resumed his seat.

I stood up : and, turning my back upon the others, arranged my tie in the cracked Paris mirror—whose irrelevant imperfections, happening to bisect my image, bestowed upon me the mask of a syphilitic Creole. I was a little startled : but I stared out of countenance this unmannerly distortion, and then turned about, remaining standing.

James Joyce was by now attempting to untie the crafty housewifely knots of the cunning old Ezra. After a little he asked his son crossly in Italian for a penknife. Still more crossly his son informed him that he had no penknife. But Eliot got up, saying 'You want a knife? I have not got a knife, I think!' We were able, ultimately, to provide a pair of nail scissors.

At last the strings were cut. A little gingerly Joyce unrolled the slovenly swaddlings of damp British brown paper in which the good-hearted American had packed up what he had put inside. Thereupon, along with some nondescript garments for the trunk—there were no trousers I believe—a fairly presentable pair of *old brown shoes* stood revealed, in the centre of the bourgeois French table.

As the meaning of this scene flashed upon my listless understanding, I saw in my mind's eye the phantom of the little enigmatic Ezra standing there (provided by our actions, and the position of his footgear at this moment, with a dominating stature which otherwise he scarcely could have attained) silently surveying his handiwork.

James Joyce, exclaiming very faintly 'Oh!' looked up, and we all gazed at the old shoes for a moment. 'Oh!' I echoed and laughed, and Joyce left the shoes where they were, disclosed as the matrix of the disturbed leaves of the parcel. He turned away and sat down again, placing his left ankle upon his right knee, and squeezing, and then releasing, the horizontal limb.

With a smile even slower in materializing than his still-trailing Bostonian voice (a handsome young United States President, to give you an idea—adding a Gioconda smile to the other charms of this office) Eliot asked our visitor if he would have dinner with us. Joyce turned to his son, and speaking very rapidly in Italian, the language always employed by him, so it seemed, in his family circle, he told him to go home : he would inform his mother that his father would not be home to dinner after all. Yes, his father had accepted an invitation to dinner, and would not be back after all, for the evening meal! Did he understand? To tell his mother that his father—But the son very hotly answered his father back, at this, after but a mo- ment's hesitation on account of the company : evidently he did not by any means relish being entrusted with messages. It was, however, with greater hotness, in yet more resonant Italian, that the son expressed his rebellious sensations when the imperturb- able Jimmie handed him the parcel of disreputable footwear. That was the last straw—this revolting, this unbecoming packet. Having exchanged a good number of stormy words, in a series of passionate asides—in a good imitation of an altercation between a couple of neapolitan touts, of the better order— Joyce, père et fils, separated, the latter rushing away with the shoes beneath his arm, his face crimson and his eyes blazing with a truly southern ferocity—first having mastered himself for a moment sufficiently to bow to me from the hips, and to shake hands with heroic punctilio. This scene took place as we were about to leave the small hotel.

270

CHAPTER V

First Meeting with Ezra Pound

As I have decided to get these principal introductions over first, I will postpone the sequel to my tale of the pair of old shoes. I will go back to an even remoter scene, in the Vienna Café in New Oxford Street, in order to give you my first reluctant glimpses of Ezra Pound.

I say reluctant, but that is too active an expression. Perhaps I should say it was with a complete passivity on my side, tinctured with a certain mild surliness, that acquaintance with Ezra Pound was gradually effected. But once it was in being, not in spite of quite, but with no assistance from, myself, I enjoyed that acquaintanceship immoderately. This theatrical fellow, as he first seemed to me, I found to be 'one of the best'. I still regard him as one of the best, even one of the best poets.

On the first two occasions on which we met I did not speak to him : on the second occasion he addressed a few remarks to me, but I did not reply. I did not consider it necessary to do so, he seemed in fact to be addressing somebody else. I mean that what he said did not appear to be appropriate, or to have any relevance—as a remark addressed to *me*.

'This young man could probably tell you!' was I think what he said, with great archness, narrowing his eyes and regarding me with mischievous goodwill.

There had been some question of the whereabouts of a kidnapped or absconding prostitute. Ezra was already attributing to those he liked proclivities which he was persuaded must accompany the revolutionary intellect. And he had been told that I was a 'rebel'. That I was, undoubtedly : but it did not occur to him that I might not be a *conventional* rebel, for Pound was *all* for convention, as he was all rebellion.

271

It has not to this day, I think, occurred to Ezra Pound that the authentic revolutionary (not the revolutionary when everybody else is revolutionary, but the really sinister and uncommon fellow) will rebel against everything—not least rebellion. So I did not respond with a ready grin of satisfaction at this attribution of orthodox devilry.—Misunderstanding blocked the way from the start with us.

The third time (the meeeting occurred elsewhere) I answered the hail. A bombastic galleon, palpably bound to, or from, the Spanish Main. I thought I had better do so, since we were always meeting, and going on board, I discovered beneath its skull and cross-bones, intertwined with *fleurs de lys* and spattered with preposterous starspangled oddities, a heart of gold.

Under a skull and crossed lilies, a kind heart that the bogus coronet of Raoul de la Tour Carol made nonsense of. That is what I found. Also, through sailing the China Seas (without the shadow of an academic sanction) this literary pirate had become a very passable, if unsound, sinologue. And nature had endowed him with more native taste—how exquisite it can be I have only to refer to *Cathay* in order to confound dissent—than all the Cambridge aesthetes could muster between them.

I should say that was in 1910 though I have no calendar, engagement book, old letters—nothing to tell me what the year in fact was. And how I can possibly convey the atmosphere of the Vienna Café in 1910 I do not know. I have no historical competence, even for events within my own experience. How does one make visible a hansom-cab to a person who has never seen one?

It is twenty-five years ago but it seems at an infinite distance. And the flaunting young poet from the Middle West who nervously flung himself into it is of course obliterated by the more full-blown, more recent Ezra, whom I know far better.

At that period I was an idle student, nursing dreams of obstreperous intervention in a farce or two that was going on, upon the stage where the painters acted, and where the aesthetes blinked and blahed. I had written an essay, a story, and an article, about something or other, and had started one or

272

two paintings (I never finished a painting till six months before the war and then it was not really more than a sketch). Outwardly, I have been told, I looked like a *moujik* : but if so it was a moujik who bought his clothes in Savile Row or Brook Street and his most eccentric shirts in the Burlington Arcade. If his shoes retained the loam of the wildest heaths discoverable at the time, they had been made for him in Jermyn Street. I had the tarnished polish of the English Public School, of the most gilded cafés of five or six continental capitals. And meanwhile I would lunch with an entertaining group of people who were mostly drawn from the official ranks of the great neighbouring Museum. With some afterwards I would dine in Old Compton Street. Mostly they were middle-aged scholars, with a distinguished elderly mandarin called Squire (no relation I think of 'Jack') and a few younger persons. Streatfield, a poet, who had been a friend of Samuel Butler's, was among them and his high crowning laugh partook of the orgasm. That laugh must later, when he lost his reason, have been found disturbing to his male attendant.

Yeats had sometimes been there but I had not met him yet. I have always thought that if instead of the really malefic 'Bloomsburies', who with their ambitious and jealous cabal have had such a destructive influence upon the intellectual life of England, something more like these Vienna Café habitués of those days could have been the ones to push themselves into power, that a less sordid atmosphere would have prevailed. The writing and painting world of London might have been less like the afternoon tea-party of a perverse spinster. But one cannot choose one's Government. And we have been governed, in matters of taste, by 'bloomsbury' aesthete-politicians for the two decades and a half that have elapsed since then, especially in the post-war.

It was announced one day that a certain Ezra Pound was to come in to lunch, a young American poet. I forget the circumstances and who had invited him, but I remember he was not a particularly welcome guest. Several of our party had already seen him. And it was reported that S. had pronounced him a Jew. S. had an excellent nose for Jews, it was claimed : he had a gift that enabled him to detect a Jew under almost any disguise—something like water-divining, a peculiar and uncanny gift. And S. had affirmed (and coming in at that moment S. confirmed it, with a dainty sideways nod—as he hung up his overcoat—of his large pink countenance, decorated with a powerful white moustache) that this 'young American poet' was undoubtedly a crypto-semite, of the diaspora of Wisconsin.

The newspapers did not resound with the embittered backchat of Jews and Aryans, Jews and Arabs, Jews and Blackshirts, und so weiter, and there was no reason why I should take any particular interest in a Jew.

When Pound appeared I was mildly surprised to see an unmistakable 'nordic blond', with fierce blue eyes and a reddishly hirsute jaw, thrust out with a thoroughly Aryan determination. But this moment of disillusion past, I took no further interest in this cowboy songster, said to be a young sprig of the Kahal. I turned my back: I heard the staccato of the States: I 'sensed' that there was little enthusiasm. Most of those present felt that he was indeed a Jew, disguised in a tengallon hat, I later heard—a 'red Jew' it was decided, a subtle blend, but a pukka Kosher. And when I rose to go back to the Museum he had whirled off—bitterness in his heart, if I know my Ezra. This was his first taste of the English. He had no luck with the English, then or at a later date, and was always in this country the perfect fish out of water—hardly a Jewish trait!

I think I have some understanding of Ezra Pound, and of my good friends of that time, too. And I can see how impossible it was that they should take to him. It was not their fault entirely : but on their side they felt that this was a bogus personage and they had no inducement to be 'taken in' by this tiresome and flourishing foreign aspirant to poetic eminence. Loyalty to Shelley and Keats alone would have prevented it! And what held for the Vienna Café held for Oxford too, as he later discovered. I may add that they also disapproved of Americans. Then he left England in disgust and of course England was the poorer and Rapallo not very much the richer.

Pound approached these strangers as one might a panther,

or any other dangerous quadruped—tense and wary, without speaking or smiling: showing one is not afraid of it, inwardly awaiting hostile action: But when it comes to his desire to *impress,* the panther image will no longer serve. For he did not desire to prove to the people he had come amongst that he was superior in physical strength, but that he was superior to all other intellectuals in intellect, and all poets in prosodic prowess. *They* were the spectators merely—they were of very little account. The feelings of dislike were mutual and immediate, as I could observe, and he never sought to hide the fact that he looked upon them as of very little consequence.

At the beginning in England Pound socially was a little too much like the 'singing cowboy'. He had rushed with all the raw solemnity of the classic Middle West into a sophisticated post-Nineties society dreaming of the Eighteenth century, discussing the quality of the respective cellars of the Oxford Colleges, calling their relatives' county palaces 'places' still *droppin'* their g's from time to time, for whom the spectacle of American 'strenuousness'—The Bull Moose tradition—was something that hardly any longer deserved a smile. They looked at it with a stony stare of infinite boredom.

This particular group in whose company I met him were apt to be learned too. Those were the days when a man going on a long train journey would be apt to slip in his pocket a copy of the Iliad in the Greek text: and there was after all Lionel Johnson's definition of a gentleman—a man who knows Greek and Latin. His lecture would, at that period, have introduced a much needed discipline into English literary Culture—which has in fact been demonstrated by his great ultimate influence, by Mr. Eliot's and that of others. As to learning, those possessing it usually did nothing with it, and he showed them its uses. But Pound arrived as an unassimilable and aggressive stranger; with his Imagism he became aesthetically a troublesome rebel.

It was not the fault of England nor was it his, but I hope I shall not seem sensational if I say that looking back I cannot see him stopping here very long without some such go-between as Ford Madox Hueffer.

He writes of England, in 'Pavannes and Divisions' (1918):

In a country in love with amateurs, in a country where the incompetent have such beautiful manners and personalities so fragile and charming, that one can not bear to injure their feelings by the introduction of competent criticism, it is well that one man should have a vision of perfection and that he should be sick to death and disconsolate because he can not attain it.

Although my feelings with regard to the Englishman are as different as possible from those of Pound, nevertheless I would endorse everything he says above as to their cultural delinquencies.

Professionalism even as long ago as Congreve (and that in spite of recent laughable attempts of whitewashing) was looked upon in England as something to shun and to disown. With the passage of time people have not grown *less* snobbish. Indeed, every decade seems to mark an advance upon the last in that respect.

The word *perfection* (the key word in the above quotation) has obvious professional associations. Perfection implies the highly finished product, result of competent craftsmanship, and consequently it is taboo in a society where a well-to-do class desire the fruits of craftsmanship without its toils, or in one where time is denied the workman, and what is done can only be fragmentary, superficial, hasty, in-the-rough. 'It is impossible,' wrote Pound ('Pavannes'), to talk about perfection without getting yourself much disliked. It is even more difficult in a capital where everybody's Aunt Lucy or Uncle George has written something or other.'—He recognized, as you see, that *nowhere* does it make things more comfortable to talk about perfection.

Pound did not remain the post-graduate figure of the first days. By the time of 'Pavannes' (1918) he had married, acquired a beard, grown into a sort of prickly, aloof, rebel mandarin—as it would be viewed by the world. He now knew his England very well without ever really having come to terms with it. After the First World War he suddenly departed, never to return.

Paris was Pound's next stopping place, in the long exile, after he had found that he was after all too American, or something,

276

to dwell with people 'still dominated by an Eighteenth century verbalism'—exponents of 'the opalescent word, the rhetorical tradition'. Retrospectively I am only astonished at his Kensington life enduring as it did, at the foot of what he describes as 'Rotting Hill'.

First sight of him in his Paris studio for me was a great change from the dark Kensington quarters. Having found his abode, I rang the bell. A good deal of noise was to be heard but no one answered: therefore I pushed the door, which opened practically into the studio. A splendidly built young man, stripped to the waist, and with a torso of dazzling white, was standing not far from me. He was tall, handsome, and serene, and was repelling with his boxing gloves a hectic assualt of Ezra's. After a final swing at the dazzling solar plexus Pound fell back upon his settee. The young man was Hemingway. Pound got on like a house on fire with this particular statue. There is logic in that too.—He was much more in his element in Paris. I actually believe he cooked better in Paris than he did in London—and like Sickert he is an excellent cook.

My remarks so far have not so much been aimed at estimating the value of Pound's stay in England—to himself or to the Englanders—as to bringing out something about him of primary significance where his personality is concerned. It is this: Pound is—was always, is, must always remain, violently American. Tom Sawyer is somewhere in his gait, the 'Leaves of Grass' survive as a manly candour in his broad and bearded face: the 'tough guy' that has made Hemingway famous, and the 'strenuousness' of him of the Big Stick, are modes of the American ethos with which Pound is perfectly in tune. The Good, bad, and indifferent in Americanism all goes in, to make the perfect specimen—where *that* is concerned it would be impossible to be more unselective. He exercises a sort of tribal attraction for his fellow-countrymen, over and above the effect of the glamour of his poetic genius. In his present great misfortune the sympathy has been markedly spontaneous. I suggest that the spectacle of a great American in eclipse in this way has an effect beyond the question of the welfare of American Letters.

Pound's nearest American analogue in the past is not Whitman, however, or Mark Twain, but a painter, James McNeil Whistler—the 'gentle master of all that is flippant and fine in art'. Whistler signed his pictures with a butterfly. Indeed their delicacy would not admit of the intrusion of the customary extrovert clodhopping calligraphy in the lower right hand corner, where the authorship of the work is proclaimed. Only by the unobtrusive presence of this winged insect was the artist's identity revealed. Like Pound in the literary art, it was in the extreme-orient that Whistler had discovered the fundamental adjustments of his preference. But what I would say here is how strangely in contradiction American 'toughness' and so much that is American is to the Butterfly—taking that as symbol.

Two of the most famous pictures of the last century, the *Portraits of Thomas Carlyle* and the *Mother*, were of course Whistler's. That Pound was conscious of affinity is suggested by the frontispiece to 'Pavannes and Divisions', in which he is posed in raking silhouette, his overcoat trailing in reminiscence of the Carlyle (though with swagger and rhetoric). But being an interloping American—like 'Jimmie' before him—aggressing among the sleepy islanders, ramming novelties down their expostulating throats—and so on—it would be the 'gentle master' at the easel (a 'Bowery tough' according to his disciple, Sickert, in conversation with me—tough in defence of his most gentle and defenceless art) rather than the sitter of whom Pound would be thinking: the author of 'The Gentle Art of Making Enemies', not the old sage responsible for 'Latter Day Pamphlets'.

We heard Pound just now allude to *perfection*, where he was speaking of the cult of the incompetent, which he encountered in England. And among artists of the modern age—since the time of the 'old masters' that is—there have been very few indeed who attempted perfection as did Whistler, or, I may add, attained it. Whether Pound himself, in his department of the arts, has compassed perfection in the same massive proportions will be decided I suppose in the end, one way or the other, by the 'cantos'. But certainly he has been bitten by the same inexorable bug, strained fanatically towards the same limits of human expression.

As to his present predicament, as a martyr of 'credit' economics, at least one knows (irrespective of one's personal opinion regarding those economics, and although it is small consolation for one of his oldest friends) that Pound is sincere. Once, in a moment of impatience, I used the word 'simpleton' : and—in addition to everything else—I am again impatient. Of course he is not that. But he demands *perfection* in action, as well as in art. He even appears to expect perfection, or what he understands as such, in the world of politics.

Economist Pound certainly is immeasurably more sophistic-ated than William Jennings Bryan, we know that : nor has any such electrifying cry came from him as—'Thou shalt not crucify mankind upon a Cross of Gold!' But with him Gold is a great bugbear too. Half a century has elapsed, the Problem has changed : with the contemporary prophet 'gold' would not be the magic word so much as 'debt'—and with debt, *Usury*. The universal slavery of Debt, rather than mankind's crucifixion by means of Gold, is the burden of the modern economist's jeremiad. Usury (usuria—usura) sometimes in one tongue, sometimes another, dominates Ezra's incantation.

> with usura
> . . .   . . .
> no picture is made to endure nor to live with
> but is made to sell and sell quickly
> *with usura, sin against nature,*
> *is thy bread ever more of stale rags*
> *is thy bread as dry as paper,*
> *with no mountain wheat, no strong flour*
> *with usura the line grows thick*
> *with usura is no clear demarcation*
> *and no man can find site for his dwelling.*
> *Stone cutter is kept from his stone*
> *weaver is kept from his loom*

WITH USURA

wool comes not to market
sheep bringeth no gain with usura
Usura is a murrain, usura
blunteth the needle in the main's hand
and stopped the spinner's cunning.

That is from Canto XLV. Usury is everywhere, as a pervasive rot, such is the teaching. If that is the sinister picture arrived at by this analytic intelligence—even though you must regard it as mistaken or perverse—and actions engaged in by him must be of an extremely different order from those undertaken by politicians.

In his attitude towards other people's work Pound has been superlatively generous. That is the most spectacular instance of the dynamic rôle of his critical sympathy : in every fact a *creative* sympathy. It extends far and wide. He does not in the least mind of being in service to somebody (as do other people it is usually found) if they have great talent. No envy of the individual is attached to the work. I have never known a person less troubled with personal feelings. This probably it is that has helped to make Pound that odd figure—the great poet and the great impresario at one and the same time. Also, he is the born teacher; and by his influence, direct and indirect, he has brought about profound changes in our literary techniques and criticism : changes, in both cases, for the better.

I consider that my second introduction has been effected. The wedge formed by Hart Street and Holborn, where they run into each other and from New Oxford Street, was occupied by the Vienna Café tottered and fell. For it was staffed and owned entirely by German or Austrians, 'alien enemies'. It could not have survived under all-British management. So it became a Bank. On the first floor was a large triangular room, with the mirrored ceiling, which reflected all your actions as if in a lake suspended above your head, surface downwards, and at a couple of tables, on the south side, these miscellaneous people would meet. It was a good club, and it was the only club of that sort in London.

I saw H. G. Wells there on several occasions. He did not belong to the circle of which I am speaking. He came independently with parties of his own. My friends observed him with something approaching horror. One of them said 'Whenever I see H. G. Wells I feel uncomfortably refined.' In looking over I saw a not particularly butcher-like, but certainly unromantic pepper-and-salt figure, springing about in a suit too tight for him, as he induced ladies into chairs and did the honours. Ezra did not become a frequent figure to this restaurant, anyhow. I saw him once, no more, at all events, beneath that ceiling of glass.

K

CHAPTER VI

First Meeting with T. S. Eliot

It is with a heavy pen, if not with a heavy heart, that I take up my narrative of my earliest 'contacts' with Number Three of my trio of eminent acquaintances, Mr. T. S. Eliot, namely. 'How can we be cheerful with the devil among us?' asks Mr. Toobad in *Nightmare Abbey*. Certainly Mr. Eliot is not the devil—I am not proposing to claim that honour for him, nor would he himself do so : 'I am no Prince Hamlet,' does not that emanation of his undergraduate days, Mr. Prufrock remark?

No. But Mr. Eliot may be regarded perhaps as not unlike the plenipotentiary of the Evil Principle in the Thomistic Heaven of the post-war—despatched there by his satanic majesty (he of the Naughty Nineties) rather as Ribbentrop is appointed to be his peace-envoy abroad by the wicked Hitler. And one's pen grows languid, it refuses to dance—it moves at a funeral pace across the paper—at the prospect of unravelling the technics of this complicated mission. It shrinks from the obligation to fix for posterity the features of this eccentric missionary. For it is nothing less than this that I have here set out to do.

Of these three friends of mine, Eliot was the second to swim into my ken—some years later than James Joyce. But he *slid* there rather than swam, as I recall the event, into my half-awakened consciousness. A sleek, tall, attractive transatlantic apparition—with a sort of Gioconda smile. I looked up one day from a brooding interval, as I sat in the narrow triangle of Ezra's flat. And there, sitting down with a certain stealth, not above a couple of feet away from me, was the author of Pru-frock—indeed, was Prufrock himself : but a Prufrock to whom the mermaids would decidedly have sung, one would have said, at the tops of their voices—a Prufrock who had no need to 'wear the bottom of his trousers rolled' just yet; a Prufrock who would 'dare' all right 'to eat a peach'—provided he was quite sure that he possessed the correct European table-technique for that ticklish operation. For this was a very attractive young Prufrock indeed, with an alert and dancing eye—*moqueur* to the marrow, bashfully ironic, blushfully *tacquineur*. But still a Prufrock!

Pound's flat was a rendezvous for translantic birds of passage. I had not the slightest idea what manner of newcomer had entered the room with Ezra, who had gone to answer the bell, nor did I at all care of course. For these people came and went as the nationals of a distant State drift through a legation. The prepossessing, ponderous, exactly-articulated, drawl, made a sleepy droning in my ear, as if some heavy hymenopter, emitting a honeyed buzz, had passed in at the Kensington window.

The interest I took in any of Ezra's friends was very small, also I entertained a most healthy suspicion of all Pound's enthusiasms—was I not one of them myself? So upon encountering another I experienced a certain embarrassment.

Ezra now lay flung back in a typical posture of aggressive ease. It resembled extreme exhaustion. (Looking back, I believe he *did* over-fatigue himself, like an excitable dog, use his last ounce of vitality, and that he did in fact become exhausted.) However, he kept steadily beneath his quizzical but self-satisfied observation his latest prize, or discovery—the author of *Prufrock*. The new collector's-piece went on smiling and growling out melodiously his apt and bright answers to promptings from the exhausted figure of his proud captor. Ezra then gave us some preserved fruit, of which it was his habit to eat a great deal.

The author of this poem had, I believed, already been published. But Pound had the air of having produced it from his hat a moment before, and its author with it simultaneously, out of the same capacious headpiece. He blinked and winked with contemplative conceit and contentment, chewing a sugared and wonderfully shrunken pear : then removed his glasses to wipe off the film of oily London dust that might have collected—but really to withdraw as it were, and leave me alone with Mr. Prufrock for a moment.

Then, that finished, Ezra would squint quickly, sideways, up at me—'grandpa'-wise, over the rims of his glasses. With chuckles, and much heavy fun, in his screwed-up smiling slits of eyes, he would be as good as saying to me in the Amos and Andy patter of his choice: 'Yor ole uncle Ezz is wise to wot youse thinkin. Waaal Wynd damn I'se tellin *yew*, he's lot better'n he looks!'

A mania like Pound's to act as a nursery and lying-in establishment—*bureau de renseignment* and unofficial agency for unknown literary talent did involve the successive presence of numbers of people. These I would find either groping around in the dark in the large middle-room of the flat—even playing the piano there; or quite often seated where Mr. Eliot was now installed. The situation therefore was one for which a regular convention existed, of quizzical dumbshow on the part of the incorrigible host, and stony stares back from me.

This very small room, in which Mr. Eliot had alighted, and in which he sat placidly smiling, was, allowance made for the comic side of Ezra's manic herding of talent, a considerable place. Dorothy Shakespeare had become Dorothy Pound and of course was in this dwarf room, too, nodding, with a quick jerk of the head, unquestioning approval of Ezra's sallies, or hieratically rigid as she moved delicately to observe the Kensingtonian Tea ritual. (Long habit in the paternal mansion responsible, she was a good turncoat *bourgeoise,* who wore her red cockade with a grim peasant gaucherie.) In any event, all social transactions were necessarily *intime.* One at a time was their rule for genius.

Mr. Eliot would presently be taken to a much larger place—where there would be more than just a crowded little triangle to sit in: not so important, yet an essential part of Ezra's exiguous social machine. For those not familiar with the hills and valleys of London, the event with which I opened took place practically at the foot of Notting Hill. Now almost at the top of that hill stood a squarish Victorian mansion, of no great size but highly respectable, within whose walls Ford Maddox Ford (known then as Hueffer) lived and entertained with Violet Hunt. A gate in a tall wall gave access to it, and

284

standing in the centre of a patch of grass, just visible from the pavement, was a large carving of Ezra by Breszka. Mr. Eliot would have to be taken there.

A number of people were to be met, certainly, belonging to the literary, theatrical, and occasionally monied, world at Hueffers (as it is better to call him, rather than Ford): for he was unspeakably gregarious. But Mr. Eliot would be taken around there primarily to be shown to Hueffer. The latter gentleman in all probability thought he wrote poems like *Prufrock* just as well if not better himself. A sort of Wild West turn, at whose hyperborean antics he could smile—that would be one thing. But it would be quite another for what was, as he saw it, a kind of Harvardian Rupert Brooke to make claims upon his tolerance. Such I imagine might be the situation arising from such a contact. But by South Lodge Mr. Eliot would have to pass, as part of initiatory proceedings.

There is no exacter manner available to me of dating my first encounter with Mr. Eliot than by stating that before the first number of *Blast* I did not know him, and he was not known I think to others: but that before the second number I knew him. *Blast No.* 1 was published in June 1914, Blast No. 2 in July 1915. In No. 2 I printed some poems of his *Preludes and Rhapsody on a Windy Night*. The last of the Preludes (No. 4) contains especially fine lines which I have often seen quoted.

> *I am moved by fancies that are curled*
> *Around these images, and cling:*
> *The notion of some infinitely gentle,*
> *Infinitely suffering thing.*
> *Wipe your hand across your mouth, and laugh;*
> *The worlds revolve like ancient women*
> *Gathering fuel in vacant lots.*

It is not secret that Ezra Pound exercised a very powerful influence upon Mr. Eliot. I do not have to define the nature of the influence, of course. Mr. Eliot was lifted out of his lunar alley-ways and fin de siècle nocturnes, into a massive region of verbal creation in contact with that astonishing didactic intelligence, that is all. *Gerontion* (1920) is a close relative of *Prufrock*, certain matters filtered through an aged mask in both cases, but Gerontion technically is 'school of Ezra.'

The didactic vocation was exercised by Ezra, unfortunately, in the void (with the exception of such a happy chance as his association with his fellow-countryman Mr. Eliot)—in a triangular box, as we have seen, practically at the foot of Notting Hill. Between Hueffer and himself there was a solid bond. Ezra 'believed in' Ford, who knew what he was talking about, praised the other's verses to the skies. And Ezra regarded it as typical—and very justly—that Hueffer should find no support in England for the *English Review*.

Although I bring the scene to life in which Mr. Eliot at that stage of his career found himself, it is the scene, and not Mr. Eliot I recreate.

Knowing the principal figure in it still so well does not make the recreation easier—though you would perhaps suppose it would. Some of these figures do not change much : others do. For instance, in 1938 when I was painting Ezra (the picture is now in the Tate) he swaggered in, coat-tails flying, a malacca cane out of the 'nineties aslant beneath his arm, the lion's head from the Scandinavian North-West thrown back. There was no conversation. He flung himself at full length into my best chair for that pose, closed and was motionless, and did not move for two hours by the clock. Ezra was not haggard, he looked quite well, but was exhausted.

'Go to it Wyndham!' he gruffled without opening his eyes, as soon as his mane of as yet entirely ungrizzled hair had adjusted itself to the cushioned chair-top. A reference to my portrait of Mr. Eliot, painted some months earlier, produced the remark that now I had a 'better subject to work from'. A mild and not unpleasing example of gasconade. But that was how I always found Ezra, full of bombast, kindness, but *always* in appearance the Westerner in excelsis. On the tips of his toes with aggressive vitality, till he dropped, or as good as. (A note here I should like to add : I have had experience of Ezra for a long time : in some respects he does not forget the teaching of Chinese sages.)

With Mr. Eliot it has always been quite the opposite. Appear-

286

ing at one's front door, on arriving at a dinner-rendezvous (I am thinking of the late thirties, not his more vernal years of course) his face would be haggard, he would seem at his last gasp. (Did he know?) To ask *him* to lie down for a short while at once was what I always felt I ought to do. However, when he had taken his place at a table, given his face a dry wash with his hands, and having had a little refreshment, Mr. Eliot would rapidly shed all resemblance to the harassed and exhausted refugee, in flight from some Scourge of God. Apparently a modest reserve of power, prudently set aside, would be drawn on. He would be as lively as ever he could be or any one need be—for of course it is not necessary to fly about on the tips of one's toes with one's scarf and coat-tails flying.

Immediately after World War One—I had not long left a military hospital and was restarting with a new studio—Mr. Eliot himself is, for me, much more distinct. For instance we went to the Loire and Brittany together—that holiday involving a meeting, the first for both of us, with James Joyce in Paris: after a stay at Saumer, and then the Breton coast in the Golfe de Vannes region.

The intermediate years—since he first sat in Pound's toy room—had greatly matured Mr. Eliot. The 'Gioconda' period seemed a thing of the past, the saturnine vein was strongly fed with the harsh spectacle of the times. He was an American who was in flight from the same thing that kept Pound over here, and with what had he been delected, as soon as he had firmly settled himself upon this side of the water. The spectacle of Europe committing suicide—just that.

The Hollow Men (of 1925) is generally considered Mr. Eliot's most successful attempt to make the paralysis and decay concrete for his contemporaries, in drained-out cadences and desiccated vocables. The date of the *Hollow Men* takes one on to the times when I was often with Mr. Eliot at the Schiffs, in Cambridge Square and Eastbourne, and in relaxation of a household where we were very much spoiled by our hosts, for my part for the last time I saw Mr. Eliot in a mood that was very young. There he would read his latest work. Even then in the early 'thirties, however, the haggard and exhausted mask of which I spoke earlier was seen nothing of. I must get back without delay to the foot of Notting Hill, in the first twelve months after the 'lights had gone out in Europe'.

Pound possessed in Miss Harriet Weaver, a very substantial auxiliary indeed. Her little office in Adelphi rather than South Lodge would be a place worth visiting for Mr. Eliot. Sympathy, as much as ambition, would cause him to prefer the active Quaker lady, editress, to the ex-editor Ford Madox Hueffer.

The Egoist was Miss Weaver's paper, but at the period of which I write you would rather have supposed that it belonged to Ezra Pound. *The Egoist* also on occasion published books. And the old files of *The Egoist* contain much work of Mr. Eliot's. This, I should suppose, was the first place where his work appeared in England. The way was also smoothed by Pound for *Prufrock's* debut in book form. So, for all his queerness at times, in spite of anything that may be said of Ezra, he is not only *himself* a great poet but has been of the most amazing use to other people. Let it not be forgotten for instance that it was he who was responsible for the all-important contact for James Joyce—namely Miss Weaver. It was *his* critical understanding, *his* generosity, involved in the detection and appreciation of the literary genius of James Joyce. It was through him that a very considerable sum of money was put at Joyce's disposal, at the critical moment.

Such is the career-side of Mr. Eliot's association with Ezra Pound. But he met in his company Imagists and others, several of those who at a later time wrote for him in *The Criterion*—Gould Fletcher, Aldington, Flint. And when I spoke of Ezra *transacting* his social life, there was nothing social for him that did not have a bearing upon the business of writing. If it had not it would have been dull. He was a man of Letters, in the marrow of his bones and down to the red follicles of his hair. He was a born revolutionary, a Trotsky of the written word and painted shape. Where he detected the slightest hint of a fractious disposition, expressing itself in verse or pigment, he became delirious. It was the schoolmaster—the missionary who instructed the incipient how to construct the infernal machine—he would spare no pains. He breathed Letters, ate Letters, dreamt

Letters. A very rare kind of man. To fall into the clutches of this benevolent mentor was not the making of Mr. Eliot—for he had already begun making himself, after quite a distinct fashion in Prufrock and other pieces. Here was a stiffening. Here was a variety of transformation, technical and otherwise, which it is not my specifically non-critical function to indicate.

Had it not been the earliest period of Mr. Eliot's life in literary circles in England, some account of which was required, the background would not have been dominated by one figure, as in this certainly has been the case. It always seems to be in this little triangular room, practically at the foot of Notting Hill, that I see Mr. Eliot. I recall entering it, for example, when on leave (a *bombardier*). Mr. Eliot was there—in the same place as the first time (there was nowhere else to sit however). After a little I found him examining me, his head to one side. I asked him what there was about me that puzzled him. He was wondering, he answered, whether the short hair suited me or not. (Before the army it had been thick and long?) My point is forcibly brought out by the fact that, at that time, I had no idea where Mr. Eliot lived. He appeared—he often was to be found—in the triangle, the supreme figure of Ezra a few feet away of course.

CHAPTER VII

An 'Age Group' meets Itself

The three principal figures on the narrative side of this book being now presented to you, in the guise that they first presented themselves to me, I will proceed with the famous tale of the old pair of shoes.

James Joyce, having disposed of his foreign-bred offspring, Ezra's embarrassing present, and his family arrangements for the evening, turned to us with the air of a man who has divested himself of a few minor handicaps, and asked us where we would like to dine and did we know Paris well, or would we commit ourselves to him and allow him to conduct us to a restaurant where he dined, from time to time, not far from where we were just then, and at which it was possible to get a good meal enough, though he had not been there lately.

We replied that we would gladly go with him to the restaurant he mentioned; and so he led the way in a very business-like fashion : he bustled on ahead of us—if the word bustled can be used of a very spare and light-footed cosmopolitan gentleman : he selected a table, took up the Menu before we had sat down, asked us what we liked, inspecting the violet scrawl to ascertain what was available in the matter of *plats du jour*. And before we could say Jack Robinson he had ordered a large and cleverly arranged dinner as far as possible for all palates, and with a great display of inside knowledge of the insides of civilized men and the resources of the cuisine of France, discovering what wines we were by way of liking if any. And he had asked for a bottle to start with to introduce the soup. And so on, through a first-class French repast, until we had finished, he pushed on, our indefatigable host : then, at a moment when we were not paying particular attention, he called for the bill : and before either of us could forestall him, he had whisked out of his breast pocket a handful of hundred-franc notes, and paid for this banquet; the wine, the liqueurs, the coffee, and added to it, it was evident, a lordly pourboire. Nor was it ever possible for T. S. Eliot or myself to pay for the smallest thing from that time onwards.

If we were in a taxicab with James Joyce, out he would spring in front of us. And before even we reached the pavement the fare was settled and the cabman was pocketing a disproportionately massive tip: whereas in a café no beer or coffee, whoever had ordered it, was ever paid for by anyone but the eminent recipient of the parcel of old shoes. Nor was there any means, whether that of physical violence or urgent persuasion, to redress this in the long run most burdensome balance in favour of us.

We had to pay his 'Irish pride' for the affair of the old shoes. That was it! He would not let us off. He was entirely unrelenting and we found it impossible to outmanoeuvre him.

Eliot and myself agreed that short of paying for meals before they were ordered, or knocking Joyce down every time he rushed forward to settle the taxicab fare, and holding him down while the other paid, there was no means of escaping. Ours was the female rôle of economic exemption, with its attendant humiliation, if regarded from the ancient standpoint of masculine convention. When alone with me Joyce would occasionally relax to the extent of allowing me to pay for an occasional drink of my own, never his, however. And even this was much later on.

Towards T. S. Eliot Joyce maintained a punctilious reserve. In alluding to him, with me, he would say 'Your friend Mr. Eliot,' as if Eliot had been an obscure family friend, with whom I happened to be travelling, and who, out of polite humanity, must be suffered to accompany us. As to mentioning his writings, or as to ever a passing reference to him as *a poet*— that was the last thing that it ever occurred to Joyce to do, it seemed. Eliot perhaps had been accepted as the messenger sent by Ezra Pound with a pair of old shoes; to whom, if you like, out of courtesy to the good if misguided Ezra, Joyce offered hospitality. I was a different matter. But then, in any case, it was not I who had been the bearer of old shoes!

What part the old shoes really played in the comedy I do not know. Contemptuous, tolerant, discreetly correct, the author of *The Portrait of the Artist* did not seem best pleased with what was not a pleasantry, but something else, of course—though exactly *what* it might be I am unable to decide. I do not suppose, for instance, that, in a spirit of heavy mischief, Ezra in fact calculated, in handing Eliot the securely wrapped-up parcel, upon these *particular* social effects. Or had he perhaps? Why no : it would have taken a different mind from that of Pound to foresee the stilted occasion, the ceremony of the handing over of the brown-paper parcel; that atmosphere of highly continental or cosmopolitan formality, of Irish social pomp, of solemnly-smiling transatlantic reticence, on the part of this biliously handsome paladin, and myself there genuinely uninterested at the unpacking, an unmoved observer! On the contrary I believe this little matter arose from the romantic charity of a man who, on a certain side, is unsusceptible to the influences of the external world of human stimulus and response. It was the work of a charitable egotist.

When I remarked that James Joyce betrayed no knowledge of the identity of 'Your friend Mr. Eliot', that statement demands some qualification. There was, indirectly, one occasion, during our first meeting, upon which he showed that he was conscious of Eliot's existence, apart from the fact of his happening to be travelling in France in my company.

This was when, as we sat together in the restaurant to which he had taken us (having breathlessly and with overpowering host-at-all-costly resolution ordered a full-course meal) he said to us—toasting us obliquely and ever so airily as he tasted his Château La Tour Rose with lung and tongue at once—'It appears that I have the melancholy advantage of being the eldest of the band,' or words to that effect. Band was not the word, nor group, but I cannot recall it nearer than this. He referred, of course, to the literary band, or group, comprised within the critical fold of Ezra Pound—the young, the 'New', group of writers assembled in Miss Weaver's *Egoist* just before and during the War. And of course Pound, Joyce, Eliot and myself

292

were all within about five years of each other in the matter of age. At that time I imagine Eliot was about thirty, Joyce about thirty-six and I a year or two younger than him. So far as the classification of people by ages goes, we did certainly make, or we do make if you like a perfect 'age-class'.

Surely the vanity of classification, however, was never better exemplified, than in the persons of these four *Zeitgenossen*! We are all familiar with the solemn groupification that occurs every year or so of, usually, a half-dozen 'poets' or artists, introduced to the world by their impresario as the team chosen (by him if not by destiny) to represent the absolutely newest generation. To-day these teams age and disintegrate with alarming rapidity. But new ones take their place. And always the rationale of their assemblage is that their members were all born of women about the same time.

Well, sure enough, the birth years of Mr. Pound's little circle, including Mr. Pound himself, were 'all sprinkled up and down', as Eliot once remarked to me, 'the Eighties of the last century'. And if being born in a stable makes you a horse, why then being born in the same years is liable, perhaps, to make you an identical human product. A mechanical theory at the best, for the purposes of the literary pigeonholing of a complex society this method is useless. According to this simple-hearted rule, Herr Adolf Hitler is as like as two peas with any Cantonese or Peruvian born at the exact minute of the Eighties of the last Century at which Herr Hitler saw the light—irrespective of place, traditions, individual ancestry, glandular, nervous, and other bodily make-up—race, religion and what not! Here we have the time-philosopher's classification with a vengeance!

But in the first place, even the *time* factor does not accord with this classification. In the Atlas Mountains to-day, or in the Tibetan hinterland, the inhabitants are anything but *Zeitgenossen* of the citizens of Chicago or of Fascist Rome. They are existing in what is the equivalent of our European feudal age. They are the contemporaries of Bayard and La Palice—or of Roland and Oliver—much more than of Litvinov and Count Ciano.

So, as to the little age-group implicitly recognized in James

Joyce's remark—with a solemn sidelong wrinkling of the nose and eye, meant for that busy Manager, and propagandist, Ezra —four people more dissimilar in every respect than himself, myself, Pound and Eliot respectively, it would be difficult to find. There is only one sense in which any such a grouping of us acquires some significance—we all got started on our careers before the War. This was, I believe, an advantage. In other respects, Joyce brought up by the Jesuits—in Ireland—in the 'Celtic Twilight'—trained as a medico—thereafter exiled in Trieste and Switzerland, and becoming an Italianate Irishman: what a different set of circumstances are those to the origins for instance and early environment of Eliot? Born under the shadow of the famous New England puritanism, but transplanted to a city south of the Mason and Dixon Line, returning to Harvard and sent into another hemisphere to get a polish at Oxford, and subsequently drafted to Germany to finish this complicated process of training. Hardly can you compel such disparities at all into a class. Substitute place for time, and suppose two people born upon the same square foot of ground, one in the age of William the Conqueror and one in 1937—one a Negro and one a Norman. It would be in vain to classify them according to identity of *place,* and hope for any fruitful results.

CHAPTER VIII

Our Lady of the Sleeping-Cars

Eliot and myself remained in Paris for some days, I forget how many. All of our time was passed in the hospitable company of James Joyce. Paris might have been his demesne, though he had only been there a month—he only knew a few streets at that period and would lose himself between Invalides and the Chamber of Deputies and was uncertain of his whereabouts even in the Latin Quarter, once he was off his beat.

Our stay was one long fête. Except for our hotel bill—which he made no attempt, as far as I know, to settle—we lived free of charge. A party would be suggested by us: and although of course Joyce paid for it, it was still *our* party. And then we could not refuse to accept a return banquet, to cap our banquet; when, in the nature of things, and hoping that *this* time we might outwit this implacable *payer,* we proposed yet another meeting—on our own ground, at some restaurant of our own choosing; but always with the same result.

To the last Eliot was treated distantly, as I have said. And this did not make these transactions any the more palatable for 'poor Tom'.

'He does not take much notice of me!' he drawled one day, with sardonic resignation, when we were discussing the problem of how to stand our eminent colleague a glass of beer—agreeing, of course, that in fact it was a feat beyond our powers, for, with the best grace we could, we had admitted defeat by this time. 'But *you* might I should have thought do something about it,' he said, with heavy melancholy mischief.

'I have expostulated with him in private and in public,' I answered. 'He does not appear to understand. He thinks he is obliged to pay. He has some idea that he *must.*'

I encountered, a little later on, a similar phenomenon to this in Venice. There I met Mr. Francis Meynell for the first time. I was introduced to him by Osbert Sitwell, at a large café in the Square of St. Mark's one evening. There were about ten people at our table I should think, and I was astonished to find after a time that Mr. Meynell always paid for the successive rounds of drinks.

On expressing some reluctance to continue under this régime of enigmatical patronage, and making some expressive movement, indicative of my intention to break the spell, I was stopped by Osbert Sitwell, who whispered, in a purring, nasal, *chuchotement* which gives a special flavour to that gentleman's asides, that it was 'no use'.

This puzzled me still more. And as Osbert Sitwell remarked that I was still not satisfied that all was as it should be, he explained, still under his breath, that Francis Meynell felt obliged, on account of his political opinions, to be responsible for the bill. Mr. Meynell was 'very sensitive' that was all I really understood. He was an outstanding Radical, so it was a case of *noblesse oblige*.

The logic of what he told me appeared entirely satisfactory to Osbert Sitwell, and I raised no further objections, though completely mystified.

Here at all events is what looks like a clear case of the same sort of fixed idea; namely that refreshments *must* be paid for by one member of a party and by no other member : indeed that drinks must be stood to all within sight : that there is *a duty* to do so, imposed upon a particular person.

As to what I am persuaded was the true motive of the embarrassing liberality on the part of James Joyce, to return to that, it never I think, occurred to Eliot to allow for the emotional weight of the Pair of Old Shoes. He put it down to an attack of objectionable openhandedness, to which, as an Irishman, he supposed, Mr. Joyce was probably subject; and which our presence stimulated to an unprecedented degree. Joyce was showing off, he was probably always showing off : and his native aggressiveness caused him to affect to be icily unaware that he was in this way entertaining, nay over-entertaining, an angel, an angelic, an archangelic poet of great promise, with

296

a brood of brooding Prufrocks behind him.

'I find our friend,' said I, 'very affable and easy don't you, if a shade stilted?' But Eliot found him definitely burdensome, and *arrogant*. Very arrogant.

'I do not think he is *arrogant*,' I said, astonished at this description of Pound's proud protégé, who seemed to me to be a civil, unassuming man enough, of agreeable and accommodating manners, except for his obsession regarding economic independence, which was harmless after all. If he really got a kick out of dashing on the tips of the little patent leather shoes (so unlike those delapidated stogies dispatched by Ezra) towards the desk of a restaurant and putting us under obligations, according to suburban money-canons, well, there was no great harm at all.

'He may not seem so!' Eliot answered, in his grim Bostonian growl. 'He may not seem arrogant, no.'

'You think he is as proud as Lucifer?'

'I would not say Lucifer!' Eliot was on his guard at once, at this loose use of the surname of the Evil Principle.

'You would not say Lucifer? Well I daresay he may be under the impression that he is being "as proud as Lucifer", or some bogtrotting humbug of that order. What provincials they are, bless their beastly brogues!'

'Provincials—yes!' Eliot agreed with contemptuous unction. 'Provincials.'

'However he is most polite.'

'He is polite.'

'I have never succeeded in getting out of the door *behind* him, have you? He is very *You First*. He is very *After you!*'

'Oh yes. He is polite, he is polite enough. But he is exceedingly arrogant. Underneath. That is why he is so polite. I should be better pleased if he were less polite.' Eliot was very grim.

'I personally don't care if he *is* arrogant—all I ask, in the words of the New England literary chanty, is "a little goddarned seevility and not much of that!" But I should be surprised if he is really arrogant.'

'No-o?' Eliot was impressed by my persistence. 'You may of course be right. It doesn't matter.'

'Not much really.'

I puzzled over this charge of 'arrogance'—it was quite a new reading for me of this perhaps after all enigmatical discovery of Ezra's, who only a few hours before had sung us a love song, all about a young lady who was ill, who indeed was dying, whose death would be the heartbreak, the despair, of the male voice, all of the most disarming passionate bel canto.— I could not see, frankly, where the arrogance came in. This Dublin gondolier might be poor and proud, but he could not be arrogant. That did not go with gondolier.

There was one occasion when Joyce did not pay for our food; but that was because it was not in a restaurant but in a private house. It was when he took us to the house of a friend of his, a Belgian journalist. This Belgian journalist's name it will not be necessary to mention, but a French mulatto lived at his flat as the lover of his wife, so he said, and he was very ribald in our presence about it.

'Daniel, vous savez, couche avec ma femme!' he announced at lunch. 'Ah salaud va!' he apostrophized the mulatto. 'Dis! Tu couches avec ma femme, n'est ce pas, Daniel?'

We looked astonished, out of politeness. Joyce raised his eyebrows with extreme detached urbanity, and most courteously wrinkled up his brow in a bland perplexity.

'Mais oui!' our host continued, noting our response. 'She doesn't want me to say that, but he does sleep with her all the same. Isn't it true Daniel, you old blackguard? Isn't it true? *Don't* you sleep with my wife? Of course you do.'

Daniel, the mulatto cuckoo-in-the-nest, who worked as a clerk in the War Ministry, and was a small quiet, dark-complexioned gentleman, of the most correct *abord,* turned upon the dully-blushing french Hausfrau, expostulating.

'Mais non, mais quoi! c'est trop fort! Ecoutez Madame!' he began to protest, without disturbing himself very much it is true. 'Cannot you contrive to prevent your husband from making these assertions?'

'Moi!' the wife asked. *'Moi!'*—pointing helplessly at a

comfortable Eighteenth Century bust that protruded over her plate. 'Do so if you can yourself monsieur. Don't ask me to I beg of you!'

The husband was jubilant. He laughed like a cuckolded hyena. With a crazy zest at the exposure of this curious little triangle which he sheltered beneath his roof, he plunged into analysis. At all costs he must show off the curiosities of this exotic *ménage à trois*.

'Do you know why Daniel appeals to her?' he shouted at us, beaming fiercely upon his wife. 'Can you guess how it is he comes to fascinate her?'

We sat abashed, conveying by our silence that we were incapable of hazarding a guess.

'Can't you see? It is plain enough however. C'est parcequ'il est nègre! Evidement! *It is because he is a nigger!*'

He threw himself back in his chair to enjoy our discomfiture at this masterly solution of the conundrum. He carried his eyes from the downcast face of Daniel, busy with his food, to ours, likewise evading his triumphant stare.

'They all fall for niggers. All! No it is no use protesting Emmeline! They are all the same. All women. Yes—*and those who protest most that they have a horror of a horrid black skin* —they are those who secretly like niggers the best! It's a fact.'

Daniel half rose in his place, waving a napkin, as if as a signal of distress.

'Ma-dame!' he vociferated indignantly. 'Really your husband to-day is beside himself! Can you do nothing about him? Is it impossible to curb him?'

'Quite impossible, as you know,' the wife answered. 'He is incorrigible. It is *ces messieurs* that excite him. I have never seen him so excited.'

'Nor I—happily!' Daniel shrugged his strictly horizontal African shoulders, and slowly resumed his seat, with a sedate *moue,* and *en hochant la tête,* casting a rapid glance of comprehensive protest which included *us.* As if we, as guests, were *en fin de compte,* in some way responsible for our host. He may have considered that we were encouraging him. I alone responded to this uncalled for glance of the outrageous mulatto, who, as a fact, was merely a colonial French métis, or an African Jew, from Alexandria perhaps.

'Our host is wrong about the negro,' I remarked.

'How *wrong!*' roared the Belgian, in indignant amazement. 'How am I wrong?'

'Some women prefer blonds,' I replied.

'Jamais!'

'It is only the Blond Beasts among our *Frauenzimmer* who care for the Black Man,' I declared.

'Tu as tort! Ah! Mais tu as tort!'

'No. Your wife is of a type who prefers a barbers-block in sugar-blond, complete with lemon moustaches of spun silk. That is *her type*. I do not say she does.'

The Belgian was uproariously grateful for this contribution to the discussion.

'My wife? A blond? She vomits at a blond!' he stormed. 'She loves only the tang of the African integument. A dash of the tar brush she *insists* on. It is a fact.'

'He is mad!' remarked his wife.

'And yet all the time she affects to find niggers repulsive! You will not credit it. And *what is more*, she *believes* what she says! That is what is extremely curious.' He gloated over this paradox. 'She really is persuaded that all coloured men are distasteful to her! N'est ce pas, c'est curieux? It is odd is it not? Tiens! I would not mind betting—I will *swear* she was surprised just now to hear that she slept with Daniel. Yes yes! She does not know that she does. I will swear it. She is hardly conscious of it. She thinks he lives here because he is a friend of *mine*. But he—Daniel now, *he* knows all about it. He is deep, is Daniel.—Thou art deep, is it not, Daniel! Speak!'

'I shall have to go,' said Daniel. 'If I stop here much longer I shall think I have got into an asylum for the alienated.'

'Asylum. Yes. Asylum.'

'I'm not particular,' objected Daniel. 'But I like a little method in people's madness. Even nonsense has its rules.'

'Daniel! You are a deep dog. Dirty and deep, Daniel. Are you not ashamed of being an aphrodisiac? Speak! Cauchemar!'

And so he went on for some time. This strange Belgian

300

confided in me, on several occasions, that recently he had contracted the habit of making love *to his wife*. It was a new experience. This had occurred since he had become possessed of a Russian mistress. This girl was well known in the quarter under the title of 'Nôtre Dame des Wagons-Lits'. She was called Nôtre Dame des Wagons-Lits because it was reported that during the communist revolution in Russia she had been shunted in a Wagon Lit, in which she was of course escaping, into a siding at a provincial station. The town had just been captured by the Red Army. While marooned in the siding, an entire bolshevik regiment—some said an army corps—had outraged her. She had after this startling experience escaped to Paris, to study art and sit in cafes, pointed out to newcomers as Our Lady of the Sleeping Cars. There more regiments deployed. In spite of her morose ugliness, she continued to be the victim of mass-ravishment. Or so she said; for her celebrated contretemps in Russia there was only one witness, herself. The Belgian regarded himself somewhat in the light of a uniquely honoured general-officer bringing up the rear, but very proud of his blowsy conquest, with her infantile jewish eyes of watery blue, her tremendous sombrero and heirloomish ear-rings of barbaric bric-à-brac.

As to Daniel, well he was tremendously proud of Daniel. He was persuaded that his domestic triangle was of a very chic geometry indeed. Daniel was a cult of his entirely and in more ways than one. It was really he who had succumbed to the 'Nigger'. I always believed, when I knew him better, that his wife was innocent of any interest, even, in Daniel, whom she suffered as a lodger of her husband's, but otherwise would have far preferred as an occasional visitor, rather than as a permanent unpaying pensionnaire. Really it was the husband over whom he had cast the spell and (intellectually) subjugated. Of this the wife was doubtless well aware. For he had an inordinate admiration for Daniel as a poet. This was expressed with even more vehemence than that displayed in showing him off as the conqueror in this connubial field.

'Il est un grand poète!' he would thunder, bearded in the French fashion, of stocky flemish build, straddling in front of one. 'Mais oui, mais oui—un très grand poète!'

On one occasion he stopped, as we were walking up the hill of Saint Michel, and asked me if I knew what Daniel had written—the greatest thing Daniel had ever written? Did I know it? I confessed that I did not. He then glared at me, and I leant against a tree.

'Vous ne le savez pas!' he said, dropping his voice.

He told me that it was in Daniel's latest book of verse. I bowed my head. He fixed me with his eye then and solemnly repeated the following two lines:

*Ai-je cru un seul instant
Dans la realité du monde!*

I still leant against the tree, smoking my pipe. '*Thus* I confute it?' my pipe seemed to say to him, in Johnsonian defiance. For he took a step towards me, peering up at me with an alarming steadfastness, as if I had questioned the unreality of the world, and the genius of Daniel, in the same rebellious breath.

'Ai-je cru un seul instant,' he whispered, scarcely trusting the accents of the Muse to his coarse organs of speech, 'dans la realité du monde!'

'C'est bien beau!' I said.

'C'est fou!' he bellowed, the eyes starting out of his head. He dropped his voice again. 'C'est formidable!' he rolled out, in a sullen roar.

We proceeded, in silence, up the street. He stopped once more.

'C'est fou!' he said again.

'En effet!' said I.

*'Ai-je cru un seul instant
Dans la realité du monde.'*

said he.

I wagged my head. And we proceeded up the boulevard. But in matters of aesthetic James Joyce and this Belgian man of letters did not see eye to eye. The latter had shrewdly realized that Joyce was a big noise, just beginning in his own corner of

302

this 'unreal' world of ours, and he had, I believe, translated a chapter of *Ulysses*. He had the gift of tongues, and once had functioned as a guide in his early days in Paris. Joyce had become acquainted with this ex-Cooksman for some propagandist or publicity purposes; because he had written, or was about to write, dope for the Paris newspapers; but whenever they discussed any matter of literature or art they clashed, invariably: and on one occasion, I remember Joyce very severely reciting back at him the ordinances of Aristotle:

'by pity and terror, etc.'

which he had by heart (out of Butcher's translation, for use I suppose on such occasions).

This singularly enraged our sturdy Belgian journalist. The mere name of Aristotle was quite sufficient to upset him for an entire evening. He would burst out from time to time until we left in the small hours: 'Vous et votre Aristote, James Joyce! You and your Aristotle!'

But Joyce stood his ground, or Aristotle's. His manner was cold and distant. His superiority tried the patience of the emancipated cicerone.

'Moi—je m'en fou d'Aristote!' he vociferated. 'What do I care for Aristotle? What has Aristotle got to do with the life going on in the street outside here—tell me that!'

'Why should he have nothing to do with it?' responded Joyce, with the quiet superiority that distinguished him, in his staid, copybook French.

'Why *should* he? What *has* he! To hell with Aristotle! All you English are the same! There you sit, the three of you. Aristotle means nothing to you, you talk about that sort of thing. Even the best of you. Yes even you, Wyndham Lewis— *you* are quite capable of talking to me about Aristotle!'

'No I am not!' I cried immediately. 'There I must defend myself! I should never dream of doing such a thing!'

CHAPTER IX

Cantleman's Spring-mate[*]

Cantleman walked in the strenuous fields, steam rising from them as though from an exertion, dissecting the daisies specked in the small-wood, the primroses on the banks, the marshy lakes, and all God's creatures. The heat of a heavy premature Summer was cooking the little narrow belt of earth-air, causing everything innocently to burst its skins, bask abjectly and profoundly. Everything was enchanged with itself, and with everything else. The horses considered the mares immensely appetising masses of quivering shiny flesh; was there not something of 'je ne sais quoi' about a mare, that no other beast's better half possessed? The birds with their little gnarled feet, and beaks made for fishing worms out of the mould, or the river, would have considered Shelley's references to the skylark —or any other poet's paeans to their species—as lamentably inadequate to describe the beauty of birds! The female bird, for her particular part, reflected that, in spite of the ineptitude of her sweetheart's latest song, which he insisted on deafening her with, never seemed to tire of, and was so persuaded that she liked as much as he did himself, and although outwardly she remained critical and vicious: that all the same and nevertheless, chock, chock, peep, peep, he was a fluffy object from which certain satisfaction could be derived? And both the male and the female reflected together as they stood a foot or so apart looking at each other with one eye, and at the landscape with the other, that of all nourishment the red earth-worm was the juiciest and sweetest! The sow, as she watched her hog, with his splenetic energy, and guttural articulation, a sound between content and complaint, not noticing the untidy habits of both of them, gave a sharp grunt of sex-hunger, and jerked rapidly

[*] *Cantleman's Spring Mate* and *War Baby* which follows it were not included in the original edition of *Blasting and Bombardiering*

304

towards Him. The only jarring note in this vast mutual admiration society was the fact that many of its members showed their fondness for their neighbour in an embarrassing way: that is they killed and ate them. But the weaker were so used to dying violent deaths and being eaten that they worried very little about it.—The West was gushing up a harmless volcano of fire, obviously intended as an immense dreamy nightcap.

Cantleman in the midst of his cogitation on surrounding life, surprised his faithless and unfriendly brain in the act of turning over an object which humiliated his mediation. He found that he was wondering whether at his return through the village lying between him and the Camp, he would see the girl he had passed there three hours before. At that time he had not begun his philosophizing, and without interference from conscience, he had noticed the redness of her cheeks, the animal fulness of the child-bearing hips, with an eye as innocent as the bird or the beast. He laughed without shame or pleasure, lit his pipe and turned back towards the village.—His fieldboots were covered with dust: his head was wet with perspiration and he carried his cap, in an unmilitary fashion, in his hand. In a week he was leaving for the Front, for the first time. So his thoughts and sensations all had as a philosophic background, the prospect of death. The Infantry, and his commission, implied death or mutilation unless he were very lucky. He had not a high opinion of his luck. He was pretty miserable at the thought, in a deliberate, unemotional way. But as he realised this he again laughed, a similar sound to that that the girl had caused.—For what was he unhappy about? He wanted to remain amongst his fellow insects and beasts, which were so beautiful, did he then: Well well! On the other hand, who was it that told him to do anything else? After all, supposing the values they attached to each other of 'beautiful', 'interesting', 'divine', were unjustified in many cases on cooler observation;—nevertheless birds were more beautiful than pigs: and if pigs were absurd and ugly, rather than handsome, and possibly chivalrous, as they imagine themselves; then equally the odour of the violet was pleasant, and there was nothing offensive about most trees. The newspapers were the things that stank most on earth, and human beings anywhere were the most ugly and offensive of the brutes because of the confusion caused by their consciousness. Had it not been for that unmaterial gift that some bungling or wild hand had bestowed, our sisters and brothers would be no worse than dogs and sheep. That they could not reconcile their little meagre streams of sublimity with the needs of animal life should not be railed at. Well then, should not the sad amalgam, all it did, all it willed, all it demanded, be thrown over, for the fake and confusion that it was, and should not such as possessed a greater quantity of that wine of reason, retire, metaphorically, to the wilderness, and sit forever in a formal and gentle elation, refusing to be disturbed?—Should such allow himself to be disturbed by the quarrels of Jews, the desperate perplexities, resulting in desperate dice throws, of politicians, the crack-jaw and unreasoning tumult?

On the other hand, Cantleman had a more human, as well as a little more divine understanding, than those usually on his left and right, and he had had, not so long ago, conspicuous hopes that such a conjecture might produce the human entirely, if that there were to be brought off. His present occupation, the trampling boots upon his feet, the belt that crossed his back and breast was his sacrifice, his compliment to the animal.

He then began dissecting his laugh, comparing it to the pig's grunt and the bird's cough. He laughed again several times in order to listen to it.

At the village he met the girl, this time with a second girl. He stared at her 'in such a funny way' that she laughed. He once more laughed the same sound as before, and bid her good evening. She immediately became civil. Enquiries about the village, and the best way back to the camp across the marsh, put in as nimble and at the same time rustic a form as he could contrive, lay the first tentative brick of what might become the dwelling of a friend, a sweetheart, a ghost, anything in the absurd world! He asked her to come and show him a short cut she had indicated.

'I couldn't. My mother's waiting for *me!*' In a rush of expostulation and semi-affected alarm. However, she concluded in a minute or two, that she could.

306

He wished that she had been some Anne Garland, the lady whose lips were always flying open like a door with a defective latch. He had made Anne's acquaintance under distressing circumstances.

On his arrival at Gideon brook, the mighty brand-new camp on the edge of the marsh, he found that his colleague in charge of the advance party had got him a bed-space in a room with four officers of another regiment. It had seemed impossible that there were any duller men than those in the mess of his particular battalion : but it was a dullness he had become accustomed to.

He saw his four new companions with a sinking of the heart, and steady gnawing anger at such concentrations of furious foolishness.

Cantleman did not know their names, and he disliked them in order as follows :

A. he hated because he found him a sturdy shortish young man with a bull-like stoop and energetic rush in his walk, with flat feet spread out to left and right, and slightly bowed legs. This physique was enhanced by his leggings : and not improved, though hidden, in his slacks. He had a swarthy and vivacious face, with a sort of cunning, and insolence painted on it. His cheeks had a broad carmine flush on general sallowness. The mind painted on this face for the perusal of whoever had the art of such lettering, was as vulgar stud, in Cantleman's judgement, as could be found. To see this face constantly was like *hearing* perpetually a cheap and foolish music.

B. he disliked, because, being lean and fresh-coloured, with glasses, he stank, to Cantleman's nose, of Jack London, Summer Numbers magazines, had flabby Suburban Tennis, flabby clerkship in inert, though still prosperous city offices. He brought a demoralizing dullness into the room with him, with a brisk punctiliousness, several inches higher from the ground than A.

C. he resented for the sullen stupidity with which he moved about, the fat having settled at the bottom of his cheeks, and pulled the corners of his mouth down, from sheer stagnation. His accent dragged the listener through the larger of slums of Scotland, harrowing him with the bestial cheerfulness of morose religion and poverty. The man was certainly, from every point of view, education, character, intelligence, far less suited to hold a commission than most privates in his platoon.—Alas that the stock of gentlemen even, was so limited.

D. reproduced the characteristics of the other three, in different quantities: his only personal contribution being a senile sing-song voice from the North, and a blond beam, or partially toothless grin, for a face.

When ten days before, Cantleman had been dropped into their midst, they had all looked up, (for it was always all, they having the inseparability of their kind), with friendly welcome, as brother officers should. He avoided their eyes, and sat amongst them for a few days, reading *The Trumpet-Major*, belonging to B. He had even seemed to snatch Hardy away, as though B. had no business to possess such books. Then they avoided his eyes as though an animal disguised as an officer and gentleman had got into their room for whom, therein, *The Trumpet-Major* and nothing else exercised fascination. He came among them suddenly, and not appearing to see them, settled down into a morbid intercourse with a romantic abstraction. The Trumpet-Major, it is true, was a soldier, that is why he was there. But he was an imaginary one, and imbedded in the passionate affairs of the village of a mock-country, and distant time. Cantleman bit the flesh at the side of his thumb, as he surveyed the Yeomanry Cavalry revelling in the absent farmer's house, and the infantile Farnes Hercules with the boastfulness of the Red explaining to his military companions the condescensions of his infatuation. Anne Garland stood in the moonlight, and Loveday hesitated to reveal his rival, weighing a rough chivalry against self interest.

Cantleman eventually decamped with *The Trumpet-Major*, taking him across to Havre, and B. never saw his book again. Cantleman had also tried to take a book away from A. (a book incompatible with A.'s vulgar physique). But A. had snatched it back, and mounted guard surlily and cunningly over it.

In his present rustic encounter, then, he was influenced in his feelings towards the first shepherdess by memories of Wessex heroines, and the something more that being the daughter of a

308

landscape painter would give. Anne imbued with the delicacy of the Mill, filled his mind to the injury of this crude marsh-plant. But he had his programme. Since he was forced back, by his logic and body, among the madness of natural things, he would live up to his part.

The young woman had, or had given herself, the unlikely name of Stella. In the narrow road where they got away from the village, Cantleman put his arm round Stella's waist and immediately experienced all the sensations that he had been divining in the creatures around him; the horse, the bird, the pig. The way in which Stella's hips stood out, the solid blood-heated expanse on which his hand lay, had the amplitude and flatness of a mare. Her lips had at once no practical significance, but only the aesthetic blandishments of a bull-like flower. With the gesture of a fabulous Faust he drew her against him, and kissed her with a crafty gentleness.

Cantleman turned up that evening in his quarters in a state of baffling good-humour. He took up *The Trumpet-Major* and was soon surrounded by the breathing and scratching of his room-mates, reading and writing. He chuckled somewhere where Hardy was funny. At this human noise the others fixed their eyes on him in sour alarm. He gave another, this time gratuitous, chuckle. They returned with disgust at his habits, his peculiarity, to what he considered their maid-servant's fiction and correspondence. Oh Christ, what abysms! Oh Christ, what abysms! Cantleman shook noisily in the wicker chair like a dog or a fly-blown old gentleman.

Once more on the following evening he was out in the fields, and once more his thoughts were engaged in recapitulations.— The miraculous camouflage of Nature did not deceive this observer. He saw everywhere the gun-pits and the 'nests of death'. Each puff of green leaves he knew was in some way as harmful as the burst of a shell. Decay and ruins, it is true, were soon covered up, but there was yet that parallel, and the sight of things smashed and corrupted. In the factory town ten miles away to the right, whose smoke could be seen, life was just as dangerous for the poor, and as uncomfortable, as for the soldier in his trench. The hypocrisy of Nature and the hypocrisy of War were the same. The only safety in life was for the man with the soft job. But that fellow was not conforming to life's conditions. He was life's paid man, and had the mark of the sneak. He was making too much of life, and too much out of it. He, Cantleman, did not want to owe anything to life, or enter into league or understanding with her. The thing was either to go out of existence : or, failing that, remain in it unreconciled, indifferent to Nature's threat, consorting openly with her enemies, making war within her war upon her servants. In short, the spectacle of the handsome English spring produced nothing but ideas of defiance in Cantleman's mind.

As to Stella, she was a sort of Whizbang. With a treachery worthy of a Hun, Nature tempted him towards her. He was drugged with delicious appetites. Very well! He would hoist the Unseen Powers with his own petard. He could throw back Stella where she was discharged from (if it were allowable, now, to change her into a bomb) first having relieved himself of this humiliating gnawing and yearning in his blood.

As to Stella, considered as an unconscious agent, all women were contaminated with Nature's hostile power and might be treated as spies or enemies. The only time they could be trusted, or were likely to stand up to Nature and show their teeth, was as mothers. So he approached Stella with as much falsity as he could master.

At their third meeting he brought her a ring. Her melting gratitude was immediately ligotted with long arms, full of the contradictory and offending fire of Spring. On the warm earth consent flowed up into her body from all the veins of the landscape.

That night he spat out, in gushes of thick delicious rage, all the lust that had gathered in his body. The nightingale sang ceaselessly in the small wood at the top of the field where they lay. He grinned up towards it as he noticed it, and once more turned to the devouring of his mate. He bore down on her as though he wished to mix her body into the soil, and pour his seed into a more methodless matter, the brown phalanges of floury land. As their two bodies shook and melted together, he felt that he was raiding the bowels of Nature : he was proud that he could remain deliberately aloof, and gaze bravely, like a minute insect, up at the immense and melancholy night, with all its mad nightingales, piously folded small brown wings in a million nests, night-working stars, and misty useless watchmen. —They got up at last, she went furtively back to her home : Cantleman on his walk to camp, had a smile of severe satisfaction on his face. It did not occur to him that his action might be supremely unimportant as far as Stella was concerned. He had not even asked himself if, had he not been there that night, someone else might have been there in his place. He was also convinced that the laurels were his, and that Nature had come off badly.—He was still convinced of this when he received six weeks afterwards in France, a long appeal from Stella, telling him that she was going to have a child. She received no answer to that or any subsequent letter. Cantleman received with great regularity in the trenches, and read them all through from beginning to end, without comment of any sort.—And when he beat a German's brains out it was with the same impartial malignity that he had displayed in the English night with his Spring-mate. Only he considered there too that he was in some way outwitting Nature, and had no adequate realization of the extent to which evidently the death of a Hun was to the advantage of the world.

CHAPTER X

The War Baby

The West Berks Hotel dominated a Military Avenue. Fifty yards from its door was the Guard Room of the Flying Corps. A boy sentry marched up and down its twenty yards of covered porch. When an officer passed, he faced the front with a series of stamps, stepped forward, and slapped the pistol holster at his side. At the conclusion of this rumpus, at which he did not look, the Officer would raise his hand languidly in front of his right eye. The boy sentry then stamped loudly as though in anger, and walked fiercely up and down for several minutes as though to work off his discontent. He then stood at ease and waited for the next Officer, when the same scene was repeated.

The Hall of the West Berks Hotel was like a theatrical store. It contained a variety of military properties. There were airmen's leather helmets, perpendicular Russian infantry caps, swords of all sorts, airy khaki forage caps. The Russian army air students were as proportionately more picturesque than their slogging earth comrades as our airmen are more picturesque than more venerable corps. But with the Russians it was veritably a plumage. Long cavalry swords and scimitars hung from pegs by slender slings in gorgeous braid and bead work, with dazzling and sinuous silver tassels. There were Circassian dirks, with jewels about the handles. The gay medals, of course, were not in the hall, but hanging all over the breasts of the heroes.

Hurried bursts of expostulatory buzzing came from behind some curtains where a lounge was, a language that was like a new situation to unfamiliar ears. Impetuous or dilatory forms left now the door leading to the dining-room, now the curtains, and took vociferously or softly the road to the Bar, the bedrooms or the smoking-room. At the back of the hall was a large office, in the middle of which sat a sulkily handsome elderly flapper of twenty-four summers. A mass of dark juiceless hair hung pompously over her eyes. She was swarthy, sophistic-

312

ated and robust; sat like a big delicate watch-dog in her illuminated dug-out in the body of the Hotel. Whenever the front door
opened she shot a black glance of inquiry in the hall; sometimes
rang a bell. At present she had two glances, though; the dark
one, and a soft variety like a furtive cuddle, which she cast a
yard to the right and some fifteen yards nearer than the door,
at a long stout figure lounging at the window of her room. A
subaltern remained leaning on a ledger, his round head stuck
well inside the Hotel office, his spurred field boots at an angle
of thirty degrees with the vertical without. He was quietly
sniffing the fragrance that her handkerchief and person filled
the office with, and conversing on topics likely to fan the second
of the two glances. His eyes ran steadily and blandly over her
figure, returning from its round, that is from her ankles up to
her face again, almost always in time to absorb her recurring
glance, burning lighthouse-like, its regulation moment. Their
conversation picked its way more or less among the visitors'
accounts which she was checking.

'I can do figures with anybody now,' she said. 'It's funny,
because when I was at school I was always bottom of the class.
I was very bad at arithmetic.'

She breathed little airy numerals all over an immense page,
and then gathered them up in aggregates with attentive eye,
registering the result at the bottom of the column.

'I think your mathematical accomplishment is wonderful,'
the artillery subaltern said, looking at the centre of her loose
high-waisted skirt at the back, trying to disinter the Kirchner
beneath it: especially one Kirchner pinned to the wall in his
room, a concession to the military life, not a diagnostic of the
commonness of his mind.

'I wish I could play with figures like that.' With hopeless
intensity he gazed at her figure, the incommensurable feminine
chiffre, which also he considered it desirable to master.

But despite her tardily acquired skill, she got into difficulties,
seemingly, at the bottom of each page, until at last she was
about a couple of pounds out. She hunted back through the
columns for the slip or slips.

'What margin of error do they allow you?' her admirer
asked, delicately, lisping a little.

'Oh! nothing, none. We are supposed to get it—'

'You just stick it on to somebody else's bill?'

'Yes!'

The young man wondered if he might take it as a hopeful sign that the little airy figures for once had bested her: or whether the old arithmetical incompetence really still lingered on in the prestigious accountant.

A woman's occupation was important in deciding her quality as a sweetheart. These millions of little blue figures that she dwelt among were, he decided, quite wholesome; an abstract and inoffensive sort of gnat. They, after all, had only attacked her comparatively late in life.

'Oh! I've got Major Kirkpatrick's bill wrong! D'you know, I'm terrified of that man!'

'It's his name I expect.'

'Yes, that's it, I expect!'

A small man with a hairy, deeply fresh-complexioned, spectacled face came into the front door and drifted quickly across the hall, then towards the drawing-room, taking his coat off as he went. He wore an infantry coat, but artillery cap badge. This was probably in order to have red edges to his shoulder straps in addition to his two gold stars. Richard Beresin—the figure adhering to the ledge of the office—knew him, through having seen him at the hut where he worked with regard to a batch of men in his battery down with measles. He had a permanent job at Paynes.

'I hate that man,' the young lady had followed him with a surly eye. 'I hate that family. I don't know why.'

'It's his mother, isn't it : and his wife?'

'No, it's his mother and sister. They seem to think that we have nothing to do but run after them. I'll tell you how, for instance. All their letters come here together to the office in the morning. The sister will come down and ask for the letters. She'll say, "Oh, these are my brother's—keep them for him." She'll put them down and take her own away. The mother does the same. And the mother won't take her daughter's letters either! It's so silly. Why can't they take all their letters together? They're one family. Oh, I don't know. I hate people like that.

314

Then they go to the front door with him at night and see him off. "Good night, my *darling* boy," for fear he should go to the *left* when he ought to go to the *right!* You'll see: here they are! No, it's my *darling* this, and my *darling* that. I'm sure he does not like it. Could a man?'

'I don't know.'

'Oh, but that's *different.*'

The mistress of the Bar came into the office and sat down, saying 'Swish!'

Her elderly figure was emphasized by a slack silk jersey. She stared with an energetic smile at the subaltern. 'Perhaps I am *de trop?*'

'Don't be silly,' her colleageue said.

'Of course I know I am not young and *attractive.*' She drawled the last word. The watcher at the window was surprised at the strength of her voice.

'She is always saying that! Why are you always saying that?' the other lady asked her.

The Bar lady looked down, and affectedly picked at her dress.

'Why do you part your hair in the middle?' the subaltern asked.

'Because it's straight: like yours.'

It was black and straight, and he saw the resemblance too. Also he thought she looked rather like him in other ways. Her good-natured aggressiveness, her straight mouth, the dark creases under the eyes, were points of resemblance. He did not say this, however, because he thought that the younger woman would then also see it, and that he would not benefit by this comparison.

He had been leaning there for an hour and ten minutes, he found, on pulling his sleeve back. It was twenty past ten. Gathering himself up, he walked with the least unsteadiness— a few glasses of whisky taking advantage of his stiffness— towards his hat, cane and coat. Over his shoulder, as he left, he said 'Tra-la-la!' He went upstairs to the left.

Ten minutes later he was standing in a slack attitude, a long white bulk in front of a large glass, stroking his sides and

315

thighs, and wondering whether to immerse himself across the passage, or roll his hot, unclothed body in the sheets and cool gradually into sleep.

Next day Richard Beresin considered whether he could afford to remain at the West Berks. He found that he could not. Yet he wanted to live out of camp. The Mess was bad. A passion for civilian ease grew in him daily. Three months previously he had left hospital and was at the most boring period of the training of a new battery.

Beresin was the son of a well-to-do city merchant, and had only left Haileybury one year before the outbreak of war. His father had sent him to Paris to learn the French language. The public-school idea, its tenacious middle-class snobberies, had held him with a poor slouch and drawl for some months. Then he had grown Parisian, but kept the Anglo-Saxon prerogatives of gait and manner somewhat for the prestige they had among his French companions. In England, after six months on a holiday, he was very parlez-vous. On the other hand with the Frenchman he was a little bleak, dumb and ironical.

In the midst of a captivating and increasingly careless life, in which he had begun to cut a figure, begun to sleek himself in front of the mirror of his fellows, discover with a nimble science the resources of his civilized spots, particular physique, the war harshly and suddenly burst on him. It received a mixed welcome at his hands. He saw at once that it was no friend of his. Patron of some, bloody Father Christmas to many a Spartan child, bringing hundreds of little lead soldiers to drill and damage, toy guns and sabretaches, it was bringing him nothing, with good instinct he felt, as he first saw it. Certain things were expected of him, he was in the home of noisy Gallic nationalism—although it was, in other moods, the home of his dream of cheap elegances and pleasures. He became a soldier early in the war. Paris soon grew distant, and he looked towards it even with a grudge and a grimace. France became the 'France' of the sentimental soldier song, with its inseparable sententious 'somewhere', the romance country of death and naïf steadfastness. France with all its pageant of history was less important than this intense localized France of four years, of the

316

English imagination, with its belts of graves and trenches; this narrow gash of a France, five-miles-deep incredible landscape developing an ephemeral species. To belong to this male, elect, death-facing genus he accepted dourly as a consolation for his vision of desirable life foregone. He took all that on, as he had affected Paris. But he wasn't so sure a man and his reactions became of a more original type, more experimental. His struggle with this endless adventure that did not suit him spinning sometimes rather wildly. Meantime the years went on, and he was young enough to thrive, although thwartly, on his new destiny. In this idle, hectic existence he made the most of his short past, and developed its more flattering veins. He became a little literary—snubbed, in a schoolboy way, with an impermeable contempt, his fellows with less fortunate histories. He wore a bracelet, read Huysmans in his dug-out, wore mufti whenever opportunity offered, acquired a settled consciousness of the aristocratic idea. He began to visualize himself as a young blood—he sought in his ancestry for the bluest seeming streams, courted imaginary ghosts. His Nietzschean illusion almost broke the heart of his subservient soldier-servant. The leather of riding-breeches pipeclayed, buttons burnished, no spot on boot or belt neglected, ever, in the line, even—during pulling out or pulling in, weeks of battles, even, when all stores were lost in retreat? He was liked all the better for that. He was a gentleman. Both he and his soldier-servant saw the same popular image of a perfection.

But war grew more and more a sinister phantom. The death-line was always there, crackling, thumping away. He could not take his aristocratic ideal to his bosom, and luxuriate with it, so near to a harsh extinction.

Enteric took him to hospital for some time, however; now he was experiencing a tantalizing lease of leisure. So extravagant were his tastes that it had its stoppages and drags.

Beresin had fixed nicely his sense of what dwelling he should choose : how comfortable, spacious, and above all, not disgustingly suburban! South fronting (gaya scienza, of course) with mulberry bushes, laurels, and one rose if possible.

The village of Paynes had had its camp for a long time. A

317

dismal barrack look pervaded it. Beresin knocked at last at the door of a decent, but very, very mediocre house, whose rooms, he was sure, contained nothing colossal or comfortable. It was the best that presented itself. The landlady appeared a precarious creature. She was almost certainly never warmed by the sun. All the windows were at the front, which faced north. He made many arrangements, inquired about this and that: then surprised her by saying he 'would come back when he had considered what she had told him'. What had she told him? She did not know! She stared at his back with fear.

He left too bored to continue further, and put off his search until the following day.

At the Hotel his groom was waiting for him. It was a question of leave for this soldier, necessitated a walk down to the Battery office. Back from that, three-quarters of an hour separated him from dinner. Stripping, the evening process to which he had accustomed his orderly began. Two bath mats, a bristling loofah a jug of scented and tepid water arranged by Misrow, awaited this young, apolaustic patrician of theory. The orderly was a sleeply-looking boy with a face like an artist. He wore a truss, grumbled at military duties. Beresin lay stomach down, his white fat springing into luminous strawberry pink beneath the massage. Misrow used to grooming horses, as he got to the back of his master's thighs his free hand seized the leg behind the knee from instinct.

'What are you up to, Misrow? Are you afraid I shall kick?'
Misrow had tickled his master.

'No, sir.' Misrow smiled his quattrocento smile, and sleep seemed to be pumped out of his eyelids, like a stagnant mist, having the effect of a barber's spray, but redolent of delicate demarcated life. Beresin rolled over. The front of his body was a series of close drifts of dark hair, with a wide central vein of dull verdure. Terminating this hairy column, raised on the best thing about him, a rather rigid and disciplined neck, his round, closely-knit head was exquisite, harsh and stone-like, reminding you of a snake's sling-like extremity. The muscles gathered up beneath the skin as he moved, like the hundred parts of a child's block puzzle coming together by cinematographic magic.

He scratched his close-cropped head, slowly hissed a rag between small opaque teeth. Particularly unaffected by experimental disquiet of the senses, he yet enjoyed the rather anomalous figure of Misrow. It was incumbent on him to live up to the Nietzschean, the Greek, picture, have this what might be decadent panel occur somewhere in the series of his day's tableaux. Excuses had to be found, with subtleties to explain the rather degrading scene where we first have seen him figuring.

That night at dinner Beresin's crowning laugh reached to every corner of the extensive room. It darted like an insolent mask among the voices and sounds of all the other diners. Everyone objected to it except the Russians, who objected to nothing that wasn't Russian : several people administered the glance of annoyance. This caused him a real satisfaction. He had the mania of shocking, the love of facile challenges. Let the aristocratically-minded display at least, by a suitable arrogance, by a flouting of the bourgeois hush, that a master was present. Let no human apprehension within reach enjoy its meal until it had bitterly noted, scowled, paid its tribute.

'Richard! Richard! your howl freezes my nerves,' his companion said, not so seasoned in the insolent life as he.

'I like laughing like that. D'you know, I always feel a better man when I laugh. If I didn't laugh for a fortnight, I believe I should grow so inhuman and wicked that I should be—a criminal without a crime!'

He brought this out with eager surprise, overlapped by a doubtful and critical moment. However, it was only Nicky. When Beresin wrote, it was always on the model of pen, pencil, and poison. Charlie Peace was of course in the first rank of his heroes. The Brides in the Bath, in those sinister houses especially designed by the Great Architect of the Universe to entrap the innocently cunning, was a case he much liked discussing. Crime —as an artist he appreciated crime! For those above the law the only mates within it are those who break law in the grip of some beautiful folly! Madness alone may mate privilege; but it must be an evil (or a pretty) madness. The saint breaks out at the opposite end, loaded with more villainous chains than any central drudge. Wilde, the philosopher of the English dandy and fashionable frigid oligarch, the flower of West European democratic life, he liked better but respected less than Nietzsche. Beresin, after all, was *not* a Prussian! He had a far cunninger brand of Junker than any Nietzsche knew on which to model himself.

Now, as regards his connection with Nicky, it is necessary to say that Beresin was not a broadly comic 'aristocrat' : that is, his discourse did not divulge with a farcical grossness the hobby of his mind. You might converse with him for half an hour and not suspect him, unless you were very acute, of being an aristocrat in any way. He had good sense : bonhomie, disastrous quality for his dreams, complicated his romantic humours. On this occasion he gave Nicky, as it happened, a brief lecture, designed to improve him; to free him, as it were.

'Besides, I like getting amongst these beggars with my laugh. I made that man at the next table there purple with anger. He's getting red again now : that's because he's listening to what I'm saying! It's so stupid of him to listen! You see, Nick, here you have a lot of glum-looking cattle. You want to stir them up : show the whole mob what you think of them! If they don't like what they hear, well, Nicky, they can do the other thing! If that gentleman there wants to know what I think of his unprepossessing countenance, why shouldn't he, bless him?'

The gentleman at the neighbouring table was prodding his wife with apoplectic sentences, to avoid listening to Beresin. A rupture would hardly arrive from him, although red. Nicky grinned. He had had his first definite lesson in the school-boy creed, and had grasped the cunning truth behind Beresin's simple exposition. This truth consisted in the perception of the impunity of the bold : of how much fun and swank could be compassed without so much as a black eye! Who would not be a 'blood' on these terms, indeed, who not?—the eager, rather vain but cautious soul of Nicky considered! Beresin imparted this with the glee of life's unfortunately wasted morning, as some new-found infallible 'tweek'. Beresin had not found out these things for himself, either. A real live prancing young noble of his acquaintance had initiated him into the fine subtleties and sublimities—so cheap as really to be within the reach of the poorest—of insolence and disregard. However humble a gentleman, you need not even be able to pass for that, once you have the trick, there will always be at least a million unenlightened souls on whom to practise. You know : they don't : an accident. Therefore you have the trickster's glee, you satisfy your eternal mood—which would be exactly theirs had they the tip, not you—and your hilarity. Is it ever necessary, Nicky might heedfully have inquired, to pay with violence on your body, or with money? Yes, his noble mentor would have been compelled veraciously to reply. For instance : you have to maintain a certain style : your tips to commissionaires, to servants and so on have to partake of that redundant quality that must characterize you. In everything you are really check-mated. That must be borne in mind. You *need* the anger of the sho̤ ̣eper as much as the opinion, or imagination, of the commissionaire. It is because you are fundamentally like, as like as two peas to, your less informed, less polished brother, that you have need of him. You need to be seen by him, to keep close to or far from him. You are always a pea disguising itself from a million other peas. The other peas all know you are a pea, and love to think of a pea like themselves being a soft, subtle, clever, insolent pea! But your identity is precarious. Yes, you must be lavish; otherwise—you will receive that deadly look that one pea gives another when pretence is laid aside. You must furthermore be careful never to touch, mingle with or attack anything before first convincing yourself that it be, in fact, *a pea*. Do not be so fatuous as to interfere with a melon! it might not result in harm, but it is no fun! The whole game is constructed, all its rules made, for bodies roughly speaking, identical in volume and potentialities.

This is taking the lesson farther than Beresin would have done, and to a conclusion, or by means, too unflattering, perhaps to have furthered his end—in the event of so much instruction being considered desirable for Nicky. But had you said to Beresin with sufficient authority and the credentials of a newer or more ancient time, that all political philosophies were for the herd, one herd or another, big or little; that a man who was indeed fastidious, or superior, was not so liable to think of himself as an 'aristocrat', whether he were or not, you would soon have reversed his discipleship. He would have been a ready apostate to the romance of the junker. For all he required was an illustrious segregation, a superiority. He would imitate any figure that would satisfy the natural vanity of a young animal with an acute sense of its personal life, without worrying much about the details of your argument.

Having developed the correct atmosphere of hostility in the surrounding hotel guests, he naturally paid no further attention to them.

'I have been looking for fresh quarters.'

'Oh! Why! Isn't this all right?'

'Well, the food here, as you can judge, is abominable. The expense is appalling. I am on the way to a fresh overdraft.'

'You are leaving Miss Brunker?' That was the name of the secretary. Beresin looked towards the hall.

'I spend half my time inside that jolly old window. Snow use! She's the only civilised being here. Well, I have found nothing up till now.'

'I should have thought there were plenty of rooms—'

'Ah!' Beresin animated himself, and drawled the word at him with a vigorous, argumentative cunning. 'Ah, yes—s! But not the rooms I want. I must, my dear Nicky, have a deep, sunny, *square* room.' (He was all for a bit of cubism, was Richard.) 'A deep, elastic bed, that reminds you of the vaulting, the velvet ocean! Spongy blankets, quite new, two inches thick. I like a large mirror on slender supports. I like everything top-heavy! Then a double-basined basalt wash-hand stand.'

Nicky's face grinned hospitably for these absurdities. Beresin stopped and looked at him, encouraging his grin to keep going as though to announce that something even better was about to arrive. It arrived at the end of a minute-long repression.

'I must have a girl, too! I have needed a girl now for three weeks. It is a scandal. Just consider: for three weeks I have wanted a woman! But I want a particular kind of woman!'

322

'Are you as particular about her as you are about the room? And do you want a top-heavy one, by any chance? Because if you do, I know just the thing for you. She is a waitress down in the Flying Corps Mess—'

'No; no. I want none of your air-scullions. I want a woman so shy that she can hardly bear to be looked at. To undress her would be like tearing a shell off a living crab. Her nudity would be so indecent that I should rush out of the room, at first, in horror. She would at the same moment faint on realizing that she was there—'

'I can see you're in a bad way, old chap. Why don't you run up to London for a few days?'

'I haven't got any money. Besides, it is here, in Paynes, that that woman exists.'

'Ah, if you know that—'

'If, if—?'

Beresin laughed once more and duly disturbed the diners.

When he was with a friend and crowing, Beresin never approached a woman. He did not go near the office of the hotel on leaving the dining-room. He went and scandalized and deafened the lounge for an hour or more.

Nicky left the camp on the following day. Beresin had grown accustomed to the hotel. But, once more examining the record of his expenditure, he was forced to the conclusion that this tendency must be discouraged.

In the hour between tea and nightfall the sun appeared bitterly and mechanically above the wet landscape, and created a dreary illumination unfavourable to hope. Richard hurried out, struggling inefficiently with inconsequent regrets, disinherited tendencies, all sorts of bleak, jabbering ideas. The unlucky sky, the squalid regularities of the town, his legs' exasperating shapeliness in their lemon puttees, his isolation in this apricot-coloured damp, severe evening; this was *so* unsuccessful a 'pocket', if thinking of flying in the air, or barrage of melancholy, if turning to land war for your analogies, that it damped the very recesses of his spirit. He would have to overhaul everything because of it.

It was in Tewkesbury Avenue and in a villa named after the

god of Paynes that he found his room. Mars Villa did not face the south; it stood shamelessly, squabbly aligned with other villas, as ignorant of its more than relative bestiality as the Hottentot photographed in a row with his scowling kith and kin. But it contained what most of even such houses contain—a woman. And was not a woman what Richard wanted?— boasted that he wanted and would get. Here she was right enough. She was a particular description of woman; he was fortunate to have found her. Her lips at all times in a lurid pout of love, set in a stagnant dream, lay at the opening of the cooing cavities of her contralto physique. She appeared generally in a dull glow of extinct passion, receding from life, or some moment of early eruption, and burning away harmlessly in Mars Villa. Could she be retrospectively amorous? Had her parents watched very swarthy dying queens, and been familiar with volcanoes? By all means with volcanoes!

Whatever answers might be found to those questions at once presenting themselves along with her like a well-trained suite, Beresin now put himself in a posture of seductive aggression. He had not liked hanging on the counter of the office at the hotel like a string of sausages, nightly. Sex and his dignity—or should you say his imposed character—were at war. He gazed and gazed and gazed at Miss Brunker, and was too afraid of his ideas—his boon companions really—to act. Here was something accessible, not encompassed with commerce, in a cheaper dwelling, materializing his boast to Nicky, approved by the flashy poet within him.

The camel, however, he also has his thoughts. The young lady of Mars Villa thought her thoughts in the discomfort of her cramped female thinking space—merely so full of subterfuges and practical business of sex. She thought her thoughts rather, too, like the crew of a retreating tank, huddled in a vulnerable and by no means swift vessel, as she ascended the stairs, pursued by his blandishments, bombarded by his bark. He barked at her, delightedly and repeatedly. It impressed her very much. 'What a funny laugh!' She dreamt of it.

He took the rooms, paid in advance, and left to bring his things round without delay. That night he was scrubbed by

324

Misrow in Mars Villa. He also kissed Titsy when he came in after dinner, she pressed against the wall, her face tastefully averted, her hands clutching his in an evidently not unfriendly spasm.

'Don't! Mr. Beresin! Please! you mustn't kiss me.'

Tets' languor welled into his room when she brought his tea. He concluded that his first impression of retrospective smouldering must be due to race : by some accident a clear and unimpeded descent on one spot or town. Everything that she felt had been felt in precisely the same way so often before by her ancestral replicas (same conditions, same chemistries and atmospheres) that its mean point of energy was considerably displaced into a past not properly hers : and also her own combustion was grown mechanical and unconvincing. But still she brought with her into the room something like a rich aura of generations of passion. When he kissed her he felt as though he were at play with a fat and sceptical ghost. She blushed in a heavy sudden way, her wet lips expanded and closed, and expanded again on her lips, like some strenuous amoeba. If he looked into her eyes they appeared to open and receive him like some extremely remote stranger. Any part he attacked, then, awoke to half life, with gentle and deliberate responsive spasm. He felt that she could lie on his breast for hours or months as naturally as a plum on its stem against a wall, without restlessness. For he still had the sensation of her consuming herself constantly. All that happened when their bodies were pressed against each other was that she appeared burning away rather more quickly.

Meantime, as regards conversation, which they had when he was not playing at the sun, or more local agency of heat, they talked very much as he had talked on the window-ledge of the West Berks office. When she came in at seven o'clock to light the lamp, he would say, 'Tet, come and sit on my knee.'

Titsy, as she was called, was a diminutive of Lutitia. Tets, appeared to Beresin to sum her up.

She would look at him with a smile and slowly shake her head.

He displaced himself and put his arms round her waist. She

immediately became the plum on the wall, hanging heavily and ripely. The fruit of her breasts, which were large, was like a symbol of her entire flesh, hanging warmly and idly on the wall of her body. When his hand pressed these, her eyes fluttered and grew heavy. They were much more the essential part of her than anything else. And his enterprise was confined to that.

'Why do you kiss me?' she said one evening. 'I don't like those French kisses.'

'Are those French kisses?'

'Yes.'

'I kiss you because I don't believe too much in individuals.'

'Go hon!'

'I want to know what you taste like, and I want to keep fat.'

'You're quite fat enough.'

'Kisses take one back six thousand years. It is a delicious journey.'

'Don't be so silly.'

'But I promise you—! That's it. Kiss a woman and you become naked at once.' His talk of the crab's shell and the swooning nudity had got no farther. 'You are running wild once more and light-hearted.'

'You do say funny things sometimes.'

'Kiss me now; you will find that you are no longer in this room! It takes you much farther back than it does me.'

'Are you often taken like that?'

The 'finest story in the world' took him no further. The cheap sententious mysticism of the imperial bard recoiled before the deaf reality of this rather psychic, rather Eastern, young lady. So far did the brave Beresin get and there he unaccountably stuck. Just as the jolliest romances are apt to draw up abashed before too naked realities, so presumably his light-hearted lechery had been damped and cowed to its nursery by the contact of a full being. Then came the bolt from the blue of his marching order. He was to leave Paynes camp all at once, and to be hurried with his battery to Pitport, a two hours' journey the other side of London. They were for the East. It was the time when Batteries were rushed out before their scheduled training was complete, and before the final push overseas, they were hurried from spot to spot, saw much of England, the routine displacement retained.

Before leaving he arranged with Tets that they should meet in London if possible on the following Saturday. The next Saturday, turned out, in the event, not to be possible. Beresin had camp orderly officer to do for the week-end of his arrival. The following week they met.

Now the quickened pace, the uprooting process, the quickening of military duties, caused a change in Richard Beresin. He clung to his exquisite habits, burnished his contempt every day and held it coldly up to his fellows with politeness when he considered they had appeared mentally untidy before him. He said his daily prayers to his deities; but even a philosopher should be in some way efficacious. He was going very soon now back to War. How had he spent his spell of leisure? It was not enough of a figure that he had filled this space with to satisfy him. Not conscious of it, the animal things had their way. Why had he not Miss Brunker to his account? His apathy in Mars Villa, following on his empty-handedness in the Hotel, what compensated for the blank canvas? He became more ostentatiously the jeune seigneur that all spirited youth should be : the natural man within swelled and concentrated itself, on the contrary, in equal measure.

The kettledrums and violins gulped and stuttered, 'Come along with me, and have a Jubilee,' in the restaurant in which they ate. The members of the orchestra whistled, gave cat-calls and in some instances sat on their instruments and yelled like drunken babies. The chef d'orchestre dominated this disorder with his sharp protruding stomach and nose that never allowed you to see both his small pink-brown eyes at once. After a lawless performance, repeated three times, the band retired to eat.

'Nice place, isn't it?' Beresin said, in the rather exhausted silence that followed.

'Yes,' Tets said, 'It was nice,' her eyes directed at furs and queer female dresses.

He had to make her drink. He looked with leisurely satisfaction at her brown curls, brown eyes, brownish dress, white flower, white teeth, white gloves, and hard, bloodless face. Her beauty was as formal as a playing card, as neat and clean as a fish. Her red lips stuck out in a pulpy abstraction. She drew herself up from time to time free of her stays and sighed. They both guzzled. Bronx and Beaune, the war-wine that appears on tap, brought the right weighty cheer into their hearts.

Their kisses in the taxi on the way to the Alhambra partook of the disordinate character of the orchestra in its last bout. She arrived there in physical disarray, her eyebrows raised, eyes staring, lips in reminiscent uncontrol. She wept with laughter at the Bing Boys. Robey, with his primitive genius, flattered the mood of the evening. She did not deny the Bacchanalia its culmination. As they drove through the black streets afterwards they lay in each other's arms and sealed their unwisdom with the ultimate convulsions of love. The eating up of the pennies and the yards on the taximeter was an intense and palpable symbol of time.

The next morning Beresin found a warm mass beside him in bed, and realized, as he would have done at the presence of a pool of blood or a dead body, that the preceding evening had been marked by a human event. The mass stirred, and a cumbrous bestial scented arm passed round his body. In the middle of a thick primitive gush of hair, he found the lips with their thoughtful pathetic spasm. He looked with curiosity and uneasiness at what he found so near to him.

The corpses of the battlefied had perhaps cheapened flesh? Anyway, realities were infectious; and all women seemed to feel that they should have their luxurious battles, too; only they were playing at dying, and their war was fruitful.

'Willie, do you love me a little bit?'

What should he say? He loved her as much as he loved a luscious meadow full of sheep, or the side of a tall house illuminated by a sunset, or any pleasant sight or sound that he might meet. But that is not what women mean by 'do you love me?' He understood that. They mean, 'Do you think that perpetual intercourse with me for the rest of your life would be a nice thing?' That was hardly a question to put to a sentimental theorist of nobility, a dealer in hardness. Was the mink to inquire of the panther whether he would always kiss so nicely, while he was giving the mink a preliminary lick before devouring his prey?

However, he answered softly enough, for he was sentimental in more ways than one, although more dangerous in love than in theory!

A woman was for him a conventional figure, and an inferior, to be treated like all other inferiors. When the moment pointed to a display of chivalry she changed at once to a figure of romance, and she became your superior. But social standing again controlled the scope and likelihood of this vacillation. He remembered Nietzsche's useful dissection of 'l'homme passionné' and what the world called 'passionate'; and that he had said that a fine woman was undoubtedly finer than a fine man, but was *much rarer!* He had chuckled at this big-browed old German fox's finesse.

Had he been an artist, and Corot, he would have attached himself to a series of valleys, and a certain delicate-tinted tree. But his woman, deflected from abstraction by her human admixture, would not have been Corotesque. That is clear.

It will seem, nevertheless, that this young man could not afford, as a Corot could, to disregard the results of his love, and its animal raison d'être. Corot might feel that Corot could not be improved on and display a certain large indifference as to where he scattered his seed; seeing that, however great the care he took, he was a culmination, and not likely to produce another Corot; and equally unlikely to cause women to bring forth Daumiers or Daubignys! Had Beresin reasoned too much, he would probably have been an ardent theorist of a more sifted hygienic stock.

Back in Pitport, he forgot his week-end with Tets in exactly the same spirit that the majority of men forget their dreams. He was imbued with a sense of the speed of events. There was a whirl behind him and there was nowhere time to look steadily at anything. Time had become as material as a taxicab. The battlefield was his destination, wherever he was for the moment. Death was extremely busy and he was in the ten-league queue, pass or not pass. He shifted and shuffled nearer.

He wrote to Tets and arranged meetings. She wrote nice and quite literate letters, with a stereotyped nonchalance of tone.

Two weeks later he felt a desire to exhaust a little more his idyll with Tets. The rawness of his raptures jarred on his memory. He wished to continue if not complete their miniature love. Tets had to be seen.

She came up from Paynes obediently. Her retrospective ardour now appeared, flatteringly, to apply to *him*. He did not have any longer to imagine dying indigo queens. He found her above his expectations as he met her on the platform. He had not had a very distinct negative of her. He approved of his fellow animal, and rapt her into a hectic bluster of cheap music, excessive food, bad drink, purse-proud spectacles, dominated by some small ape, specializing in comic hysteria. With her, he deliberately chose the vulgarer sites and scenes contemptuously, to keep her in her place. That she should in any way be appearing to share his finer life would have been inappropriate. He liked relegating her a little more than he would, in any event, unconsciously have done, to the places where coarse things prevailed.

For two days they wallowed breathlessly. She appeared perpetually in a sort of mesmerized inattentiveness. She hurried, excited and a little unhappy, along with him, her eyes staring away, clouding, crying, dark rings coming under them. His eye fixed on her person like a small blasting flame, and he did not leave her till the end of the second day, when that illumination had burnt itself down and grown normal. His train left before hers, and he left her crying, sitting like a child sideways on a seat and shaking.

His equanimity gave way to discomfort as he watched this sight. Had he really been immersing in a harsh, seething brutality what was fundamentally a *child?* Objectively men are so small, and startle each other by pictures of weakness. This last picture, as he left the Tets show for good, remained an emotive key in his mind as regards this last sweetheart.

A fortnight later Beresin sailed for the East. He did not go into action for some time. He was lucky when he did. He was

330

away for eighteen months. Letters from Egypt reached Tets, short notes describing odds and ends of life in war time. Her second letter announced a complication. Tets must expect a child. Slowly growing, henceforth, from a speck, until it became an appreciable human cloud of new being, Beresin was faced with a complex and weird monument to his parting licence. Something had been started that nothing could arrest, in Tets' case, and with him away so far. From what he knew of her, he accepted the girl's indication of him as father. He wrote her what he considered with reason a plain and friendly letter; he enclosed a cheque for ten pounds, which he recommended her to husband.

'I cannot marry you when I get back. But I will keep the child. Write me what money you need.'

He saw the figure sitting sideways on the seat and crying. It was to this figure he wrote. That had been a sort of foreshadowing of the child. The moving adult mass in the bed, so much larger and more formidable, had cast up, as a parent does, the little dressed derelict crying on the platform, a temperate atom of everyday life. Tets was small and pathetic. He was patronizing with his larger manifestation (an equivalent of which Tets equally possessed) Tets' smaller physical manifestation.

Beresin derived acute satisfaction from the sight of this diminutive pathos: the small, in fact, in this case, almost synonymous with the Beautiful. So no virtue can be alleged on account of his pity. The letter brought not much consolation to Tets. She divined a very tough self-preservative instinct behind the promises, pity and ten-pound note. She shrank herself up into a child again and wept, although there was no one (except perhaps her more mature and formidable self) to see it. The burning-away process that Beresin had conceived as characteristic of Tets, now set in no longer as the visual preserve of the perspicacious. Everyone near Mars Villa could note her diminishing on the one hand, as she grew on the other. From two sides now, retrospectively and ultrospectively, she guttered away. She was sent to London for the most scandalous stage of her pregnancy.

In Africa Beresin found that he had more than singed himself in contact with the peculiar flame that gnawed away at Tets. In the form of Tets herself he began to be devoured by it in turn. The big white scented mass recollected, made a Thébaide of his dug-out. He was snug as a beetle in the midst of a trencher full of dough. His enthusiasm for particularity did not stand out against the eloquent attacks of his animal spirits. Extreme homesickness, in the first place, was a thing he was as susceptible to as anyone could be to sea-sickness. The distance intervening between himself and his attachments made him giddy, as though the troop-ship had mounted to Egypt, instead of later-ally progressing through the waves. Tets also dominated and engulfed the composite picture of his harem—of Caroline, Maisie, Maud and Billie. What a pass to have come to! He goes out on the female hunt; lodges in his trap, incidentally: now he is being slowly devoured by his prey. He finds himself toying absentmindedly with—what is this? A marriage ring! He calls in Paris, with its painted sweetmeats, to his aid. Entire cafés full of boon-companions and of women are emptied into his dug-out. Then again he looks round at the Black and the Brown. They, as we all know, help you along with the White. But much more than that, this caviare of a dark and acrid skin is the test, surely, of whether your palate is a noble, an adventurous palate, or a plebeian one! This was perhaps the bitterest pill. Beresin could never bear to think of that failure! Without the presence of mind, ever, when in face of this discom-fort, to reflect on the quality of the 'mets' and therefore the extent of his disgrace, he was simply blackened in his own eyes for ever, ethiopianly blackened.

There was one, only one, thing he could remember with equanimity from this time: one little flash of the true stuff. It was when at the moment of perhaps his supreme discomfort—the second chronologically—he seized his cane and beat the vociferous young negress who was the cause of it.

'You nasty black baggage! Take that on your horrible hide! And that and that! I don't like you! You're all dressed up and nowhere to go! How dare you! Take *that!*'

Except for that masterly gesture, even at the moment when he was being ignominiously certified as possessed of bourgeois senses, and with grave disabilities for inclusion in the ranks of the elect, except for that it was a period of complete eclipse of his self-esteem. Then, he was at present associated with two or three genuine dooks, as an officer. One of these nobles did not like him, and abused him to the other younger nobles. What could it be? Beresin wondered. Was it a further judgment on him, like the discomfort of his senses at the hands, or lips, of the Negroid and the Nautch? Was it now the turn of Blue Blood itself, as it had been a moment before of Black, to turn him down; or for him to be unqualified to mix with? Beresin in the presence of the real thing was shy. The actual breathing, walking flower to which so many doctrines, Nietzches and Gobineaus, reverently point: this magical, masterly thing? Could the flesh and blood of the disciple be expected to support that sight with equanimity? He was awed at the polish and purity of the vocables, of the exquisite vowels, when two of the nobles were talking together. Ah, but his middle-class enunciation—? Then the attitude of mind—so free, so cynical—how well calculated to allure the Philosopher, and make him place Truth somewhere where she could learn such beautiful manners! The short, scrubby physique, the thoroughly villainous stupidity of the noble, who was also his colonel, and enemy, appeared to him in the highest sense, peculiarly, attributes. The stupidity, which he also saw, was the divine stupidity of the Noble! The physical commonplace—which he noted— how characteristic, paradoxical, and in fact the 'real thing'!

Here were fresh despondencies, then, that threw him back more yet upon the female presence which was the twin domination in his life. And these two masters that destiny had bestowed on him were at war. Or rather, was it not a Master and a Mistress? The Mistress did not also move in quite the same circles as the Master, the prancing noble; friction ensued, therefore, where possession of Richard was in question. Billie and Caroline had been other forms of Tets. But Tets was enthroned; for although one of several, she was softly sculpting a Totem, whereas others had not had that art—or craft.

He wrote her a sort of love-letter. It was a sort of one because it was wrung with repugnance as well as passion. Oh, why was not the Home-girl a Haristocrat? Then she would have been as likely, as well as vigorous, a nymph as could be found on the banks of an English stream. No, nothing but a *sort* of a love-letter could be written; a tentative, shame-faced, blowing hot and cold missive. It blew hot in parts, where the endearments came to be written. He told her what a romantic bore the Desert was; that Suez was a sink of ennui. He wished that she were there! He could do with—he divagated and dreamt almost obscenely. So much amassed idleness, heat, and the staring red inflammation of youth! He tied the letter up with the others and it went on its nebulous errand.

In return, he got a letter from Lutitia's parents informing him in injured and more or less injurious terms that their daughter was dead.

He received this bitter communication in his dug-out, on the North-west frontier, while he was engaged in censoring the men's letters. They could be summed up in the hackneyed type of man's letter, 'Dear Ma, this war's a fair bugger,' with the interminable, piteous 'in the Pinks.' The one he was actually looking through kept referring to Kate's apparently well-known penchant for soldiers. Kate was certainly the writer's sister and he seemed strongly to dislike the thought of her frequenting any man of the same calling as himself and friends. Beresin was wondering if Driver Lawrence had some past English guilt on his mind, or whether it was from sheer dislike of and a form of vengeance on his comrades. Ma, even, too, was addressed fiercely, and would seem to have been not quite free from similar tendencies.

Beresin's irony was chastened by the arrival of his own letter.

Now the ghost that his senses had brought all the way from England to vegetate in his dug-out or hut was dead. There was an eerie feeling in it; he looked at the two photographs placed neatly on a shelf five feet above the ground. One still smiled, but he felt now that they were objects of ill-omen. They were shortly after put back in his kit-bag. He was sorry; but it did not make him reflect. That night, lying in his camp-bed, he remembered that the night before he had been luxuriating in the anticipation of sleeping with Tets again when the distant leave to England came; practically sleeping with her there, in fact, for a moment and to some extent, while all the time she was dead. The child received a little tentative thought. The parents shortly received a cheque from him for £40.

And the year passed, chiefly in Mesopotamia; when he came home he was much the worse for wear, after dysentery. At his request, Tets' mother brought her daughter's child up to London. He waited for her uneasily at his hotel. He occupied an unnecessarily handsome room, and stood in the full glory of impeccable mufti. At their last meeting he had settled up with Mrs. Stapledown for board and lodging.

The mother was surprisingly silent and looked at him in an uncertain way, several different interests and opposite emotions cancelling one another on her face.

'How do you do, Mrs. Stapledown? You don't know how upset I was. I was dreadfully upset. I loved your daughter. You don't believe me, I expect? No? I intended—Ah! this is our baby? What a jolly little baby! I don't know what to say to you! I'm afraid you—'

He took the child in an embarrassed way. The feeling of this warmth, and the weight of the springy, limp object—warmth and weight *his,* like his own hands—pleased and embarrassed him still more.

'Yes; I do! I'm a mother. I loved my girl. You have done wrong, *very wrong,* Mr. Beresin.'

She stood rather breathless, her eyes shining.

The clumsy way she was being held increased the baby's alarm at the stranger. The face puckered slowly, and sitting helplessly on his knee she began to howl. He recognized at once in the child the Tets touch. The little convulsive crab-like being sat there on his knee like a transfigured Tets.

He shyly and slowly pedalled it up and down on his knee. There was a moment full of embarrassing innuendoes when he had to give it back to Mrs. Stapledown.

'Never mind, my precious, then!—there—!' The grandmother also appeared to be substituting Tets for the infant.

Beresin helped regularly with the rearing of the child, and saw it fairly often. For the first year and a half it was, with its reveries, its dead white face and beauty of minuteness, very affecting. It had the same unusual interest at that stage as Tets promised when he first saw her. The horrible gift of speech had not descended on it.

He got it called Veronica, for it to have a name similar to Lutitia's. But when Veronica grew big she lost her beauty. The pulpy and stormy little totem became a dull human being, with whom decay set in early. She was unnecessarily robust with a mania for exploiting the beauty of smallness! She would attempt to stimulate interest, cause pity, or induce amusement, by mincing or conducting herself in babyish style, to mesmerize you into seeing her 'en petit'.

From Beresin's point of view it was lamentable. It was as though she had divined, in the telepathy of her infant state, the cause of the father's infatuation, and his more distant emotion at her mother's helplessness, and attempted, with a coarseness not even elephantine, and a bitter lack of tact, to perpetuate it.

The whole of their future relations, beyond the first years of babyhood, were struck by what seemed like a blast of God's irony. Also she was the homeliest description of woman. No aristocrat could have had a less appropriate child!

CONCLUSION

The New Guy who's got into the Landscape

Conclusion

We now come to 1926. I was practically *always* underground by then—buried in the Reading Room of the British Museum or out of sight in some secret workshop. And then, on top of the General Strike, was published the first of my non-fiction books, *The Art of Being Ruled*.

The title of this book speaks for itself. I had attacked the problem of government. But it is important to notice that it was advice to 'the ruled' that was tendered, not to those who do the ruling. It was instruction for people in the gentle art of keeping the politician at bay. That was what would be called a 'Leftwing' book. I'm doing to-day just what I was doing in 1926, when I began. I am trying to save people from being 'ruled' too much—from being 'ruled' off the face of the earth, as a matter of fact.

Anyhow, in 1926 I began writing about politics, not because I like politics but everything was getting bogged in them and before you could do anything you had to deal with the politics with which it was encrusted. And I've got so bepoliticked myself in the process that in order to get at *me*, to-day, you have to get the politics off me first. That's one of the things I've tried to do in this book.—However, when politics came on the scene I ring down the curtain; and that was in 1926. That was when politics began for me in earnest. I've never had a moment's peace since.

I don't know how such a book as this ought to end : I feel inclined just to shut it down now. But I'm told, by people who seem to know, that I ought to drag in the present (Autumn 1937, time of writing). And I did, in my Introduction, rope in, in a desultory way, these latterdays.

The Zeitgeist, as I said three hundred pages back, is getting clear of the wash, or the undertow, kicked up by the Great War; we've got a new Zeitgeist, almost. It's almost as if a new guy had got into the landscape. I can hear him and smell him—there are new crepitations in the air, as yet unexplained. I believe he will be a great improvement, from my point of view, on the last one.

I picked up a newspaper just now to call to mind what was happening to us: I mean really big things. The usual triplets and 'doodles' bulked large. A Star called Taylor is mobbed by stenographers. 'Jim-and-Amy'—Jack Doyle and Mrs. Dodge-Godde: that is what bulks largest, the customary figures of our Free Press carnival. But I cut them out and concentrated on our Foreign Secretary at Geneva. Apologizing, I found him, about Great Britain's not being able to make war until 1942. A lot of small peoples would unfortunately have to put up with a lot more tiresomeness on the part of tyrants till then, it just couldn't be helped. It *sounds* as nonsensical as a 'doodle'. But it is a life-and-death doodle. It's big stuff—it's history. It's not just a child playing about, though you'd suppose it was at first sight.

What I like about the new Zeitgeist is that he's stopped paying any attention to all that—to Anthony Eden and Jack Doyle, Broadribb and Hore Belisha. He's settling down to wait, like the rest of us. Since he can do nothing in spite of the fact that he's the Zeitgeist, to alter things, he is making himself at home in this long long 'pause' (to use Blum's word).—Nothing can happen till 1942, I suppose he argues. Then there'll be another Zeitgeist.

In my own particular field there's not a great deal doing—except for doodles. In painting and writing what might be called a doodledum obtains.

Among those who have become great public figures in the course of the last ten years, Mr. Auden heads the list. Is I *the new guy who's got into the landscape*. No: but he's got the technique of a new guy. I like what he does. He is all ice and woodenfaced acrobatics. Mr. Isherwood, his *alter ego*, is full of sly Dada fun, too. Both pander to the unuplifted, both flirt robustly with the underdog, but both come out of Dr. Freud's cabinet.

I am the most broadminded 'leftwinger' in England. If I

have mentioned these Marxian playboys first, it is not out of bias for the rebellious mind. It is because the right-wing never 'creates', for some reason, in England. For impressive literary output, in Great Britain as in America, you must go to the Radical camp. France is quite different, of course. There the traditionalist is often a passably inventive fellow : there is no rule. But with us the Shaws, Huxleys, and Lawrences are all out for the rich man's blood, and I don't blame them.

This is not an accident, though. It is the historic attitude of the Anglo-Saxon. Also in England it is a domestic necessity : the rich man is so stupid here.—I of course, being an artist as well, have an acute personal dislike, even, for the British rich-man. It could not be otherwise. As to the rich-man's wars, you know what I think of them.

To body forth my optimism regarding the Zeitgeist 1937 is a little difficult. I cannot give him a name. If we turn to publicists and the sort of active men whose profession is letters, there are many hints of a change in which we could, I think, detect the presence of the Zeitgeist. There is an agreeable alteration in accent. Words fall with a more businesslike, a bleaker click.

There is a group of inkslinging clubmen : I don't know much about them, except that a number of them are papists : such names as Bryant, Hollis, Barnes, come to my mind. The very names are reassuring, and have a businesslike ring : this lot, although mostly orthodox party-men and devoted to the interests of privilege and property, express themselves very well. They often state a dubious case with a laudable lack of humbug. (Humbug is of course the besetting sin of my radical friends—only Shaw escaped.)

England has no Hemingway, but if it had he would come out of a Club. A group of matter-of-fact reporters and lighthearted clubmen-journalists will do for us perhaps, someday, what the Middle-West did for the New World. The West End and the Middle-West stand for the same thing.—I just mention Hemingway to show you the sort of thing I am talking about. Every Anglo-Saxon community should have its Hemingway to disinfect it of its inveterate 'uplift', and provide a background of insensitiveness and alertness.—And *then,* of course, you need something else to dekiplingize you afterwards of your Hemingway!

Mr. Douglas Jerrold stands out from the hardboiled crowd : he is the brains of the Right. I think he is the Sotelo of English right-wingery. As the legitimate successor of Belloc and Chesterton he occupies a significant place in English letters, and brings with him also a brilliant narrative gift which should declare itself in successes in the theatre, if one could be found to put on a romantic tory farce. What I like about him is the dashing manner in which he throws his politics down, like jaunty ultimatums, and then turns his back. But like Mr. T. S. Eliot, his politics are French rather than English. He would possibly have flourished better in the land of the *Action Française* or of the *Acción Popular*. And his co-religionist, Father D'Arcy, the extremely brilliant Master of Campion Hall, is a 'continental' figure, too, picturesque not only because a Jesuit. He happens to be one of the most characteristic heads in my portrait gallery (see illustration), as well.

Another portent—all by himself—is Mr. Malcolm Muggeridge. He is young and very very odd : for he is 'left-wing', as much as I am, and yet he is not silly. I rubbed my eyes when I first caught sight of Mr. Muggeridge. I really thought I was dreaming. I didn't think Mr. Muggeridge was real.

It is not, however, in any individual that you must look for the kind of thing I have been announcing, and which I think I have distinctly perceived. Look closely at the written word. It is rather the new smells and colours of the words men use you have to look out for—the *gait* of the sentences, the tone of the voice. (Didn't you know that words could *smell*? Read Mr. Joad!)

However, this is enough about a system of things, which, although joined to the Great War (the main subject of my book) by the 'post-war', is really a distinct division of Time, which it would require another book to describe properly.— The Great War is a magnet, the 'post-war' its magnetic field. It is my belief that we should try to neutralize it. We do not want to be drawn back into *that*. The 'post-war' is the link between to-day and the War. And the free movement of particles we

342

can detect everywhere at present, again, is an extremely encouraging sign. It looks almost as if the magnestism was getting weaker.

I ought to say something striking now that should epitomize all that you've been hearing about, since I first showed you a scowling Bombardier upon a distant parade ground at a Dorsetshire Camp. Yet one can't epitomize *oneself*. An attempt to do so would only lead to one's appearing either too pleased with oneself or not pleased enough.

The many external adventures which I have attempted faithfully to set down are of no great importance, except in so far as they determine the actions of what is inside. For obviously my *raison d'être* is inside. Everyone's *raison d'être* is what he is best at. And my long suit is not *action,* in the ordinary sense.

I am not averse at moving about. The body moves about a good deal, in obedience to the laws of life, and I encourage it to do so. But as its business is to mark, learn and inwardly digest, and *not* to hit people in the eye, or poise itself upon the brink of precipices (I am very firm about that—I never let it go above 10,000 feet) its adventures are *my* adventures, not the other way round.

Still I hope I may have entertained you, here and there, for it is amazing the number of different sorts of things I have done. And I hope that, in addition to the entertainment—as my sight is keen, as nothing escapes my eye, and as I may claim a respectable measure of common sense, with which to interpret the 'bag' brought to me, daily, by this formidable eyesight—it may be that, in this amusing way by following my body round, as we have done, some portion of my experience may have passed over into you.